Designing Indicators for a Plural Legal World

Designing Indicators for a Plural Legal World engages with the role of quantification in law, and its impact on law and development and judicial reform. It seeks to examine how different institutions shape and influence the making and use of legal indicators globally.

This book sheds light on the limitations of existing quantification tools, which measure rule of law because of their lack of engagement with plural legal orders and countries in the Global South. It offers an alternative framework for measurement, which moves away from an institutional look at rule of law, to a bottom-up, user-centred approach that places importance on the lives that people lead, and the challenges that they face. In doing so, it offers a way of thinking about access to justice in terms of human capabilities.

Siddharth Peter de Souza is a post-doctoral researcher at the Tilburg Institute for Law, Technology and Society, Tilburg University, The Netherlands. He was previously a researcher at the Chair of Public Law and Comparative Law, Humboldt University, Berlin. He has co-edited *Mutinies for Equality: Contemporary Developments in Law and Gender in India* with Tanja Herklotz (Cambridge University Press, 2021), *Technology, Innovation and Access to Justice: Dialogues on the Future of Law* with Maximilian Spohr (2021) and *Crowdsourcing, Constructing and Collaborating: Methods and Social Impacts of Mapping with World Today* with Nida Rehman and Saba Sharma (2020).

GLOBAL LAW SERIES

The series provides unique perspectives on the way globalization is radically altering the study, discipline, and practice of law. Featuring innovative books in this growing field, the series explores those bodies of law which are becoming global in their application, and the newly emerging interdependency and interaction of different legal systems. It covers all major branches of the law and includes work on legal theory, history, and the methodology of legal practice and jurisprudence under conditions of globalization. Offering a major platform on global law, these books provide essential reading for students and scholars of comparative, international, and transnational law.

Series Editors

M. E. A. Goodwin
Tilburg University

Randall Lesaffer
KU Leuven & Tilburg University

David Nelken
King's College London

Han Somsen
Tilburg University

Books in the Series

Intimations of Global Law
Neil Walker

Legalized Families in the Era of Bordered Globalization
Daphna Hacker

Transnational Sustainability Laws
Phillip Paiement

The Sociology of Law and the Global Transformation of Democracy
Chris Thornhill

Designing Indicators for a Plural Legal World

Siddharth Peter de Souza

CAMBRIDGE
UNIVERSITY PRESS

CAMBRIDGE
UNIVERSITY PRESS

University Printing House, Cambridge CB2 8BS, United Kingdom

One Liberty Plaza, 20th Floor, New York, NY 10006, USA

477 Williamstown Road, Port Melbourne, vic 3207, Australia

314 to 321, 3rd Floor, Plot No.3, Splendor Forum, Jasola District Centre, New Delhi 110025, India

103 Penang Road, #05–06/07, Visioncrest Commercial, Singapore 238467

Cambridge University Press is part of the University of Cambridge.

It furthers the University's mission by disseminating knowledge in the pursuit of education, learning and research at the highest international levels of excellence.

www.cambridge.org

Information on this title: www.cambridge.org/9781316514894

© Siddharth Peter de Souza 2022

First published 2022

Printed in India by Avantika Printers Pvt. Ltd.

A catalogue record for this publication is available from the British Library

ISBN 978-1-316-51489-4 Hardback

Cambridge University Press has no responsibility for the persistence or accuracy of URLs for external or third party internet websites referred to in this publication, and does not guarantee that any content on such websites is, or will remain, accurate or appropriate.

For Mama and Dada
Tigers in my corner

Contents

Acknowledgements

I would like to thank my supervisor Professor Philipp Dann for being a supportive and engaged mentor throughout my doctoral studies at Humboldt University, Berlin. To the team at the Chair of Public Law and Comparative Law, Smarika Lulz, Dr Tanja Herklotz, Maxim Bönnemann, Thomas Dollmaier, Dr Konrad Vossen, Dr Michael Riegner, Medha Srivastava, Juliane Brauer and Corinna Roudani, thank you for being open and collaborative over these years with your feedback and comments. Lisa Hahn and Dr Larissa Vetters helped me think through my project with a socio-legal lens and worked with me through demystifying methods and making them fun. Thanks to several others who have been part of the Chair including Gabriel Noll, Katharina Wommelsdorf, Katharina Hufgard, Freya Schramm, Hoa Vuong and Nadja Baumert. Thanks also to Professor Mattias Kumm for his feedback and suggestions on the thesis.

I would like to thank Amos Helms and Pankaj Madan from the Konrad Adenauer Stiftung for supporting my research with a doctoral scholarship. The generosity of the foundation helped make studying and living in Berlin possible.

This research was initially influenced by my time at the Max Planck Foundation for International Peace and Rule of Law and a very special thanks is due to Dr Tilmann Röder for being available to discuss my project over the years. I have also benefitted from my time as a judicial clerk in Delhi; thank you also to Justice S. Muralidhar for his engagement and advice. During the PhD I had an opportunity to have many useful discussions in India when I conducted exploratory interviews with Dr Melvil Pereira, Ms Sharifa Khanam, Dr V. Geetha, Dr Usha Ramanathan,

Ms Patricia Mukhim, Dr Jeuti Barooah, Professor Gassah, Professor Vidhu Verma, Professor Sudhir Krishnaswamy, Professor Sitharamam Kakarala, Professor Siddharth Swamninathan, Professor Arun Thiruvengadam, Professor Nehsat Quaiser, Professor Mohan Gopal, Professor Alito Siqueira, Professor Sasheej Hegde, Justice B. S. Chauhan and Dr Aparna Chandra. These discussions helped me gain further insights into understanding the landscape of judicial data in India, and the place of legal pluralism in India's judicial architecture.

During a research stay at the Centre for Socio-Legal Studies in Oxford, I had very insightful conversations with Professor William Twining on how to shape my research as a dialogue with existing work on legal indicators. I am also thankful to Professor Fernanda Pirie, Professor Jonathan Wolff, Dr Tania Burchardt, Dr Surabhi Ranganathan and Professor David Nelken for making time and offering generous feedback during my research stay in the UK. Thank you to Professor Yash Ghai and Mr Waikwa Wanyoike for their time and advice in understanding constitution making and legal pluralism in Kenya. Thank you also to my colleagues at Tilburg University where I have completed the work on this book, and especially Professor Linnet Taylor for her support. Thank you also to Professor Morag Goodwin and Professor David Nelken for their feedback while including the book in the Global Law Series, and to the great team at Cambridge University Press, Qudsiya Ahmed, Anwesha Rana and Aniruddha De, for their wonderful support. Thanks to Shamoli Barreto for the painting that is used on the cover.

Thank you Patsy, Merlin and Usha for being my Berlin family, and for all their generosity in making me immediately feel welcome and supported in a new city. Thank you to Marja for her support. I am grateful to Pravesh and Rashmi, my in-laws who gave up their study for me in Delhi and who have been full of encouragement and humour as I have navigated working through the book. Thank you to Dhulari and Anastasia, for all their care and reinforcement during my writing in Goa.

My sisters Gayatri and Roshni have been a source of constant cheer and affection knowing when to motivate, when to listen and when to nudge, and I hope to play the same role as they work through their PhDs. Their support has been invaluable and I thank them very much for being there and seeing me through this project.

Saba and I have journeyed through our PhDs together and I am very happy we did so. She has been a sounding board for many of my ideas, provided comfort for many anxieties with the research, and been a source of motivation by finishing her PhD before me (despite all my bold predictions of finishing before). Her companionship and love have been instrumental throughout these past few years.

My parents Peter and Ligia are the reason why I first thought of doing a PhD. Their confidence, support and love every step of the way has given me the freedom to work on things that I enjoy and in the process explore the life of the mind. None of this would have been possible without having them in my corner, and I am very lucky to have them as interlocutors and buddies. I dedicate this book to them.

1

Introduction

A multi-stakeholder Task Force on Justice that brought together United Nations (UN) member states, civil society and international organizations in 2019 released a report that estimated a global justice gap of 5.1 billion people.[1] This number, which makes up over two-thirds of the world's population, was estimated to be of those people who are without meaningful access to justice. The gap has three dimensions that looked at the living conditions of people, matters of dispute resolution and opportunity deprivation to lead a secure life. First, at least 253 million people live in conditions of extreme injustice, of which 12 million are stateless, 40 million work in conditions of modern slavery and 203 million live in conditions of such insecurity that it is difficult to pursue justice. Second, over 1.5 billion people are unable to resolve their justice disputes on account of challenges of the civil or administrative system or unresolved criminal matters. Third, over 4.5 billion people are excluded from political, economic and social opportunities that are provided by the law on account of being unable to access a legal identity, lack of land tenure and informal employment. These are startling figures, which indicate the sheer magnitude of the challenge that confronts those working to address barriers to access to justice. This large exercise also demonstrated a move towards quantifying justice, as a method to articulate these barriers in order to emphasize the urgency

---

[1] Task Force on Justice, *Justice for All Report: Final Report* (New York: Center on International Cooperation, 2019), 18, https://www.justice.sdg16.plus/report (accessed 2 July 2019).

for action. Rule of law indicators and measurement frameworks[2] have become increasingly popular and widely used to evaluate the capacities of legal systems. This is so because *inter alia*, indicators are seen to increase the diagnostic capacity of policy makers to identify bottlenecks in the legal system,[3] enable empirically based solutions for justice reform, and enhance the capacity of civil society to monitor justice delivery. By examining regional variations among various legal systems, analysing elements of state practice and law making, and drawing linkages between access to justice, good governance and democratic validity, these indicator frameworks speak to the question: is the rule of law increasing globally? Through the data collected and subsequently analysed, these indicators are used to indicate and signal a way to assess the state of justice and legal institutions around the world.[4] In doing so, as I will discuss in the course of this book, these indicators acquire considerable power through their ability to frame, highlight and make concepts knowable that are otherwise abstract and theoretical.[5]

The processes of building indicators for measuring justice systems raise several critical issues, such as the role that they play to build a global law project, which would aspire to establish common rules and universal guidelines for the functioning of dispute resolution systems.[6] The methods through which these tools are standardized as unambiguous measures for otherwise complex and dynamic problems raise questions about the power

---

[2] Please note that the terms 'measurement frameworks', 'quantification tools' and 'indicators' are used interchangeably in this book.

[3] 'Justice systems' and 'legal systems' are used interchangeably in this book to relate to the different types of institutions, users, procedures and values that make up the system through which justice is delivered.

[4] Sally Engle Merry, 'Measuring the World: Indicators, Human Rights, and Global Governance', *Current Anthropology* 52 (2011): S83–S95.

[5] Steffen Mau, *The Metric Society: On the Quantification of the Social* (Cambridge: John Wiley & Sons, 2019); Sally Engle Merry, *The Seductions of Quantification: Measuring Human Rights, Gender Violence, and Sex Trafficking* (Chicago: University of Chicago Press, 2016); Debora Valentina Malito, Gaby Umbach and Nehal Bhuta (eds.), *The Palgrave Handbook of Indicators in Global Governance* (Cham: Springer, 2017).

[6] Benoît Frydman and William Twining, 'A Symposium on Global Law, Legal Pluralism and Legal Indicators', *The Journal of Legal Pluralism and Unofficial Law* 47, no. 1 (2015): 1–8.

relations at play between those measuring and those being measured.[7] A poor conceptualization of indicators also has implications at a political, economic and social level, since they are not just instruments of knowledge but also instruments of governance.[8] These implications can be seen in the way human rights violations are identified, the quantum of foreign aid to be given is determined in development programming, and how justice sector reforms are recommended.[9] Researching these frameworks will give us an idea into how the methodology and concepts used in the indicators are developed, how the information from the indicators is applied, and how the data and findings influence the proposals for reforming the delivery of justice and legal institutions around the world.

Indicators from the bottom up

This book addresses the study of legal indicator frameworks as they relate to contexts of plural legal orders consisting of state and non-state justice systems. Through its attention to debates of legal pluralism, the book inquires whether existing indicator frameworks perpetuate a particular notion of a well-functioning justice system and investigates whether these

---

[7] Merry, 'Measuring the World'; Kevin Davis, Angelina Fisher, Benedict Kingsbury and Sally Engle Merry (eds.), *Governance by Indicators: Global Power through Classification and Rankings* (Oxford: Oxford University Press, 2012); Richard Rottenburg, Sally E. Merry, Sung-Joon Park and Johanna Mugler (eds.), *The World of Indicators: The Making of Governmental Knowledge Through Quantification* (Cambridge: Cambridge University Press, 2015).

[8] See generally Kevin E. Davis, Benedict Kingsbury and Sally Engle Merry, 'Introduction: Global Governance by Indicators', in *Governance by Indicators: Global Power through Quantification and Rankings*, ed. Kevin Davis, Angelina Fisher, Benedict Kingsbury and Sally Engle Merry, 3–28 (Oxford: Oxford University Press, 2012).

[9] Merry, 'Measuring the World'. See generally Sally Engle Merry, Kevin E. Davis and Benedict Kingsbury (eds.), *The Quiet Power of Indicators: Measuring Governance, Corruption, and Rule of Law* (Cambridge: Cambridge University Press, 2015). In Chapters 2–3, I will examine the impacts that indicators have as instruments of governance and knowledge and how they are used by international organizations, development agencies and civil society organizations to develop policies and programs as part of their development efforts. These include organizing capacity-building training for legal officials, developing new legal and administrative procedures and designing new institutions.

indicators advance a state-centric form of measurement grounded in western normative considerations. The book explores whether legal indicators are able to capture local legal systems that already exist in plural legal orders or whether the targets and values that they prescribe are inapplicable to the contexts of plural legal worlds. The book offers an alternative path to developing indicators that maps the experiences and realities of justice users and how they resolve their grievances through plural and competing dispute resolution processes.

In the ensuing chapters, I explore whether the current discourse on legal indicators offers holistic articulations of how justice systems function or, if instead, it offers an institutional approach to justice that does not take sufficient account of the aspirations of the justice user. I will also explore how procedural and substantive considerations of justice are balanced when evaluating justice systems through indicators, and if these indicators also account for the cultural considerations that arise in plural legal orders.

A core aspect of this book is to examine how indicators capture the legal needs of people from plural legal orders and countries in the Global South by examining the language, concepts, ideas and narratives that emerge from these regions.[10] I will explore the realities of how the law and dispute resolution work in practice in contrast with how they are constructed in existing indicator frameworks. In doing so, I seek to study whether the indicators construct standards that reflect a global consciousness or whether they instead seek to impose a particular jurisprudential discourse that perpetuates certain norms and institutions.

In the course of the book, I reflect on how indicators and metrics have become pervasive in the shaping of understandings of legal systems. In this context of the widespread use of indicators, I argue that it is important to not just critique indicators but persist and offer a different strategy to show that the construction of indicators can be developed to account for plural and diverse legal contexts and social worlds. This is why I introduce the idea of persistence in the book, which is a strategy to engage with dominant

---

[10] I will examine the Global South as a political and epistemic space which is in contestation with the Global North over what is valuable, significant, inclusive and fair. It is relational. Because there is a Global North, there is a Global South. As a space, it is where the marginalized and invisibilized acquire voice and dignity in distinct and multifaceted ways. Therefore it is not a geographical area but a philosophy of justice with a plurality of knowledge and lived experiences.

understandings of indicators, and offer a different framing that aims to be more representative and inclusive. I do this by arguing that more diverse and varied voices and concepts must be included which pluralize the conversation around legal indicator frameworks and find place in their development. In doing so, I argue for building indicators that are built in a more grounded and reflexive manner, and that integrate the messiness of how it is realised.

This book unfolds through three steps of analysis to address the following central aims:

1 It examines the impacts of quantification in law, and how indicators have emerged as an important device and vocabulary for understanding legal systems.
2 It discusses the lack of an engagement with questions of legal pluralism and epistemologies of the South in the development of legal indicators, and how this results in a myopic understanding of how legal systems function in diverse contexts.
3 It draws together the above and recommends a bottom-up framing of indicators to advance an approach of measuring access to justice in resolving disputes by using a Justice Capabilities Framework.

After a brief introduction to signpost some of the arguments for the use of indicators in the law, I provide brief explorations of the three steps of analysis in this book.

Indicators and the law

A key argument for the use of indicators in law is that both within the same jurisdiction and between jurisdictions there is a lack of vocabulary and tools for comparison to understand and evaluate the institutional challenges that constrain the delivery of justice. This includes the efficiency of judges, independence of courts, experiences of users, and accountability and transparency of procedures and practices in these institutions. Indicators help evolve a 'common understanding' and a 'shared sense' of the complexities and challenges that confront a legal systems by determining the contours of terms such as 'access to justice' and 'rule of law', and establishing how such concepts can be measured.[11] A crucial aspect to this process is to

---

[11] Canadian Bar Association, 'Access to Justice Metrics: A Discussion Paper', 2013, http://www.cba.org/CBAMediaLibrary/cba_na/images/Equal%20Justice%20-%20

understand if it is possible to 'make access to justice a quantifiable concept instead of a broad aspiration'.[12] This ability to standardize multifaceted phenomena unambiguously and impersonally, by labelling and naming them, is one of the key influences and powers of an indicator.[13]

The rise in legal indicators can be attributed, among other things, to the increased globalization of legal systems, the universalization of human rights, increasing judicial borrowing and donor investment in building legal systems, and a more economic and management based outlook to the functioning of legal systems.[14] With the globalization of legal systems, indicators are used as devices to justify the pollination, and in most cases transplantation of ideas and values, because of the perception of their rigour and neutrality.[15] As Porter has argued, 'quantification is well suited for communication that goes beyond the boundaries of locality and community', and hence it can logically be seen as a technical tool to further a particular project in different contexts.[16] In this regard, one part of this technical outlook, which will be developed later in this book, is the role of formalism in law, and how the prominence of the state in legal systems and its ways of regulating and governing have an influence on the development of legal indicators and their subsequent use in evaluation.[17]

Microsite/PDFs/Access_to_Justice_Metrics.pdf (accessed 28 September 2018).

[12] Martin Gramatikov, Maurits Barendrecht and Jin Ho Verdonschot, 'Measuring the Costs and Quality of Paths to Justice: Contours of a Methodology', *Hague Journal on the Rule of Law* 3 (2011): 349–379.

[13] Nehal Bhuta, Debora Valentina Malito and Gaby Umbach, 'Introduction: Of Numbers and Narratives—Indicators in Global Governance and the Rise of a Reflexive Indicator Culture', in *The Palgrave Handbook of Indicators in Global Governance*, edited by Debora Valentina Malito, Gaby Umbach and Nehal Bhuta, 1–29 (Cham: Springer, 2017); Merry, Davis and Kingsbury, *The Quiet Power of Indicators*.

[14] Tor Krever, 'Quantifying Law: Legal Indicator Projects and the Reproduction of Neoliberal Common Sense', *Third World Quarterly* 34, no. 1 (2013): 131–150. In Chapters 2–4, I will examine how indicators are playing an increasing role in impacting how decisions are being made due to their capacity to influence how information is framed and distributed.

[15] See generally Malito, Umbach and Bhuta, *The Palgrave Handbook of Indicators*.

[16] Theodore M. Porter, 'Preface', in *Trust in Numbers: The Pursuit of Objectivity in Science and Public Life*, vii–xii (Princeton: Princeton University Press, 1995), ix.

[17] David Restrepo Amariles, 'Legal Indicators, Global Law and Legal Pluralism: An Introduction', *The Journal of Legal Pluralism and Unofficial Law* 47, no. 1 (2015): 9–21.

The first large-scale projects of building legal indicators began around the 1970s where Merryman and Friedman, in association with the United States Agency for International Development (USAID), attempted to understand how law and legal institutions functioned in the development process. They sought to build 'a new body of theory and method—a "social science" of law and development—to provide the intellectual framework for effective study, research and understanding'.[18] One of the objectives of the project was to study legal systems quantitatively.[19] From the 1980s, the World Bank began developing measurement tools with the purpose of promoting neo-liberal markets, increasing fiscal discipline, free trade and limited state intervention through projects such as the Country Policy and Institutional Assessment exercise, which is a planning tool to assess a country's effectiveness in utilizing development assistance.[20] In its framework, it conceived of law as being a tool for economic development and offered a comparative and quantifiable study of legal systems around the world by focussing, at a macro level, on whether legal systems protected property rights and ensured legal certainty.[21] More recently, projects such as the ease of doing business index and the governance indicators of the World Bank, where the functioning and measurement of legal reform are seen from the purview of governance, have increasingly been used as illustrations of how the rule of law is conceived. These frameworks are used as benchmarks in order to evaluate the regulatory environment for business activity as well as the deficit in governance measured in terms of accountability and transparency. However, with the growth of a policy impetus on the rule of law being essential for economic growth and the eradication of poverty and sustainable development,[22] the rule of law is

---

[18] John Henry Merryman, 'Law and Development Memoirs II: SLADE', *The American Journal of Comparative Law* 48, no. 4 (2000): 713–727.

[19] Ibid.

[20] David Restrepo Amariles, 'Transnational Legal Indicators: The Missing Link in a New Era of Law and Development', in *Law and Policy in Latin America*, ed. Pedro Borges Fortes, Larissa Boratti, Andres Palacios Lleras and Tom Gerald Daly, 95–111 (London: Palgrave Macmillan, 2016).

[21] Ibid. See also Philipp Dann, 'Institutional Law and Development Governance: An Introduction', *Law and Development Review* 12, no. 2 (2019): 537–560.

[22] United Nations General Assembly, 'Declaration of the High-Level Meeting of the General Assembly on the Rule of Law at the National and International Level A/

now also being seen as an end in itself.[23] As a concept, therefore, the rule of law is now being understood as a measurable value that can be studied independently rather than as a subset of governance or democracy.[24]

From this discussion, I wish to show—through particular episodes—how law has been increasingly quantified and a vocabulary has emerged around it.[25] In the following chapters, I will conduct an assessment of six prominent indicators that measure the rule of law, which are developed by different organizations: the World Justice Project Rule of Law Index, the Democracy Barometer, the World Bank Worldwide Governance Indicators, the United Nations Rule of Law Indicators, the Ibrahim Index of African Governance, and the Hague Model of Access to Justice. The assessment of these indicators will provide an insight into how the rule of law is conceptualized in these different tools, as well as explore the methods through which data are collected and assessed. In analysing these factors, I will investigate whether certain qualities of justice systems are idealized and given prominence over others, and what the implications of such decisions can be on evaluating the institutions and people's experiences with justice in resolving disputes.

The impacts of quantification in law

In order to understand the impact of quantification, the book investigates the advancement of indicator frameworks that have emerged as critical vocabulary for understanding concepts such as the rule of law, access to

---

Res/67/1', 2012, A/Res/67/1, https://www.un.org/ruleoflaw/files/A-RES-67-1.pdf (accessed 7 May 2020).

[23] David M. Trubek and Alvaro Santos, 'Introduction: The Third Moment in Law and Development Theory and the Emergence of a New Critical Practice', in *The New Law and Economic Development: A Critical Appraisal*, ed. David M. Trubek and Alvaro Santos, 1–18 (Cambridge: Cambridge University Press, 2006).

[24] René Urueña, 'Indicators and the Law: A Case Study of the Rule of Law Index', in *The Quiet Power of Indicators: Measuring Governance, Corruption, and Rule of Law*, ed. Sally Engle Merry, Kevin E Davis and Benedict Kingsbury, 75–102 (Cambridge: Cambridge University Press 2015).

[25] This book does not seek to provide a history of legal indicators but rather a socio-legal exploration of the use and impact of these tools as they relate to contexts of legal pluralism.

justice, freedom, governance and democracy and in evaluating how legal systems function across the world.

Through an examination of the concepts and methods that indicators adopt, this book will study the politics that indicators promote and the silences that are reinforced as a result of their development and deployment. It will also ask questions about the narratives that emerge from these indicator frameworks and the impact that such narratives have on law and development reform. For instance, if legal indicators are designed to capture the data that focuses on factors such as the number of cases pending, the number of judges per population, the speediness with which cases are resolved, the independence and accountability of judicial institutions and the resources allocated for the judiciary, then through such factors one can deduce that there is an emphasis on rule-of-law institutions and how they function. This hypothetical indicator, for instance, would explore how institutions work, how effective the administration is and what the hindrances and barriers to justice are, as seen from the supply side or an institutional perspective. This empirical evidence would, in turn, determine how policy makers who use indicators should respond. I study such lifecycles of indicators and examine the impact they have on the people, institutions and regulations that are influenced by them.

A starting point of this exploration is to examine the key arguments that critics of the use of quantification in the law have raised, and review these critiques through an analysis of how indicators project particular meanings, offer a sense of trust, and have the power to influence actions and decisions.[26] I have sought to systematize different critical perspectives on indicators because these offer an important vocabulary for the evaluation of different challenges, whether in terms of power structures, epistemological diversity or policy application that emerge through the construction, development and deployment of indicators. This thematic organization of the challenges of indicators is purposeful, as I seek to engage with the concerns that indicators bring and use this as a basis to offer a response. After offering a more general critique of indicators, I then move into specific concerns that emerge in the use of legal indicators for contexts with legal pluralism.

---

[26] Chapter 2 provides an overview of different critiques based on previous work that examined how indicators impact and influence ways of seeing and knowing the world.

The absence of an engagement with legal pluralism

For numerous people living around the world, transactions and interfaces with justice involve interacting with multiple legal systems that have different capacities, rules and criteria for legitimacy.[27] The existence of legal pluralism as a matter of ordinary practice has been a challenge for development practitioners for many years.[28] This is because it is seen as a limitation towards building societies based on a strong state and the rule of law. With the repeated failure of development interventions that focus on an institutional, top-down approach to justice reform, greater attention is now being paid to legal empowerment to better capture the heterogeneity of justice users.[29]

I engage with the concept of rule of law as it is designed in legal indicators and study whether it is productive as a framework and concept for measurement of dispute resolution in plural legal orders. I assess how the concept of rule of law has been used in development cooperation work, including the promotion of rule of law for judicial reform and institution building. I, thereafter, examine a turn to legal pluralism in development cooperation work and the implication that this has for the concept of the rule of law.[30] I argue that debates on the rule of law in the context of law and development reform will also have an impact on discussions surrounding

---

[27] John Griffiths, 'What Is Legal Pluralism?', *The Journal of Legal Pluralism and Unofficial Law* 18, no. 24 (1986): 1–55.

[28] Brian Z. Tamanaha, Caroline Sage and Michael Woolcock (eds.), *Legal Pluralism and Development: Scholars and Practitioners in Dialogue* (Cambridge: Cambridge University Press, 2012); Julio Faundez, 'Legal Pluralism and International Development Agencies: State Building or Legal Reform?', *Hague Journal on the Rule of Law* 3, no. 1 (2011): 18–38.

[29] Brian Z. Tamanaha, 'Introduction: A Bifurcated Theory of Law in Hybrid Societies', in *Non-State Justice Institutions and the Law: Decision-Making at the Interface of Tradition, Religion and the State*, ed. M. Kötter, Tilmann J. Röder, Gunnar Folke Schuppert and Rüdiger Wolfrum, 1–21 (London: Springer, 2015); Peter Albrecht and Helena Maria Kyed, 'Introduction: Non-State and Customary Actor in Developing Programs', in *Perspectives on Involving Non-State and Customary Actors in Justice and Security Reform*, ed. Peter Albrecht, Helene Maria Kyed, Deborah Isser and Erica Harper, 3–22 (Rome: IDLO and DIIS, 2011).

[30] Ronald Janse, 'A Turn to Legal Pluralism in Rule of Law Promotion?', *Erasmus Law Review* 6 (2013): 181–190.

legal indicators because these tools are used to evaluate justice systems globally.[31]

Consequently, I deconstruct how the rule of law is described in legal indicators to offer an analysis about their utility to evaluate plural legal orders.[32] In terms of legal indicators, I explore whether the conceptualization of the rule of law is limited to encoded civil and criminal law or whether it also includes other forms of law such as religious, traditional or community law, and how effective this broader concept is to work with. An understanding of the application of the concept of rule of law, whether described to cover the maintenance of law and order or more broadly cover issues of accountability, non-arbitrariness and human rights standards,[33] offers an exploration into what could constitute a shared sense and set of values that can then be transferable and meaningful across social and cultural contexts.

I examine how the rule of law as a concept places an overwhelming importance on the presence and influence of the state and whether this institution's role in the delivery of justice sometimes monopolizes the conceptualization of legal indicators. In connection with this, the roles different communities and space play in influencing norms accepted in the administration of justice, and whether these influences are included in an understanding of the rule of law indicators and in choosing its factors are also discussed. In investigating the rule of law as a concept, I also explore the potential for access to justice to be a more expansive concept, within which indicators for measuring how disputes are resolved in plural legal systems can be built. In this context, the book analyses whether access to justice can focus not just on institutions like the state, but also on people and their experiences, and by doing so, explore ways in which justice is realized beyond the state-centred

---

[31] Merry, 'Measuring the World'; Frydman and Twining, 'A Symposium on Global Law'.

[32] I draw from Ralf Michaels' arguments of the role that 'law', the 'state', the 'community' and finally 'space' play in a resolution of disputes in plural legal systems. See Ralf Michaels, 'Global Legal Pluralism', *Annual Review of Law and Social Science* 5, no. 1 (2009): 243–262.

[33] See generally Wolfgang Merkel, 'Measuring the Quality of Rule of Law', in *Rule of Law Dynamics: In an Era of International and Transnational Governance*, ed. Michael Zürn, André Nollkaemper and Randy Peerenboom, 21–47 (Cambridge: Cambridge University Press, 2012); Martin Krygier, 'The Rule of Law: Legality, Teleology, Sociology', in *Relocating the Rule of Law*, ed. Gianluigi Palombella and Neil Walker, 45–70 (London: Hart Publishing, 2008).

justice system. To do this, the notion of access to justice as a framework that can capture the anxieties, claims and capabilities of different people as they resolve a dispute and evaluate the different stages of a dispute resolution process will be developed.

Building indicators from below

An interesting conclusion from the Task Force on Justice report that quantified the justice gap was the turn towards a more bottom-up approach to understanding which justice problems matter most to people, finding ways for greater participation of people in socio-economic life, and investing in systems and institutions that respond to the justice needs of people.[34] This focus on capturing bottom-up narratives and user stories is one that is critical to the re-imagination of a legal indicator framework offered in this book. In the following chapters, I look at how indicators can be constructed so that the framing of legal needs reflects divergent narratives and also takes into account different concepts and values in a dispute resolution process that are central to understanding justice at a global level.

I argue that this approach is necessary because although global legal indicators are constructed with the purpose of meeting transferable global standards, this does not often materialize. In addition to the place of legal pluralism in the design of indicators, as I will argue subsequently, the struggles of people are not adequately represented in terms of how they negotiate the resolution of their disputes. I will investigate how—in a move towards developing indicators that are transferable and global—values, concepts and struggles that exist outside state-centric legal systems are not given prominence. As a result, the idea that law can be approached beyond its technocratic constructs and its formal institutional frameworks is not given adequate weight in the design of legal indicators, and neither is the perspective and experiences of the justice user.

Through focussing on experiences from the bottom up, and by placing emphasis on the demand perspectives of users, which is what users experience in the justice delivery process, this book poses the challenge of whether it is possible for the legal struggles of a plural legal world to be captured and reflected in a legal indicator framework. I explore this through the development of a framework to measure and understand how people

---

[34] Task Force on Justice, *Justice for All Report*, 69.

engage with barriers to access to justice given the institutions and other constraints that limit their choices. This book argues that it is important to choose methods in the development of legal indicators that allow for policy interventions that are contextual and reflective of a global plurality, and that respond to the legal struggles in people's lives.

Drawing on the capability approach of Amartya Sen and of Martha Nussbaum, I aim to build a framework to track the different capabilities that would enable an individual to have better and more meaningful access to justice while resolving their disputes in plural legal orders.[35] With a need to understand how disputes are resolved in their plurality, the book will explore the choices people make when they resolve a dispute and the experiences they face throughout various stages of a dispute resolution process. In this regard, I suggest that the measurement of justice is not just about the efficiency of institutions and the administration of justice but also about the choices justice users make and the capabilities that they require to find resolutions to their grievances. The proposed framework will examine ways to focus on people instead of institutions, and places emphasis on their needs, which impact their security, stability and safety of a dispute resolution process.

Questions, design and challenges

The book raises the following questions: first, what is the role of quantification and indicators in law, legal systems and legal reform, and how can we understand the impact of these tools on the social worlds around us. Second, how do indicators influence the nature of rule-of-law programmes, in particular its promotion around the world. Consequently, the book flags the important need to deconstruct the rule of law as a concept in itself, and to examine its productiveness for legal indicators. Third, at an epistemological level, it explores how we can infiltrate the dominant vocabulary of legal indicators that is from institutions in the Global North to represent voices from the Global South. Fourth, it asks who we measure for when we measure how disputes are resolved in legal systems, and how we can understand the plural nature of choices before individuals when

---

[35] Amartya Sen, 'Introduction: Development as Freedom', in *Development as Freedom*, 3–12 (Oxford: Oxford University Press, 2001); Martha Nussbaum and Amartya Sen, *The Quality of Life* (Oxford: Oxford University Press, 1993).

they use legal systems. Fifth, it asks whether it is possible to represent the resolution of legal disputes as a messy, contested process, rather than one that is neatly categorized in institutional offerings, and if so, how such a framework can be developed.

To achieve these goals, the book adopts a multi-layered strategy, where it deals with conceptual, empirical as well as epistemological questions.[36] It is an interdisciplinary project that draws from literature in law, sociology, development studies and design, and seeks to integrate these different perspectives to offer a more rounded perspective of justice measurement.[37] This is because the nature of the question of quantification and its implication on law and social worlds requires several lenses for investigation.[38] This book examines and deconstructs prominent legal indicator frameworks that undergird these assessment tools in terms of the concepts employed and the methodology used, and seeks to understand whether the legal indicator frameworks reflect the aspirations and challenges of people and the barriers to justice they encounter in their everyday lives.

Due to the intersecting nature of the questions, the book draws from understandings in legal theory of concepts such as the rule of law, the nature of law and the ways in which legal systems coexist in plural societies with differing levels of authority and legitimacy. In order to draw on these debates, the book adopts a socio-legal exploration of law, institutions and practices in their social, economic and political contexts.[39] It goes beyond doctrinal constructs of texts and rules to instead investigate how the law is shaped in its interactions with societies and how it in turn shapes the organization of societies.[40] During this foray into the social worlds of the

---

[36] See generally Boaventura de Sousa Santos, *Toward a New Legal Common Sense: Law, Globalization, and Emancipation* (Cambridge: Cambridge University Press, 2002).

[37] Sanne Taekema and Wibren van der Burg, 'The Incorporation Problem in Interdisciplinary Legal Research, Part 1: Theoretical Discussions', *Erasmus Law Review* 8, no. 2 (2015): 39–42.

[38] William H. Newell, 'A Theory of Interdisciplinary Studies', *Issues in Integrative Studies* 19 (2001): 1–25, https://our.oakland.edu/handle/10323/4378 (accessed 4 December 2020).

[39] See generally Naomi Creutzfeldt, Marc Mason and Kirsten McConnachie, *Routledge Handbook of Socio-Legal Theory and Methods* (Oxon: Routledge, 2019).

[40] Reza Banakar and Max Travers, 'Introduction to Theory and Method in Socio-Legal Research', Social Science Research Network, 2005, SSRN Scholarly Paper ID 1511112, https://papers.ssrn.com/abstract=1511112 (accessed 18 February 2018).

law, an opportunity arises to explore the nature of the interactions that take place between individuals and institutions.[41] This is particularly important because the book examines the many ways in which legal indicator frameworks construct and impact the world they inhabit, and how their development and deployment have far-reaching consequences.[42]

For this purpose, this book relies on design theory, where prominence is given to the justice user and the criticality of user-centeredness in legal systems.[43] This is important since one of the departures in this book is that when thinking about the law we must think not just of the text and the institutions that give it power and sanction, but shift our focus to people and their ways of using the legal system.[44] Design offers an opportunity to think in terms of what is valuable to an individual (both as a single person and in interactions with the community) when they navigate a legal system.[45] It offers an exploration of what is useful and usable when resolving a legal dispute as seen from the perspective of the person who finds it most urgent and necessary.[46] As Escobar has argued, we need to design in a manner that we are able to fit together many worlds.[47] If we do this, many life and social worlds, which were erased through colonialism and other hierarchies of power, are represented through acknowledging different space and time.[48]

---

[41] Lisa Hahn and Siddharth de Souza, 'Self-Reflecting, Constructing and Positioning: Intersecting Debates in Socio-Legal Studies', Rechtswirklichkeit, 14 March 2019, https://barblog.hypotheses.org/2988 (accessed 7 December 2020).

[42] See generally Roger Cotterrell, 'Why Must Legal Ideas Be Interpreted Sociologically?', Journal of Law and Society 25, no. 2 (June 1998): 171–192.

[43] See generally Donald A. Norman, 'The Psychopathology of Everyday Things', in The Design of Everyday Things, 1–36 (New York: Basic Books, 1990).

[44] Siddharth Peter de Souza, 'Towards a User-Centered Engagement with Law', Südasien-Chronik/South Asia Chronicle 2018, no. 8 (2019): 238–291, https://edoc.hu-berlin.de/handle/18452/20489 (accessed 31 July 2019).

[45] Amanda Perry-Kessaris, 'Legal Design for Practice, Activism, Policy, and Research', Journal of Law and Society 46, no. 2 (June 2019): 185–210.

[46] Margaret Hagan, 'Legal Design as a Thing: A Theory of Change and a Set of Methods to Craft a Human-Centered Legal System', Design Issues 36, no. 3 (2020): 3–15.

[47] Arturo Escobar, Designs for the Pluriverse: Radical Interdependence, Autonomy, and the Making of Worlds (Durham: Duke University Press, 2018).

[48] Boaventura de Sousa Santos, 'Legal Plurality and the Time-Spaces of Law: The Local, the National, and the Global', in Toward a New Legal Common Sense: Law, Globalization, and Emancipation, 99–120 (Cambridge: Cambridge University Press 2002).

This book will reflect on the idea of design justice, which is understood as a method to 'rethink design processes, (to) center peoples who are normally marginalized by design and uses collaborative, creative practices to address the deepest challenges our communities face'.[49] Drawing on this idea, the book offers an approach to measuring justice that is grounded in a framework that elevates voices, concepts and experiences that are not afforded sufficient prominence in macro-level institutional approaches to evaluating justice systems.

Much of the research for this book has involved examining secondary material. This allowed a mapping of the existing theoretical landscape for conceptions of the rule of law and access to justice to document the realities of plural legal systems, identify the basis for an audit culture in law, explore the legal needs of people around the world and consider the technicalities that come into play when operationalizing the capability approach. The book, therefore, builds on the existing literature but attempts also to introduce new keywords, through which the debate on quantification in law can be understood within a more inclusive and plural framework. At an epistemological level, it begins by examining the power of these indicator frameworks and their use in silencing, marginalizing and subsuming significant legal populations. It does so by drawing on research at the intersection of law and development. At an empirical level, because the book also offers to build a new indicator framework, it examines data from legal needs surveys,[50] which are surveys that help understand where people go when they resolve disputes and what challenges they encounter. It draws on many ethnographic case studies of non-state justice systems (NSJS) in order to illustrate how plural legal systems operate. The book looks at a wide variety of cases of NSJS around the world, ranging from cross-country studies to single-site ethnographic works.[51] These cases offer

---

[49] 'Read the Principles', Design Justice Network, https://designjustice.org/read-the-principles (accessed 4 May 2020). See also Sasha Costanza-Chock, *Design Justice: Community-Led Practices to Build the Worlds We Need* (Cambridge, MA: MIT Press, 2020).

[50] Pascoe Pleasence and Nigel Balmer, *Legal Needs Surveys and Access to Justice* (Paris: OECD, 2018), https://iris.ucl.ac.uk/iris/publication/1620815/1 (accessed 7 August 2019); HiiL, 'HiiL Justice Dashboard: Justice Data at Your Fingertips', https://justice-dashboard.hiil.org/ (accessed 6 May 2020).

[51] These are systems based on religion, custom, community and tradition that engage with the state at different levels of recognition. These include studies such as Danish Institute for Human Rights, 'Informal Justice Systems: Charting a Course for Human

rich diversities, values and criteria of how disputes are resolved in forums within and outside the state. Additionally, constitutions that consider legal pluralism, and engage with it in practice, are also studied to examine the nature of different legal systems.

India is used as a case study to illustrate the argument for a different kind of quantification tool.[52] As an illustration, India allows for three possibilities: first, to examine how contestations, bargaining and competing choices play out for users in a plural legal system; second, to track what data is being collected; and third, to offer a picture that captures both the dominant narrative as well as its subversions because of India's colonial history and the resistances to it.

This book, therefore, provides a framework to think about, critically question and creatively rework the abundance of existing material on indicators and assessment tools, and the conceptual frameworks underpinning them. It provides the groundwork and methodological approach for measuring access to justice in plural legal contexts and the tools for its application. The goal of the framework is also to be useful for policy design when engaging in rule of law reform and to be reflexive and cognizant of the epistemic pluralities around how law is materialised.

Structure of the book

As this book aims to build an alternative framework for legal indicators, the key starting point of the study is to investigate the different critical

---

Rights-Based Engagement', UNDP, UNICEF and UN Women, 2013, http://www.undp.org/content/undp/en/home/librarypage/democratic-governance/access_to_justiceandruleoflaw/informal-justice-systems.html (accessed 7 December 2017); Kalindi Kokal, *State Law, Dispute Processing and Legal Pluralism: Unspoken Dialogues from Rural India* (London: Routledge, 2019); M. Kötter, Tilmann J. Röder, Gunnar Folke Schuppert and Rüdiger Wolfrum (eds.), *Non-State Justice Institutions and the Law: Decision-Making at the Interface of Tradition, Religion and the State* (London: Springer 2015); Mark Goodale, *Anthropology and Law: A Critical Introduction* (New York: NYU Press, 2017); Fernanda Pirie, *The Anthropology of Law* (Oxford: Oxford University Press, 2013); Miranda Forsyth, *A Bird That Flies with Two Wings: Kastom and State Justice Systems in Vanuatu* (Canberra: ANU E Press, 2009).

[52] Chapter 4 provides a detailed assessment of how justice is measured in the Indian context.

perspectives on indicators. Chapter 2, '"Meanings", "Trust" and "Power": Critical Perspectives on Legal Indicators', defines legal indicators and briefly looks at how, and for what purposes, these frameworks have emerged. It will provide a detailed reflection of the various meanings that can be found when looking at indicators. It discusses the trust that numbers and quantification generate by examining notions of reliability. It also questions the implications that follow the standardization of contested concepts. It showcases the power of indicators to influence policy ad behaviours through numbers.

Chapter 3, 'Rule of Law Promotion, Legal Indicators and Legal Pluralism', locates the study of legal indicators within a discussion of rule of law promotion. It explores how rule of law reform has emerged as a technocratic framework that attempts to transplant particular ideas and frameworks across the world and cautions about the limitations of such an approach. Legal pluralism, and the presence of contesting legal systems, represents an important fulcrum in the disposal of disputes, particularly in the Global South. The chapter investigates how the concept of rule of law travels in plural legal systems. It also provides illustrations from cases of rule of law indices to show how these frameworks offer an incomplete narrative on the state of justice delivery because they do not consider questions of legal pluralism and ideas of justice from the Global South. Thereafter, the chapter argues why it may be productive to engage with the concept of access to justice and the challenge that arises when multifaceted meanings are attached to an understanding of the concept. It makes connections between legal pluralism and access to justice, and offers a distinct way of defining the concept in contexts where there are multiple actors, forums and authorities that claim legitimacy for the resolution of legal disputes.

The main argument of Chapter 4, 'Epistemic Diversity and Voices from the Global South: Countering the Managerial Implications of Measuring Justice', is for the need to build contextual indicators, which, rather than imposing a standardization of complex phenomena, instead attempt to integrate the messiness of law in action into the framework. By offering arguments that counter the managerial aspects of indicators through a case study from India, this chapter sets out to offer a bridge that addresses the views of the critiques while also offering a conceptual method for building plural legal indicators that are conscious of different epistemologies of knowledge, and that acknowledge legal pluralism.

While the previous three chapters have, in different ways, challenged indicators and their role in development, Chapter 5, 'A Capability Approach to Access to Justice in Plural Legal Systems', builds on these foundations to develop a framework of indicators, which considers legal pluralism as a central influence for understanding access to justice through the lens of the capability approach. It explores the transition from measuring institutional performance to assessing user capabilities and identifies a basic set of capabilities that can help transform different stages of the dispute resolution process through operationalizing the capabilities approach. It then goes on to develop a Justice Capabilities Framework (JCF) that is conscious of people's experiences, needs and aspirations, and examines how such framework works when navigating and resolving disputes.

Chapter 6, 'Conclusion', draws together and presents the key arguments and contributions from this research on measuring justice in a plural legal world at three levels—methodological, epistemological and substantive. It concludes by offering a future agenda for action.

2

'Meanings', 'Trust' and 'Power'

Critical Perspectives on Legal Indicators

In late 2017, India climbed a sharp 30 places in the World Bank's Ease of Doing Business rankings.[1] The rankings were discussed and celebrated as testament to the manner in which the Indian government, under Prime Minister Narendra Modi, had effected policy change to improve the trade, tax and economic climate in the country.[2] The prime minister himself tweeted that it was the outcome of a multi-sectoral reform agenda of his government.[3] A few months later, the Centre for Global Development (CGD) produced a study, which stated that India's rise in the rankings was closely related to a change in the methodology adopted by the World Bank rather

---

[1] World Bank, *Doing Business 2018: Reforming to Create Jobs*, 2018, https://www. doingbusiness.org/content/dam/doingBusiness/media/Annual-Reports/English/ DB2018-Full-Report.pdf (accessed 17 December 2020).

[2] 'Big Thumbs-up to Modinomics: India Jumps 30 Places to 100th Rank in Ease of Doing Business Report', *Economic Times*, 31 October 2017, https://economictimes.indiatimes. com/news/economy/indicators/big-thumbs-up-to-modinomics-india-jumps-30-places-to-100th-rank-in-ease-of-doing-business-report/articleshow/61363995. cms?from=mdr (accessed 17 December 2020).

[3] Chowkidar Narendra Modi (@narendramodi), 'Historic Jump in "Ease of Doing Business" Rankings Is the Outcome of the All-Round & Multi-Sectoral Reform Push of Team India', Twitter, 31 October 2017, https://twitter.com/narendramodi/ status/925371481437044737/photo/1?ref_src=twsrc%5Etfw%7Ctwcamp%5Etweete mbed%7Ctwterm%5E925371481437044737&ref_url=https%3A%2F%2Fwww.cgdev. org%2Fblog%2Fchange-world-bank-methodology-not-reform-explains-indias-rise-doing-business (accessed 16 May 2019).

than a result of sustained reform in India.[4] This study closely followed a rare admission by the former World Bank chief economist Paul Romer, who questioned the integrity of the Ease of Doing Business ranking, which he argued had been politically motivated. He spoke, in particular, of the case of Chile where the ranking appeared to favour Sebastian Pinera over Michele Bachelet in the presidential race.[5]

The CGD also showed that the fall in rankings of Chile during the time of Bachelet was due to methodological tinkering and not an outcome of any laws or policy changes by the government.[6] On recreating the Ease of Doing Business ranking using a consistent methodology and fixed sample of countries from 2006–2019, the study showed that the performance in Chile had in fact not been as volatile as in the official ranking.[7]

In both the instances of India and Chile, the rankings were seen as objective measures, backed by the influence of the World Bank. They were then used by political actors and rivals as election planks to dismiss rival political visions, performances and abilities to reform. The reasons for their use were that the rankings produced a sense of authenticity and certainty about the state of the country at that point in time. It provided a justification for making sense of the otherwise nebulous concept of 'ease of business' by creating criteria that could form a set of rankings. These cases illustrate how the use of numbers in the form of indicators have the power to tell stories,

---

[4] Justin Sandefur and Divyanshi Wadhwa, 'A Change in World Bank Methodology (Not Reform) Explains India's Rise in Doing Business Rankings', Center for Global Development, 5 February 2018, https://www.cgdev.org/blog/change-world-bank-methodology-not-reform-explains-indias-rise-doing-business (accessed 29 December 2018).

[5] Christopher Woody, 'The World Bank Says It Will Redo Its Competitiveness Rankings after Unfairly Influencing Them for Years', Business Insider, 13 January 2018, https://www.businessinsider.in/the-world-bank-says-it-will-redo-its-competitiveness-rankings-after-unfairly-influencing-them-for-years/articleshow/62491966.cms (accessed 29 December 2018); Michael Riegner, 'Cheating Chile', Völkerrechtsblog, 19 January 2018, https://voelkerrechtsblog.org/cheating-chile/ (accessed 29 December 2018).

[6] Justin Sandefur and Divyanshi Wadhwa, 'Chart of the Week #3: Why the World Bank Should Ditch the "Doing Business" Rankings—in One Embarrassing Chart', Center for Global Development, 18 January 2018, https://www.cgdev.org/blog/chart-week-3-why-world-bank-should-ditch-doing-business-rankings-one-embarrassing-chart (accessed 16 May 2019).

[7] Ibid.

build narratives and affect changes in behaviours—a matter that will be investigated further in this chapter.

Indicators have become a framework to communicate and organize different phenomenon that are often central to everyday life, whether matters of the economy, business, corruption, democracy, governance or human development.[8] These tools help to explain concepts and make them knowable by breaking down complex situations, making connections, and thereby reducing ambiguities by providing answers to otherwise fuzzy issues.[9] Indicators have been used as forms of evaluation because it is argued they offer objectivity and neutrality in their portrayal of different phenomena, which are then used to build consensus across several disparate stakeholders.[10] However, as the cases above demonstrate, the process of translation of concepts into acceptable standards is not one that takes place without debate or contestation, hidden and not so hidden political agendas and economic imperatives. The challenge, therefore, when studying indicators is not just with the choice of assumptions being made to build the indicators but also with the taxonomies institutions, resources and expertise that are used to support the development of these frameworks.[11]

What are these different influences when developing indicators and what are their points of conflict? Who are the stakeholders invested in quantification and what are their interests? How do these framers of indicators arrive at particular frameworks? What knowledge do they draw upon? What are the methods used to build indicators? Is there any scepticism

---

[8] Wendy Nelson Espeland and Mitchell L Stevens, 'A Sociology of Quantification', *European Journal of Sociology/Archives Européennes de Sociologie* 49, no. 3 (2008): 401–436.

[9] Richard Rottenburg and Sally Engle Merry, 'A World of Indicators: The Making of Governmental Knowledge through Quantification', in *The World of Indicators: The Making of Governmental Knowledge through Quantification*, ed. Richard Rottenburg, Sally E. Merry, Sung-Joon Park and Johanna Mugler, 1–33 (Cambridge: Cambridge University Press 2015).

[10] William Davies, 'Spirits of Neoliberalism: "Competitiveness" and "Wellbeing" Indicators as Rival Orders of Worth', in *The World of Indicators: The Making of Governmental Knowledge through Quantification*, ed. Richard Rottenburg, Sally E. Merry, Sung-Joon Park and Johanna Mugler, 283–306 (Cambridge: Cambridge University Press 2015).

[11] Rottenburg and Merry, 'A World of Indicators'; Sally Engle Merry, 'A World of Quantification', in *The Seductions of Quantification: Measuring Human Rights, Gender Violence, and Sex Trafficking*, 1–33 (Chicago: University of Chicago Press 2016).

voiced in the use of such quantifiable frameworks? How are these questions addressed? Addressing these questions demands examining political and social factors that impact the development of indicators.

The focus of this chapter is to synthesize the discussions on the use and the development of indicators as tools of construction, narration and knowledge generation. It aims to distil, from varied opinions, a composite critique outlining how existing assumptions, practices and philosophies around the use and spread of indicators have been questioned, and the different concerns raised during the lifecycle of the indicator. It goes without saying that there are diverse voices, many unique and distinct, that have interrogated indicators, and therefore even an exercise of assembling diverse views is bound by limitations. This chapter provides broad organizing themes to understand the direction of the critique and to suggest particular ways of unpacking it. From an examination of the literature, three aspects of 'meanings', 'trust' and 'power' embodied in legal indicators emerge as critical challenges in the discourse. These factors assume importance when one examines the networks of influence that indicators create at the time of their development, their use and impact thereafter, and will be discussed in the course of this chapter.

While there are many different types of indicators in use, the focus in this study will be on international or global legal indicators—those that are used for the measuring of human rights, the rule of law, governance and access to justice, among other factors. These are international in the sense that they are used to measure, in a comparative perspective, the performance of states and the functioning of their legal systems.[12] After an examination of these indicators, in later parts of this book, I will examine how effectively these indicator frameworks evaluate plural systems, and also how they incorporate epistemologies, values and concepts from the Global South. In undertaking this project, which examines the world of legal indicators and the effects of quantification, the goal is not just to map out the network that an indicator constructs but also to identify the implications that it has in knowledge generation, the impact on the constituency it serves and the broader politics of its use. Doing so will provide a platform on which to

---

[12] David Restrepo Amariles, 'Supping with the Devil? Indicators and the Rise of Managerial Rationality in Law', *International Journal of Law in Context* 13, no. 4 (2017): 465–484.

examine how to engage with indicators, both politically and pragmatically, as the later chapters will do.

The next section will briefly define an indicator, and in particular the forms of legal indicators and their networks, in the backdrop of what has been called an 'audit explosion' where there is a constant demand to evaluate.[13] The third section will explore the meanings and the symbolism behind indicators to foreground how such symbolism becomes critical. The fourth section will look at why there is trust in numbers, and what this means for associated aspects of transparency, accountability and fairness. The final section will introduce the idea of the power behind indicators and the different ways in which the use of indicators demands particular behaviours and responses.

The emergence of indicators

Cooley argues that three trends have led to the explosion of international ranking systems: the use of performance evaluation in social and political life, the increase in information technology and open data platforms, and the growth of global governance networks.[14] These factors are a result of living in a connected, globalized and regulated world. This chapter builds on the work of Merry[15] and Davis et al.,[16] who discuss the impact of indicators in terms of knowledge, which undergirds the naming and the development of categories, which then become lenses to assess the world, and through governance and regulation, which speaks of how indicators are tools of management and assessment through which countries are held to account for their performances. In the course of this section, I will provide

---

[13] Michael Power, *The Audit Explosion* (Oxford: Oxford University Press, 1999).

[14] Alexander Cooley, 'The Emerging Politics of International Rankings and Ratings', in *Ranking the World: Grading States as a Tool of Global Governance*, ed. Alexander Cooley and Jack Snyder (Cambridge: Cambridge University Press, 2015).

[15] Sally Engle Merry, *The Seductions of Quantification: Measuring Human Rights, Gender Violence, and Sex Trafficking* (Chicago: University of Chicago Press, 2016).

[16] Kevin E. Davis, Benedict Kingsbury and Sally Engle Merry, 'Introduction: The Local-Global Life of Indicators: Law, Power, and Resistance', in *The Quiet Power of Indicators: Measuring Governance, Corruption, and Rule of Law*, ed. Sally Engle Merry, Kevin E. Davis and Benedict Kingsbury, 1–24 (Cambridge: Cambridge University Press 2015).

definitions of indicators, examine some key aspects that influence their development and briefly outline some aspects of the influence of indicators.

Indicators as tools for comparing and description

Examining the word 'indicators' etymologically suggests that 'to indicate' is to point or to detect but not to explain, which is to mean that while indicators can provide a guide to action, they are not able to provide depth or detail.[17] This is reflected in the fact that indicators are built for the purpose of combining several elements together into one single statistic.[18] They attempt to transform multifaceted and complicated ideas into standardized measures by using principles of 'integration', where the sum of the parts provides greater value than individual elements, and 'parsimony', where there is an emphasis on clarity and simplicity.[19] Davis et al. have defined indicators as 'a named collection of rank-ordered data that purports to represent the past or projected performance of different units generated through a process that simplifies raw data about a complex social phenomenon.'[20] Indicators are tools of construction as well as description, which allows for representing, naming and comparing different worlds. In doing so, they give structure and make complex and messy phenomena knowable.[21]

Indicators offer an opportunity to evolve a common language through defining concepts to facilitate conversations in an otherwise multi-layered world. A key aspect of this is that they are able to produce commensurability, which is where a common metric is used for comparison between different

---

[17] Theodore M. Porter, 'The Flight of the Indicator', in *The World of Indicators: The Making of Governmental Knowledge through Quantification*, ed. Richard Rottenburg, Sally E. Merry, Sung-Joon Park and Johanna Mugler, 34–55 (Cambridge: Cambridge University Press 2015), 34.

[18] Martin Gramatikov and Malini Laxminarayan, 'Weighting Justice: Constructing an Index of Access to Justice' Tilburg University Legal Studies Working Paper No. 18/2008, 2009, https://papers.ssrn.com/abstract=1344418 (accessed 28 September 2018).

[19] Ibid.

[20] Davis, Kingsbury and Merry, 'Introduction', 6.

[21] Nehal Bhuta, Debora Valentina Malito and Gaby Umbach, 'Introduction: Of Numbers and Narratives—Indicators in Global Governance and the Rise of a Reflexive Indicator Culture', in *The Palgrave Handbook of Indicators in Global Governance*, edited by Debora Valentina Malito, Gaby Umbach and Nehal Bhuta, 1–29 (Cham: Springer, 2017).

units.[22] Indicators do so by providing equivalences where commonality is found despite difference through the use of categories that classify and encode particular phenomenon.[23] By creating equivalences across different aspects, building a classification about what, in a phenomenon, can be categorized and what cannot, and finally coding these individual cases into the categories, indicators enable data to be collected which can be compared.[24] This data is then used to represent a particular concept or phenomenon by embarking on a process of standardization and benchmarking, so that the concept can then be counted and evaluated.[25] For example, the Ease of Doing Business rankings examine aspects such as procedures for starting a business, getting credit, systems of taxation and investor protection, among others. By identifying these different factors, in essence the rankings are able to identify which factors are important when making an assessment of a country's business environment. This assessment thus makes an abstract concept actionable.[26] Indicators can play multiple roles, including judging the performance of different states, providing tools with which to monitor performance, tools with which to advocate change, and tools of branding and marketing.[27] Each of these roles can be seen in the cases of India and Chile on the Ease of Doing Business rankings where indicators, at different junctures, performed one of these functions: ranking India and Chile on a scale, suggesting whether their economies were worth

---

[22] Wendy Nelson Espeland and Mitchell L. Stevens, 'Commensuration as a Social Process', *Annual Review of Sociology* 24, no. 1 (1998): 313–343.

[23] Sally Engle Merry, 'Conclusions', in *The Seductions of Quantification: Measuring Human Rights, Gender Violence, and Sex Trafficking*, 207–222 (Chicago: University of Chicago Press 2016).

[24] Gramatikov and Laxminarayan, 'Weighting Justice'; Bhuta, Malito and Umbach, 'Introduction'.

[25] Espeland and Stevens, 'Commensuration as a Social Process'; Espeland and Stevens, 'A Sociology of Quantification; Alain Desrosières, 'Introduction: Arguing from Social Facts', in *The Politics of Large Numbers: A History of Statistical Reasoning*, 1–15 (Cambridge, MA: Harvard University Press, 1998).

[26] World Bank, 'Doing Business Rankings', https://www.doingbusiness.org/en/rankings (accessed 13 September 2019).

[27] Cooley, 'The Emerging Politics of International Rankings'; Judith G. Kelley and Beth A. Simmons, 'Politics by Number: Indicators as Social Pressure in International Relations', *American Journal of Political Science* 59 (2015): 55–70.

investing in, and providing tools for marketing and change by evaluating them over time and across geographies.

Indicators have been used as devices to build knowledge of how to govern by determining ways to classify populations, determine economic performance or analyse policy change.[28] Foucault argued that analysing the 'conduct of conduct' would enable one to evaluate how particular methods and rationalities are structuring possible actions.[29] Drawing on this notion, Davis, Kingsbury and Merry have argued that indicators have become 'technologies of global governance' because they are now part of the architecture of international institutions that order the world we live in.[30] As Sokhi-Bulley suggests, statistics operate as technologies of governmentality as they are able to influence the ways in which institutions govern. Using the example of the European Union Fundamental Rights Agency, she argues that statistics make rights visible, engineer trends, push particular identities—like who is classified as a victim, who is a guardian—and highlight what can be called best practices.[31]

In this regard, what needs to be emphasized is the method in which an indicator is developed. This includes the process through which a particular concept is quantified, how interconnections are made between disparate aspects within a concept and what choices lead to absences and silences in the choice of categories in order to come up with an indicator, that is what is prioritized and what is ignored.

Developing an indicator

Indicators are designed to be objective and neutral. However, this is rarely the case since the development of indicators is not just a technical or objective process, but also involves 'interpretative decisions about what

---

[28] Desrosières, 'Introduction'; Geoffrey C. Bowker and Susan Leigh Star, 'Introduction: To Classify Is Human', in *Sorting Things Out: Classification and Its Consequences*, 1–32 (Cambridge, MA: MIT Press, 2000).

[29] Mitchell Dean, 'Putting the Technological into Government', *History of the Human Sciences* 9, no. 3 (1996): 47–68; Thomas Lemke, *Foucault, Governmentality, and Critique* (London: Routledge, 2015).

[30] Kevin E. Davis, Benedict Kingsbury and Sally Engle Merry, 'Indicators as a Technology of Global Governance', *Law and Society Review* 46 (2012): 71–104.

[31] Bal Sokhi-Bulley, 'Governing (Through) Rights: Statistics as Technologies of Governmentality', *Social and Legal Studies* 20, no. 2 (2011): 139–155.

to quantify, how to categorize it, and how to label it'.[32] These are political decisions that require calculations on what to include and exclude, how to quantify concepts where there are contradictions in views and how to incorporate different viewpoints.[33] This process of commensuration changes the terms in which concepts are talked about, how they are valued and how one can engage with what is valuable.[34]

One of the means of ensuring transferability is the process by which complex concepts are simplified to their common denominators by reducing uncertainty and introducing standardized ways of understanding and representing them. This process, which prioritizes commensurability, often results, instead, in an 'erasure of narratives' of the experiences of persons being evaluated so as to ensure adaptability of indicator frameworks to other contexts.[35] In such a process where decisions are made on what to include and exclude, it is important that the process by which narratives are chosen are transparent and not opaque because otherwise the ways in which indicators are inferred and interpreted can be subject to misrepresentation, especially when they are used in the contexts for which they are not built.

The development process of indicators involves a series of stages where broad ideas and concepts are converted into reliable measures. In addition to determining the usefulness and accuracy of indicators to represent legal contexts and situations, understanding the background and assumptions that go into developing indicators is equally important.[36] The relevance of unpacking these factors is to understand the decisions that go into defining the purpose, evolving the conceptual framework, and analysing and establishing a method of evaluation. Davis, Kingsbury

---

[32] Rottenburg and Merry, 'A World of Indicators', 11.

[33] Lorenzo Fioramonti, 'The Politics of Statistics', in *How Numbers Rule the World: The Use and Abuse of Statistics in Global Politics*, 1–9 (London: ZED Books, 2014).

[34] Debora Valentina Malito, Nehal Bhuta and Gaby Umbach, 'Conclusions: Knowing and Governing', in *The Palgrave Handbook of Indicators in Global Governance*, ed. Debora Valentina Malito, Gaby Umbach and Nehal Bhuta, 503–512 (Cham: Springer 2017).

[35] Wendy Espeland, 'Narrating Numbers', in *The World of Indicators: The Making of Governmental Knowledge through Quantification*, ed. Richard Rottenburg, Sally Engle Merry, Sung-Joon Park and Johanna Mugler, 56–75 (Cambridge: Cambridge University Press 2015).

[36] Tor Krever, 'Quantifying Law: Legal Indicator Projects and the Reproduction of Neoliberal Common Sense', *Third World Quarterly* 34, no. 1 (2013): 131–150; Davis, Kingsbury and Merry, 'Introduction'.

and Merry trace the trajectory of indicator development and outline four distinct steps: conceptualization, production, use and impact.[37] I briefly discuss them here.

The first step of *conceptualization* is the process by which the indicator is named and given an overall identity. In this step, there is a theory of social change backing it, including a clear theoretical position. At this point the categories of measurement and tools for analysing data are also developed. Davis et al. argue that while conceptualizing an indicator, aspects such as the actors and institutions involved in building the indicators, the relevant expertise of the developers, the temporality and period within which it is developed, and finally the resources used and sourced assume importance.

Production, the second step, is where the concept is connected with the data, whether available or generated, and thereafter presented and packaged in an accessible manner. Whereas conceptualization is about defining issues and building categories, production is more pragmatic and involves making compromises with the concepts depending on data available to populate such an indicator framework. The question of importance here is understanding how compromises are made, how far are they influenced by the data, and why is it that there is a lack of particular kinds of data.

The third step of *use* is where the indicator is treated as a source of knowledge and thereafter used to form a basis for action. This aspect of use is the basis for policy frameworks and action by different agents such as governments, corporations or international financial institutions.[38] Finally, the fourth step is a review of the *impact and effects of* indicators and refers to, for example, how the performance of countries on indicators such as on corruption, or indicators on public accountability, become a reference point

---

[37] Davis, Kingsbury and Merry, 'Introduction'. Please refer to pages 10–16 of the introduction of the book on *The Quiet Power of Indicators*, where these steps in the development of an indicator are detailed.

[38] María Angélica Prada Uribe, 'The Quest for Measuring Development: The Role of the Indicator Bank', in *The Quiet Power of Indicators: Measuring Governance, Corruption, and Rule of Law*, Benedict Kingsbury, Kevin E Davis and Sally Engle Merry, 133–155 (Cambridge: Cambridge University Press 2015).

for whether these countries are able to apply for foreign aid, or negotiate trade agreements.[39]

Underlined in these different stages is commensuration and ensuring the validity of the measurement, meaning that the background ideas must then be converted into systematized and specific concepts that can then be made into indicators and scores.[40]

Indicators, by virtue of interpreting complex situations and producing a particular framework within which to understand them, contribute towards creating new knowledge and information. As they develop, they become a system of knowledge and a technology of governance, through which 'problems are conceptualized and solutions imagined'.[41] Through tools like surveys, graphs and other statistical methods that go into making indicators, this phenomenon is then represented as information and knowledge.[42] These practices not only make knowledge of the subject possible but also visible, as they make it into calculable forms.[43]

The development process of building indicators offers an opportunity to understand how, at the time of conceptualization, production, use and impact of these frameworks, a series of decisions are made by those who develop indicators, which in turn determine their lifecycle and impacts. In the next few sections, I will examine the implications of the development and use of indicators by looking at the potential for indicators to convey meaning, how they evoke trust and the kind of power they yield.

---

[39] Nikhil K. Dutta, 'Tradeoffs in Accountability: Conditionality Processes in the European Union and Millennium Challenge Corporation', in *The Quiet Power of Indicators: Measuring Governance, Corruption, and Rule of Law*, ed. Benedict Kingsbury, Kevin E. Davis and Sally Engle Merry, 156–196 (Cambridge: Cambridge University Press 2015).

[40] Robert Adcock and David Collier, 'Measurement Validity: A Shared Standard for Qualitative and Quantitative Research', *American Political Science Review* 95, no. 3 (September 2001): 529–546.

[41] Davis, Kingsbury and Merry, 'Introduction', 1. See generally Lemke, *Foucault, Governmentality, and Critique*.

[42] Jonathan Xavier Inda, 'Introduction: Government and Immigration', in *Targeting Immigrants: Government, Technology, and Ethics*, 1–26 (Oxford: John Wiley & Sons, 2008).

[43] Sokhi-Bulley, 'Governing (Through) Rights'. For a discussion on numbers as tools of enumeration and as tools for surveying and mapping, see Jonathan Xavier Inda, 'Government and Numbers', in *Targeting Immigrants: Government, Technology, and Ethics*, 63–66 (Oxford: John Wiley & Sons 2008).

The 'meanings' of legal indicators

In this section, I explore what meanings emerge through indicator frameworks, and why they have particular impacts. I do this by examining the language and symbols of quantification and the trade-offs involved in making abstract concepts more measurable and knowable.

The language and symbols of quantification

Language plays an important role in quantification because it is not only the means through which the phenomenon to be quantified is communicated and made understandable, but also reflects the nature of the audiences and the communities that the indicators hope to engage with and represent. For example, defining the concept of the rule of law in the good governance rankings of the World Bank, as 'the extent to which agents have confidence in, and abide by, the rules of society, and in particular the quality of contract enforcement, property rights, the police, and the courts, as well as the likelihood of crime and violence',[44] makes clear that particular choices are made to mark out the rule of law to focus on issues such as matters of crime or contract enforcement. Indicators offer insight and direction in terms of what we mean by the concept through making it generalizable. Porter states that quantification is a 'technology of distance' because it helps standardize concepts so that they can be understood far away.[45] This, he suggests, is because the language of numbers imposes structures and rules, which demand discipline in order to achieve a standardized outcome [46] and in the process, these numbers supplant local cultures with rational methods.[47]

---

[44] World Bank, 'World Governance Indicators 2019', https://info.worldbank.org/governance/wgi/ (accessed 7 May 2020); Daniel Kaufmann, Aart Kraay and Massimo Mastruzzi, 'The Worldwide Governance Indicators: Methodology and Analytical Issues', *Hague Journal on the Rule of Law* 3 (2011): 220–246, 223.

[45] Theodore M. Porter, 'Preface', in *Trust in Numbers: The Pursuit of Objectivity in Science and Public Life*, vii–xii (Princeton: Princeton University Press, 1995), ix.

[46] Ibid.

[47] Theodore M. Porter, 'The Political Philosophy of Quantification', in *Trust in Numbers: The Pursuit of Objectivity in Science and Public Life*, 73–86 (Princeton: Princeton University Press 1995).

What this distance and standardization offer us are ways of presenting realities to different publics, whether states, donor agencies or civil society, in a clear, cogent and seemingly non-controversial manner.[48] In the case of the rule of law, each audience has different purposes and uses for it, either as tools of promotion, monitoring or of advocacy. However, while different audiences use indicators, not all contribute to its making, which is done largely by experts from law, policy and economics situated in the Global North.[49]

The language that is used to frame and outline indicators is a reflection of the language of the researcher or of the sponsoring institution.[50] It conveys the priorities, objectives and meanings behind the choice of phrases. In a study of the language of the World Bank's annual reports, Moretti and Pestre demonstrate how the language adopted by the bank is different from everyday language in that it is self-referential, detached and codified, such that its ambitions and goals are vague and unfocussed.[51] For example, the word 'governance' is seen to correlate with only factors that are positive, such as 'stability, progress and growth', adjectives such as global, and terms such as collaboration, and community, so much so that the authors even term the language around governance as the galaxy of governance.[52] In the report, unlike the word government, which could also be bad, governance was seen to have a more singular and positive dimension to it.

This example is relevant when we think back to the development process of indicators and the ways in which concepts are formed. Through studying language, we get an insight into a dichotomy where on the one hand, through this process of standardization, we now have a comparable concept that can be articulated using the galaxy of terms around it, but on the other hand, we lose forms of contestation, nuance

---

48 Merry, 'A World of Quantification'.

49 Merry, 'Conclusions'; Cris Shore and Susan Wright, 'Governing by Numbers: Audit Culture, Rankings and the New World Order', *Social Anthropology* 23 (2015): 22–28.

50 Urueña examines how the Corruption Perception Index was seen in an ideological context of being an obstacle to economic development. René Urueña, 'Activism through Numbers? The Corruption Perception Index and the Use of Indicators by Civil Society Organisations', in *The Palgrave Handbook of Indicators in Global Governance*, Debora Valentina Malito, Gaby Umbach and Nehal Bhuta, 371–387 (Cham: Springer 2017).

51 Franco Moretti and Dominique Pestre, 'Bankspeak', *New Left Review* 92 (2015): 75–99.

52 Ibid.

and difference that can emerge by engaging in heterogeneous concepts.[53] This would make us ask not if there is a *galaxy* of governance but *galaxies* of governance.

Desrosières argues that quantification is an activity that not only offers a reflection of the world but is also one that actively transforms and reconstitutes it through a standard set of linguistic devices.[54] He advances that the verb 'quantify' has two parts: the first is a series of conventions, such as comparisons, translations, negotiations and compromises, which leads to the numerical form being created; and the second is measurement, which evaluates the existing framework thereafter.[55]

This linguistic aspect also ties into another aspect of 'meaning', which is the symbolism from the prioritizing of particular narratives over others.[56] One of the by-products of the process of developing indicators is the manner in which the narratives of people and contexts are simplified to ensure their circulation. This results in the erasure of some narratives but also the development of frameworks that lead to new forms of narratives.[57] These narratives also have new masters, for instance the international organization or the donor agency, who then become authorities on a range of issues because they set the terms of what is being measured, how it is measured and what the knowledge generated means, and in turn influence the creation of best practices and advocate for policy changes based on this knowledge.[58] In essence, they become gatekeepers who determine reform agendas and priorities. Cooley and Snyder argue that Transparency

---

[53] Porter, 'The Flight of the Indicator'; Sally Engle Merry, 'Measuring the World: Indicators, Human Rights, and Global Governance', *Current Anthropology* 52 (2011): S83–S95.

[54] Alain Desrosières, 'Retroaction: How Indicators Feed Back onto Quantified Actors', in *The World of Indicators: The Making of Governmental Knowledge through Quantification*, ed. Richard Rottenburg, Sally E. Merry, Sung-Joon Park and Johanna Mugler, 329–353 (Cambridge: Cambridge University Press 2015).

[55] Ibid.

[56] Wendy Nelson Espeland and Michael Sauder, 'The Dynamism of Indicators', in *Governance by Indicators: Global Power Through Classification and Rankings*, ed. Kevin Davis, Angelina Fisher, Benedict Kingsbury and Sally Engle Merry, 86–109 (Oxford: Oxford University Press 2012).

[57] Espeland, 'Narrating Numbers', 56.

[58] André Broome, Alexandra Homolar and Matthias Kranke, 'Bad Science: International Organizations and the Indirect Power of Global Benchmarking', *European Journal of International Relations* 24, no. 3 (2018): 514–539.

International, for example, plays the 'roles of judges, sources of governance, advocates, and self-promoters' on matters of corruption because of their outsized influence on setting the terms of rankings.[59] The effect of playing so many different roles, beyond the obvious accountability question, is that the cultural process of creating categories, determining ways to count and presenting the numbers are all cognitive processes, which are now seen as managerial functions.[60] These numbers, which should be symbolic of the particular economic and political ideologies of those that have created them, are now positioned as universal categories, and all of their justification, validity and life are reinforced by those that have created them.[61]

As indicators, through their language, convey rigorous and objective ways of evaluating the world, another fallout is that the critique of numbers is now missing.[62] In their research, Snyder and Cooley found that because there are now rankings for issues like corruption and creditworthiness, the need for an investigation to independently analyse situations, and study whether there are challenges, have been substituted by numbers, which give a ready answer for the state of the world.[63] The example from India of the rise in the Ease of Doing Business rankings were so symbolic that the prime minister started measuring reform by saying that he aimed for the country to be in the top 50 positions in the future.[64] It appeared that his focus was not on a need to provide a reform agenda that was tailored to the needs of the country but rather one that would facilitate a rise in India's position on this ranking. Numbers can be so persuasive that any nuanced

---

[59] Jack Snyder and Alexander Cooley, 'Conclusion', in *Ranking the World: Grading States as a Tool of Global Governance*, ed. Alexander Cooley and Jack Snyder, 178–193 (Cambridge: Cambridge University Press 2015), 189.

[60] Davis, Kingsbury and Merry, 'Introduction'; André Broome and Joel Quirk, 'Governing the World at a Distance: The Practice of Global Benchmarking', *Review of International Studies* 41, no. 5 (2015): 819–841.

[61] André Broome and Joel Quirk, 'The Politics of Numbers: The Normative Agendas of Global Benchmarking', *Review of International Studies* 41, no. 5 (2015): 813–818.

[62] Snyder and Cooley, 'Conclusion', 179.

[63] Ibid.

[64] PTI, 'Narendra Modi Wants India among Top 50 on Ease of Doing Business Index, Double Economy to $5 Trillion', *Hindustan Times*, 19 November 2018, https://www.hindustantimes.com/india-news/narendra-modi-wants-india-among-top-50-on-ease-of-doing-business-index-double-economy-to-5trillion/story-n9da7OmAzAJQQzfuxyOeTP.html (accessed 15 March 2019).

disagreement with them is difficult. In fact, when an unemployment report from the National Statistical Commission in 2018–2019 showed record unemployment in India around election time, the Government of India did its best to suppress the release of the report.[65] This would have provided a potentially contradictory narrative to the positive reports from the Ease of Doing Business rankings and would have been detrimental to the government's narrative on the robustness of the Indian economy.[66]

The trade-offs in the development of indicators

The development of indicators by virtue of standardizing and simplifying different concepts requires that certain trade-offs be made when building and producing a particular concept into a measurable form. Trade-offs are an important aspect of creating meaning through quantification because they lay out how choices are made in pursuit of delivering quantifiable values. Espeland articulates that this trade-off is between matters of simplification and elaboration, where the former is concerned with creating technologies that are easy to follow, are concise and thereby comparable, while the latter examines what kind of narratives emerge through the numbers and how these narratives affect, impact and govern those that are measure.[67] Thinking through this dichotomy is important because it helps to articulate the scope of measure as well as what is excluded and included, and how these different decisions create an impact. The World Justice Project, in its Rule of Law Index, has an indicator on 'informal justice'. It has not, for several years, collected data to measure informal justice because in the methodology the project argues that doing so is too complex a task given the different manifestations of informal justice systems across the world, and would be difficult to compare.[68] This decision on data collection

---

[65] Nidheesh M. K., '"Jobs Report Can't Be Called a Draft, It Is Final Once I Approve It"', *Mint*, 11 February 2019, https://www.livemint.com/news/india/the-jobs-report-can-t-be-called-a-draft-it-is-final-once-i-approve-it-mohanan-1549824555045.html (accessed 15 March 2019).

[66] Kaushik Basu, 'India Can Hide Unemployment Data, but Not the Truth', *New York Times*, 1 February 2019, https://www.nytimes.com/2019/02/01/opinion/india-unemployment-jobs-blackout.html (accessed 13 September 2019).

[67] Espeland, 'Narrating Numbers', 56–61.

[68] World Justice Project, 'Advancing the Rule of Law Worldwide', https://worldjusticeproject.org/ (accessed 6 November 2020).

on informal justice will also be discussed in later chapters, but I have mentioned it here to highlight the fact that the developers of the index made a choice to prioritize comparability over elaboration.

The second dimension of trade-offs is in regard to the methodological decision on the weights of different factors. These weights are decided on the basis of particular normative assumptions and, as a result, have a subjective dimension.[69] The weighing of particular factors is also not just a technical decision but also a political one, resulting from existing ideologies of who is designing and developing the indicators, and the priorities that they place on certain dimensions.[70] Do these decisions emerge from normative considerations or due to empirical considerations? If it is the former, and it has not been indicated, then what more can be done to ascertain more information on this? It is clear that there is a need for a transparency in the development of indicators.[71]

The third dimension of the trade-offs is between building categories that can be universal or local, and the potential for what can or cannot be translatable. The challenge here is to find a way to make it possible to account for a plurality of experiences and yet measure abstract simplified concepts. While the first dimension of trade-offs examined the impact of narratives as simplified devices versus complex ones, this is more focussed on how universalized meanings emerge through quantification.[72] It offers

---

[69] Snyder and Cooley, 'Conclusion'. See Michael Freudenberg, 'Composite Indicators of Country Performance: A Critical Assessment', working paper no. 2003/16, OECD, 2003 https://www.oecd-ilibrary.org/science-and-technology/composite-indicators-of-country-performance_405566708255 (accessed 22 May 2020). He argues that change in weights can mean that a country does better or worse on a particular ranking. He uses the case of developing an index for innovation performance to demonstrate the impacts of weights.

[70] Salvatore Greco, Alessio Ishizaka, Menelaos Tasiou and Gianpiero Torrisi, 'On the Methodological Framework of Composite Indices: A Review of the Issues of Weighting, Aggregation, and Robustness', *Social Indicators Research* 141 (2019): 61–94.

[71] See also OECD checklist: OECD and Joint Research Centre European Commission, *Handbook on Constructing Composite Indicators: Methodology and User Guide* (Paris: OECD, 2008), https://ictlogy.net/bibliography/reports/projects.php?idp=2308&lang=es (accessed 17 May 2019).

[72] Stefania Milan and Emiliano Treré, 'Big Data from the South(s): Beyond Data Universalism', *Television and New Media* 20, no. 4 (2019): 319–335; Rottenburg and Merry, 'A World of Indicators'; Broome and Quirk, 'Governing the World at a Distance'.

an examination into whether indicators want to study macro or micro structures, and whether they are interested in comparison such that a level of abstraction is without question or whether they examine the depth of an issue based on experiences.[73] In the case of the rule of law in the governance indicators from the World Bank, by limiting the definition of 'rule of law' to aspects of criminal law and contract enforcement, the framers seek to posit one notion of the rule of law as being entirely about law and order—a constraining rather than an enabling conception, which could also concern aspects of rights, welfare, democracy, and freedoms. How, for example, would such a measurement of the rule of law take into account the rights of people displaced by large infrastructure projects? A study by the International Consortium of Investigative Journalists 'Evicted and Abandoned: The World Bank's Broken Promise to the Poor' showed that over 3.4 million people had been economically or physically displaced by more than 1000 projects sponsored by the bank between 2004–2013, which resulted in the loss of land and livelihood.[74] Does such data on displacement also come within an understanding of the rule of law, and if not, how do we construe aspects of law and order when the lives of people are materially impacted?[75]

In the development of indicators, there are different trade-offs that contribute to and influence whether certain factors are given significance or whether they are silenced or made absent. In the next section, I explore the assumption of trust in indicators.

The 'trust' in legal indicators

Indicators are compelling quantification devices because, through processes of simplification, they are able to articulate how to make sense of otherwise complex realities. The portrayal of neatly arranged manifestations of

---

[73] Hans Krause Hansen and Tony Porter, 'What Do Numbers Do in Transnational Governance?', *International Political Sociology* 6, no. 4 (December 2012): 409–426.

[74] ICIJ, 'Explore 10 Years of World Bank Resettlement Data', https://www.icij.org/investigations/world-bank/explore-10-years-world-bank-resettlement-data/ (accessed 28 March 2020).

[75] In Chapter 3, I will explore in detail the ways in which the rule of law is constructed in indicators. I will also then examine how to build an indicator framework that considers the lives that people live in plural legal contexts.

phenomena using numbers hide the contestations that otherwise exist. This masking of contestation provides the first lens to building 'trust' through indicators because they allow for objects or phenomena to be studied devoid of the complexity around them. The second lens that relates to creating trust is the notion of the reliability of numbers that are perceived as objective instruments to understand realities; they, in turn, influence behaviours that lead to a further development of trust. This implicit trust in indicators then makes the ability to critically examine them more difficult and therefore it is imperative to first find ways to recognize how indicators evoke trust, and then how to demystify this trust.

The masking of contestation

We engage with indicators through a neatly presented manifestation of a series of variables that together form a measurement device. The composition of these different variables is portrayed as the baseline from where a common understanding of different contexts, whether the rule of law, democracy or business, can be ascertained. However, even as these indicators are presented as technical and objective devices, their standardization masks many kinds of contexts and contestations.[76]

First, it is not apparent what kind of deliberations have gone into determining the usefulness of a particular concept or methodology, what objections different technical experts have raised, and what kind of conflict of interests may be hidden in the making of these indicators.[77] Rosga and Satterthwaite argue that the 'means and messiness' in the generation of numbers is erased by tabulated numbers, such that the evidence of human decision making is obscured under the garb of the neutrality of the presentation of numbers.[78] These distinctions, whether at the stage of concept formulation or at the stage of developing categories and indicators, are simply covered up by a set of numbers. As a result, these number-driven

---

[76] Theodore M. Porter, 'Introduction: Cultures of Objectivity', in *Trust in Numbers: The Pursuit of Objectivity in Science and Public Life*, 3–8 (Princeton: Princeton University Press 1995); Desrosières, 'Introduction'.

[77] Galit A. Sarfaty, 'Regulating through Numbers: A Case Study of Corporate Sustainability Reporting', *Virginia Journal of International Law* 53, no. 3 (2013): 575–622.

[78] AnnJanette Rosga and Margaret L. Satterthwaie, 'The Trust in Indicators: Measuring Human Rights', *Berkeley Journal of International Law* 27, no. 2 (2009): 253–315.

policies project a shift to the technical from the political. This also results in a move away from deliberation and discussion around contested concepts to expertise around those matters.[79] An interesting recent example of this shift was during the COVID-19 crisis, where the United Kingdom government's initial response to tackling the pandemic was to rely on models projected by its Behavioural Insights team through computer modelling and nudge theory, which suggested that the best way forward was to encourage 'herd immunity', where if enough people got infected with the virus, there would not be many new cases.[80] Soon after, however, there was a major backlash against this approach because of a study from Imperial College, which projected a high number of deaths in the UK if such an approach was followed.[81] This resulted in the UK reversing its decision and taking strict steps to monitor movement in the country along the lines of similar decisions taken by most countries in Europe.[82] In this case, technical expertise offered projections of numbers, which, in turn influenced decisions, public responses and policies—a techno-solutionism.[83] However, what this case

---

[79] Max Weber speaks of the difference between value rationality and instrumental rationality, where realities are subordinate to values in the former, whereas in the latter, they are a means to an end. See also Stephen Kalberg, 'Max Weber's Types of Rationality: Cornerstones for the Analysis of Rationalization Processes in History', *The American Journal of Sociology* 85, no. 5 (1980): 1145–1179; Krever, 'Quantifying Law'.

[80] Devi Sridhar, 'Britain Had a Head Start on Covid-19, but Our Leaders Squandered It', *The Guardian*, 23 March 2020, https://www.theguardian.com/commentisfree/2020/mar/23/britain-covid-19-head-start-squandered (accessed 8 April 2020).

[81] Neil M. Ferguson, Daniel Laydon, Gemma Nedjati-Gilani, Natsuko Imai, Kylie Ainslie, Marc Baguelin, Sangeeta Bhatia, Adhiratha Boonyasiri, Zulma Cucunubá, Gina Cuomo-Dannenburg, Amy Dighe, Ilaria Dorigatti, Han Fu, Katy Gaythorpe, Will Green, Arran Hamlet, Wes Hinsley, Lucy C Okell, Sabine van Elsland, Hayley Thompson, Robert Verity, Erik Volz, Haowei Wang, Yuanrong Wang, Patrick GT Walker, Caroline Walters, Peter Winskill, Charles Whittaker, Christl A Donnelly, Steven Riley, Azra C Ghani, *Report 9: Impact of Non-Pharmaceutical Interventions (NPIs) to Reduce COVID-19 Mortality and Healthcare Demand*, 16 March 2020, http://www.imperial.ac.uk/medicine/departments/school-public-health/infectious-disease-epidemiology/mrc-global-infectious-disease-analysis/covid-19/report-9-impact-of-npis-on-covid-19/ (accessed 19 December 2020).

[82] Sridhar, 'Britain Had a Head Start on Covid-19'.

[83] Stefania Milan, 'Techno-Solutionism and the Standard Human in the Making of the COVID-19 Pandemic', *Big Data and Society* 7 (2020), https://doi.org/10.1177/2053951720966781 (accessed 30 October 2020).

also shows is how these technical solutions are not without their messy and contradictory elements, which are masked because numbers provide the façade of authority.

Second, it is not just the preparation stages of indicators that mask conflicts, but also the collection of data itself, which is itself a political decision.[84] This can be understood in terms of the methods that are used to manage databases, the resources available to carry out and maintain statistics, and the influences on numbers both at a national and international level.[85] Along with questions of the transparency of numbers to ensure that indicators are not gamed, what is equally important is the convening power of those who generate numbers to use and impact policymaking. Developing countries often find that international organizations or developed country counterparts do not take their data seriously.[86] In the example mentioned previously of the Rule of Law Index by the World Justice Project, whereas there are criteria to measure informal justice systems, the data has never been collected because of the previously stated difficulties of doing so. If this were the case, does the indicator on informal justice exist purely symbolically? Would counting this factor impact the ranking of some countries more than others, particularly those that have entrenched plural legal systems?

As Perry-Kessaris has shown in the case of the Ease of Doing Business rankings, indicators first define the nature of what is the normative model; in this case, they gain legitimacy through the ways in which they are able to outline the contours of a productive economic environment.[87] Thereafter, once this model has gained prominence, it is then used in turn to influence the formation and development of state legal systems that meet their criteria, ignoring other systems.[88]

---

[84] Catherine D'Ignazio and Lauren F. Klein, 'Introduction: Why Data Science Needs Feminism', in *Data Feminism*, 1–20 (Cambridge, MA: MIT Press, 2020).

[85] Broome, Homolar and Kranke, 'Bad Science'.

[86] Davis, Kingsbury and Merry, 'Introduction'; Merry, 'Measuring the World'.

[87] Amanda Perry-Kessaris, 'The Re-Co-Construction of Legitimacy of/through the Doing Business Indicators', *International Journal of Law in Context* 13, no. 4 (2017): 498–511.

[88] Ibid.

Many of the critiques of legal indicators engage more closely with functions, and less with the conceptual categories that indicators use.[89] Without the potential for argumentation around concepts that are seemingly fixed, there is a preponderance of box ticking, which results in meeting checklists, rather than engaging with the costs and benefits of particular actions and categories.[90] In this regard, the legal world is considered from an objective standpoint and not from one of political struggle.[91] Working with a language of checklists implies that deeply political concepts such as freedom or equality are now measured in terms of efficiency.[92] Because efficiency is one of the underlying effects of the use of indicators, 'judgments based on values' are replaced by rational decision-making and Nelken observes that this private and elite decision-making behind the preparation of checklists is then euphemized as technical expertise.[93] An outcome of this checklist approach is that when assessing the impact of development, the burden for failure is often shifted away from donor communities, and an examination of their policies and programmes, to the implementation programmes in developing countries and their role in the lack of development.[94] In the course of this book, this study will build on unpacking and critiquing technical expertise and a functional approach that is divorced from the contestation in the development of indicators. It

---

[89] Krever, 'Quantifying Law'; David Nelken, 'The Legitimacy of Global Social Indicators: Reconfiguring Authority, Accountability and Accuracy', *Les Cahiers De Droit* 59, no. 1 (2018): 35–84.

[90] Sarfaty, 'Regulating through Numbers'; Benoît Frydman, 'From Accuracy to Accountability: Subjecting Global Indicators to the Rule of Law', *International Journal of Law in Context* 13, no. 4 (2017): 450–464.

[91] As we will discuss in the next chapter, the rule of law is a concept that is deeply contested, and one that requires debate into its antecedents, its appropriateness, and its use. In this sense, I analyse in the course of this book the ways in which different narratives and discourses have played a role in the formation of concepts such as the rule of law. See also Mark Brown, '"An Unqualified Human Good"? On Rule of Law, Globalization, and Imperialism', *Law and Social Inquiry* 43, no. 4 (2018): 1391–1426.

[92] Krever, 'Quantifying Law'.

[93] David Nelken, 'Conclusion: Contesting Global Indicators', in *The Quiet Power of Indicators: Measuring Governance, Corruption, and Rule of Law*, ed. Sally Engle Merry, Kevin E. Davis and Benedict Kingsbury, 317–388 (Cambridge: Cambridge University Press 2015).

[94] Ibid.

will also ask why it is important to question not just the thinness or the thickness of concepts but the plurality and diversity of how these concepts have been constructed to begin with.

The reliability of numbers

A by-product of the masking of contestation in the development of indicators is the belief that numbers are trustworthy and objective.[95] Nelken argues that indicators destabilize the link between the actual and the normative, such that facts, which include data aspects, are transformed into standards.[96] By offering a numerical representation of otherwise complex phenomenon, indicators are emerging as part of an accountability discourse. They provide ways to assess performance, they help to effectively communicate phenomena for those who are governed as well as those who govern and offer a tool for advocacy for the former and a check for the latter. Due to their preciseness and lack of ambiguity, they are seen as unbiased and carry the legitimacy of being rigorous and scientific.[97]

As the cache of being scientific has resulted in less debate on the conceptual categories that go into the numbers, and with indicators being seen as reliable, they are also increasingly becoming substitutes for debates and judgment. Bhuta cautions that indicators become an authority on different matters, which then substitute for engagement with issues in the public policy realm.[98]

When algorithms started being used to test recidivism (the potential of the accused to commit crimes again) in the United States, Judges ended up taking recourse to these formulae without conducting due diligence on the methodologies behind the numbers, so much so that only after investigation was it found that these systems had an ingrained machine bias that did

---

[95] See generally Theodore M. Porter, *Trust in Numbers: The Pursuit of Objectivity in Science and Public Life* (Princeton: Princeton University Press 1996).

[96] Nelken, 'Conclusion'.

[97] David Nelken, 'Whose Best Practices? The Significance of Context in and for Transnational Criminal Justice Indicators', *Journal of Law and Society* 46, no. S1 (2019): S31–S50.

[98] Ibid.

not account for race.[99] As a result, Black persons without criminal records were being misclassified in sentencing, and accused White persons with past criminal records were being under-classified and awarded lighter sentences than their Black counterparts.[100] The paradox of reliability is not that the numbers necessarily reduced human errors; it is that they project authority, engineer accountability and thus do not encounter as much scrutiny as decisions would have if they were executed through human judgment. This perception of reliability is drawn from the belief that numbers are objective and neutral, without considering the fact that these numbers are also representative of the world views and biases of those that have developed and conceptualized them.[101]

One of the outcomes of this perception of reliability and accountability is the reactivity that numbers inspire. Espeland and Sauder show in their examination of law school rankings that as numbers become forms of knowledge, they create 'social worlds' that are likely to influence expectations and behaviours of people, who are reflexive beings.[102] In this particular case, prospective students, on the one hand, made decisions regarding which universities to attend based on the school rankings, while universities on the other hand, decided on what courses to offer based on what would be better suited to the criteria of indicators. The universities ended up making decisions in order to game the rankings by adopting new strategies—changing programmes and resource allocation—all with the

---

[99] Julia Angwin, Jeff Larson, Surya Mattu and Lauren Kirchner, 'Machine Bias', *ProPublica*, 23 May 2016, https://www.propublica.org/article/machine-bias-risk-assessments-in-criminal-sentencing (accessed 16 February 2018).

[100] Ibid.

[101] Siddharth de Souza, 'Unpacking the Black Box: Addressing the "Social" to Make Construction of AI-Powered Legal Technologies More Transparent and Unbiased', *Journal of the Oxford Centre for Socio-Legal Studies*, 2018, https://joxcsls.com/2018/06/18/unpacking-the-black-box-addressing-the-social-to-make-construction-of-ai-powered-legal-technologies-more-transparent-and-unbiased/ (accessed 20 March 2019).

[102] Wendy Nelson Espeland and Michael Sauder, 'Rankings and Reactivity: How Public Measures Recreate Social Worlds', *American Journal of Sociology* 113, no. 1 (2007): 1–40. For more on social worlds that can be understood as forms of social organization which are not determined by formal structures of space or territory but rather by communication and interaction; see also David R. Unruh, 'The Nature of Social Worlds', *Pacific Sociological Review* 23, no. 3 (1980): 271–296.

purpose of maximizing rankings.[103] In addition to recognizing the kind of user choices and decisions that result from indicator frameworks and their implications for society, the methodology of how indicators and rankings are produced, it also becomes essential to examine how these numbers are circulated, interpreted and narrated in order to have an idea of the impact they have on different stakeholders.[104] We need to ask how these technical assessments influence standard settings and decision-making, and also the relations between those that govern and those who are governed by these frameworks.[105]

In the next section, we examine this aspect of reliability and trust in further detail by looking at the power behind these frameworks.

The 'power' of legal indicators

The notion of power is significant because it builds on the other two factors of 'meaning' and 'trust' by reshaping the worlds in which quantification takes place. The power in numbers argument maintains that forms of auditing or accounting are not technical or neutral, but instead are social and sometimes institutional, and carry a disciplinary power.[106]

The judgment of numbers

Desrosières asks pointedly: 'are quantitative indicators an instrument of emancipation or an instrument of oppression?'[107] This is an important question because it is a comment on the potential power dynamics that emerge through the knowledge networks created. He argues that some might say that indicators provide society with a mirror image of itself, which then enables it to improve and work towards creating more equity and justice where there are gaps. On the other hand, indicators also create

---

[103] See also Espeland and Sauder, 'Rankings and Reactivity'.

[104] See also Espeland, 'Narrating Numbers'; Malito, Bhuta and Umbach, 'Conclusions'.

[105] Davis, Kingsbury and Merry, 'Indicators as a Technology'.

[106] Michael Sauder and Wendy Nelson Espeland, 'The Discipline of Rankings: Tight Coupling and Organizational Change', *American Sociological Review* 74, no. 1 (2009): 63–82.

[107] Desrosières, 'Retroaction', 329.

benchmarking and assessment, and these can also dominate relationships, which in turn result in a culture of individualism and competition between units—for example countries or law schools—seeking to improve how they do on the rankings.[108] In the case of the law schools discussed above, we saw a manifestation of this, where there was an attempt at improving positions on ranking frameworks through designing programs linked to indicator criteria, thereby uncritically presuming that the ranking reflects an unqualified good, rather than building a program that reflects the philosophy of the school or the needs of the students. Is less attention paid to critically examining the suitability of the indicator framework because all energies are diverted to performing the best within the method laid out?

Amariles argues that legal indicators create subjectification by first creating categories according to conceptual leanings, and then filling them up.[109] The related effect of the process, through which these frameworks are developed, is akin to that of a black box. This is because while these technologies produce certainty and authority, they do so without being open to the scrutiny of the people, finances and knowledge that go into their creation.[110] The challenge of the subjective lens of the indicator is that it quickly acquires a normativity of its own due to the power of indicators as technologies of governance.[111] In the case of Albania, Smoki Musaraj narrates an incident from 2008, when the Ambassador of the United States to Albania used the language of a USAID study on corruption perceptions in Albania to express his disapproval for the local government.[112] The study demonstrated how the survey was used by the Ambassador as a device to offer what was considered to be objective and legitimate criticism, and how

---

[108] Ibid.; Cris Shore and Susan Wright, 'Audit Culture Revisited: Rankings, Ratings, and the Reassembling of Society', *Current Anthropology* 56, no. 3 (2015): 421–444.

[109] Amariles, 'Supping with the Devil?'

[110] Nelken, 'Conclusion'.

[111] Perry-Kessaris, 'The Re-Co-Construction of Legitimacy'; Mathias Siems and David Nelken, 'Global Social Indicators and the Concept of Legitimacy', *International Journal of Law in Context* 13, no. 4 (2017): 436–449.

[112] Smoki Musaraj, 'Indicators, Global Expertise, and a Local Political Drama: Producing and Deploying Corruption Perception Data in Post-Socialist Albania', in *The Quiet Power of Indicators: Measuring Governance, Corruption, and Rule of Law*, ed. Sally Engle Merry, Kevin E. Davis and Benedict Kingsbury, 222–247 (Cambridge: Cambridge University Press 2015).

the data was perceived to portray a source of expertise and knowledge.[113] However, what it also shows is the manner in which indicators provided a framework through which development knowledge and the type of society that must be promoted is advanced.[114] Indicators, by suggesting what kind of society must be created and what kind of decisions must be taken, lead to not just knowledge but also a governance effect, and a consequence is that regulatory frameworks grow from these systems.[115] An illustration of this can also be the Sustainable Development Goals (SDGs), which present a framework for the world on matters from access to justice to sustainable agriculture, education, and so on. While the ambition of the goals was reflected in intense stakeholder consultations, the process of finalizing these goals was one that was politically driven and influenced by country agendas and resulted in many changes to the ambitions, framing and definitions of goals because of the recognition that once these are adopted, they take on a life of their own.[116] This transition from subjective considerations and ways of measuring the world to normative standards creates a series of impacts, which is why the SDG process was deliberately deliberative.

The judgment that emerges from numbers manifests in myriad ways. Indicators can then play the role of tools for naming, shaming and blaming, because they provide the standards upon which decisions are expected to be made, policies are expected to be formed and outcomes are expected

---

[113] Ibid.

[114] Morag Goodwin, 'The Poverty of Numbers: Reflections on the Legitimacy of Global Development Indicators', *International Journal of Law in Context* 13, no. 4 (2017): 485–497.

[115] Nelken, 'Conclusion'.

[116] Sakiko Fukuda-Parr and Desmond McNeill, 'Knowledge and Politics in Setting and Measuring the SDGs: Introduction to Special Issue', *Global Policy* 10 (2019): 5–15. See also statement by Women Major Group as an illustration calling for deliberative discussions, which said, 'we caution against developing another set of reductive goals, targets and indicators that ignore the transformational changes required to address the failure of the current development model, which is rooted in unsustainable production and consumption patterns exacerbating gender, race and class inequities' in Global Forest Coalition, 'Intervention by the Women's Major Group on Land Degradation, Desertification and Drought at the UN OWG SDG Meeting 23 May 2013', 23 May 2013, https://globalforestcoalition.org/es/intervention-by-the-womens-major-group-on-land-degradation-desertification-and-drought-at-the-un-owg-sdg-meeting-23-may-2013/ (accessed 5 May 2020).

to be achieved.[117] For example, a study of Transparency International and its impacts in Jamaica argued that the rankings resulted in changes in government policy as these departments of government closely monitored the ranking that reflected the global market perception of Jamaica.[118] In addition to this, indicators can also be used as tools for emulation, for behavioural change and adaptation, because by prescribing standards they determine the ways in which those who are evaluated are expected to react and engage.[119]

One common illustration of the pressure for change that emerge through indicators is the question of conditionality. This is when development assistance is tied to meeting particular policy targets. These targets are developed and then measured by indicators and they in turn then determine the terms upon which funds are allocated and concessions are made.[120] The German Development Aid organization is one such organization that is now adopting a human rights approach to development cooperation, including aligning project objectives and indicators to human rights and sustainable development goals.[121] The judgment through numbers, therefore, has multifaceted effects; it results in the creation of normative ideas based on the subjective considerations of those who develop the indicators, and then has a series of consequences from blaming to emulating that are inspired by behaviours seeking to respond to indicators.

The presentation and representation of indicators

Another important power of indicators is in the representation of gaps that exist between actual performance and ideal performance. This is

[117] See generally Davis, Kingsbury and Merry, 'Introduction'.

[118] Omar E. Hawthorne, *Do International Corruption Metrics Matter? The Impact of Transparency International's Corruption Perception Index* (Maryland: Lexington Books, 2015).

[119] Davis, Kingsbury and Merry, 'Introduction'; Rosga and Satterthwaie, 'The Trust in Indicators'.

[120] Goodwin, 'The Poverty of Numbers'; Merry, Davis and Kingsbury, *The Quiet Power of Indicators*.

[121] Deutsche Gesellschaft für and Internationale Zusammenarbeit (GIZ) GmbH, 'The ABC for Human Rights for Development Cooperation', 2013, https://www.institut-fuer-menschenrechte.de/fileadmin/user_upload/Publikationen/E-Info-Tool/e-info-tool_abc_of_human_rights_for_development_cooperation.pdf (accessed 30 July 2021).

because indicators create standards that are then presented as ideals.[122] This implies that indicators determine what the aspiration for all legal systems must be, what kind of governance is important and what types of institutional apparatus is critical thereafter. In creating representations of ideals, indicators are also responsible for a process of othering: they determine what is efficient, what is worthy, and by representing a series of standards, they present the world with criteria on what functions well and what does not.[123]

These representations, however, are not neutral but contain the agendas of those that construct, fund, and promote them.[124] Due to the power of indicators and their ways of presenting concepts, there is more attention being paid to where one entity ranks in comparison to another rather than questioning how the measurements are taking place. For example, the Supreme Court of Canada used the Rule of Law Index and the rankings of Canada to describe how Canadians access the civil justice system.[125] By doing so, the court used the representations of what access to civil justice should include according to how they appeared in the Index and identified the position of Canada and the lacunae present. These rankings were used without challenging their conceptual nature or whether they were holistic or comprehensive enough to capture the Canadian context. This case shows how the representation of issues and their positioning in ranking provide quicker ways towards affecting policy responses by providing an empirical overview of the implementation gaps as determined by the indicator framework.

In Serban's study of Romania, she analyses how the rule of law indicators, including those by the World Justice Project, were referenced in a report by

---

[122] David Restrepo Amariles, 'Transnational Legal Indicators: The Missing Link in a New Era of Law and Development', in *Law and Policy in Latin America*, ed. Pedro Borges Fortes, Larissa Boratti, Andres Palacios Lleras and Tom Gerald Daly, 95–111 (London: Palgrave Macmillan, 2016).

[123] Benoît Frydman and William Twining, 'A Symposium on Global Law, Legal Pluralism and Legal Indicators', *The Journal of Legal Pluralism and Unofficial Law* 47, no. 1 (2015): 1–8, DOI: 10.1080/07329113.2015.1030210; Amanda Perry-Kessaris, 'Prepare Your Indicators: Economics Imperialism on the Shores of Law and Development', *International Journal of Law in Context* 7, no. 4 (2011): 401–421.

[124] Broome and Quirk, 'The Politics of Numbers'.

[125] Supreme Court of Canada, *Hryniak v. Maudlin* 2014 SCC 7, https://scc-csc.lexum.com/scc-csc/scc-csc/en/item/13427/index.do#_ftnref2 (accessed 19 May 2020).

the European Commission to critique Romania's commitment to the rule of law.[126] What is interesting about this case is that it is an example of how indicators are used as knowledge resources, which then have regulatory effects to determine whether Romania is meeting its standards of the rule of law as well as highlight which areas in the judicial system require reform.[127]

In this instance and in the Canadian example, the indicators are taken as prescriptions of what the rule of law should be. With the ambition of creating global standards, these numbers are used and their effects magnified without sufficient attention to the different ways in which numbers are constructed, influencing whose voices are heard, whose are silenced and whose are subsumed.[128]

Conclusion

This chapter has highlighted how indicators affect ways of knowing and seeing and how they regulate and influence behaviour in different contexts. It argued how indicators play an important role in constructing the world we live in, affecting how we understand and judge it, and how we behave and act. It has attempted to connect together different challenges of indicators both at a general level as well as in a legal context and has organized these critiques of indicators around aspects of the meanings that they generate, the trust they command and the power they wield.

The purpose of collating such a set of diverse views is to lay the foundation for a response that is embedded in engaging with critical questions that arise in the study of indicators. These challenges of indicators will be used to evaluate how indicators can be developed with plural ideas that move beyond representing only particular cultural values, political theories, and epistemic communities. The book will argue that the quantification

---

[126] Mihaela Serban, 'Rule of Law Indicators as a Technology of Power in Romania', in *The Quiet Power of Indicators: Measuring Governance, Corruption, and Rule of Law*, ed. Sally Engle Merry, Kevin E. Davis and Benedict Kingsbury, 199–221 (Cambridge: Cambridge University Press 2015).

[127] Ibid.

[128] Goodwin, 'The Poverty of Numbers'; Nelken, 'Whose Best Practices?'; Sotiria Grek, 'Prophets, Saviours and Saints: Symbolic Governance and the Rise of a Transnational Metrological Field', *International Review of Education* 66, nos. 2–3 (2020): 139–166.

process has to be more than just purely technical. Additionally, the book will explore how these processes of commensuration and aggregation of these frameworks do not just exist in isolation, but are instead backed by institutions, whether states or international organizations, or by large private entities that invest huge sums of money into ensuring that these become the dominant ways of analysing, determining and studying the phenomenon around us.

3

Rule of Law Promotion, Legal Indicators and Legal Pluralism

The promotion of the rule of law has been a major part of development assistance programmes because it is seen as a core element in the fulfilment of various aims such as economic development, peace and security, and respect for human rights.[1] Much of the effort to promote the rule of law has been focussed on strengthening the formal justice systems in countries in the Global South by executing projects such as building new courts and legal institutions, training judges and lawyers, and drafting new laws that are meant to develop the justice system by reflecting successes seen in other jurisdictions, primarily of the Global North.[2] The assumption behind such policies is that if such institutions are built, then the rule of law will automatically follow.[3] Over the years, these policies and projects which have largely focussed on building formal justice systems have cost

---

[1] Brian Z. Tamanaha, 'The Rule of Law and Legal Pluralism in Development', *Hague Journal on the Rule of Law* 3, no. 1 (2011): 1–17; Stephen Humphreys, 'Introduction', in *Theatre of the Rule of Law: Transnational Legal Intervention in Theory and Practice*, 1–26 (Cambridge: Cambridge University Press, 2010).

[2] Stephen Golub, 'Beyond Rule of Law Orthodoxy: The Legal Empowerment Alternative', Carnegie Endowment for International Peace, http://carnegieendowment.org/2003/ 10/14/beyond-rule-of-law-orthodoxy-legal-empowerment-alternative-pub-1367 (accessed 7 December 2017); Julio Faundez, 'The Rule of Law Enterprise: Promoting a Dialogue between Practitioners and Academics', *Democratization* 12, no. 4 (2005): 567–586.

[3] Katherine Erbeznik, 'Money Can't Buy You Law: The Effects of Foreign Aid on the Rule of Law in Developing Countries', *Indiana Journal of Global Legal Studies* 18 (2011): 873–900; Deval Desai, 'In Search of "Hire" Knowledge', in *The International Rule of*

billions of dollars.[4] A consistent critique of these policies has been that transplantation of legal ideas, values and institutions, without cognizance of local contexts and realities, does not work.[5] Similarly, as this chapter will show, the framing and developing of legal indicators are also influenced by legal formalism and institutional ideas of the rule of law.

Increasingly, however, there has been a shift in rule of law programming with more engagement with local dispute resolution forums such as those based on custom, religion and community practices. For the purposes of the analysis, these will collectively be called non-state justice systems (NSJS).[6] This is not to diminish or ignore the plurality among them and the diversity of their functions but to distinguish them from the state-centred justice systems, which, in this instance, include the executive, the judiciary and the legislature of a country, and their bureaucracies.

The phenomenon of 'legal pluralism' has emerged in rule of law programming because development agencies recognize the resilience of NSJS and the limits of top-down legal reform that takes place without

---

Law Movement: A Crisis of Legitimacy and the Way Forward, ed. David Marshall, 42–83 (Cambridge, MA: Harvard University Press, 2014).

4   A recent report from the United States Government Accountability office stated that 2.7 billion dollars was spent between 2014 and 2018 on rule of law assistance. See United States Government Accountability Office, *Rule of Law Assistance: Agency Efforts Are Guided by Various Strategies, and Overseas Missions Should Ensure That Programming Is Fully Coordinated* (Washington, DC: US GAO, 2020), https://www.gao.gov/assets/710/707442.pdf (accessed 30 July 2021), https://www.gao.gov/assets/710/707442.pdf (accessed 4 November 2020). An IDLO report showed that over 2.6 billion dollars was spent on legal and judicial development assistance in 2008, which was a rise from the 1.7 billion dollars the previous year and 841.5 million dollars in 2006. See IDLO, *Legal and Judicial Development Assistance* (Rome: IDLO, 2010), https://www.files.ethz.ch/isn/139312/LJAnnualReport.pdf (accessed 30 July 2021).

5   Tamanaha, 'The Rule of Law and Legal Pluralism in Development'; Martin Krygier, 'The Rule of Law: Pasts, Presents, and Two Possible Futures', *Annual Review of Law and Social Science* 12, no. 1 (2016): 199–229.

6   Danish Institute for Human Rights, 'Informal Justice Systems: Charting a Course for Human Rights-Based Engagement', UNDP, UNICEF and UN Women, 2013, http://www.undp.org/content/undp/en/home/librarypage/democratic-governance/access_to_justiceandruleoflaw/informal-justice-systems.html (accessed 7 December 2017).

cognizance of history, culture and context.[7] Development agencies have also recognized that NSJS have legitimacy and authority in particular regions around the world because they are accessible, affordable and familiar.[8]

In rule of law programming work such as building justice institutions, developing administrative procedures, or influencing the adoption of new laws, legal indicators are used as tools for auditing, measurement and accounting of the rule of law, and to measure human rights and governance.[9] These tools exist as instruments through which legal institutions and the rule of law can be evaluated. They provide a language and source of knowledge with which it is possible to assess whether institutions are functioning successfully, programmes are being implemented, change is taking place, and reforms are having an impact.[10]

With the turn to legal pluralism in development programming, I will examine whether legal indicators can be developed with concepts that account for diversity in values and institutions, acounting for how people resolve their grievances across time and space.[11] As many legal indicators are developed on some construction of the rule of law, examining the concept itself in development programming is instructive.[12] In studying

[7] These include development aid agencies from the United States, the United Kingdom and Denmark that have been supporting justice reform work and have projects on supporting non-state justice systems. See also Ronald Janse, 'A Turn to Legal Pluralism in Rule of Law Promotion?', *Erasmus Law Review* 6 (2013): 181–190.

[8] Siddharth Peter de Souza, 'Evaluating "Access to Justice" in Informal Justice Systems: A Suggestive Framework', *Max Planck Yearbook of United Nations Law Online* 19, no. 1 (2016): 469–504.

[9] Sally Engle Merry, 'Measuring the World: Indicators, Human Rights, and Global Governance', *Current Anthropology* 52 (2011): S83–S95. See also Mila Versteeg and Tom Ginsburg, 'Measuring the Rule of Law: A Comparison of Indicators', *Law and Social Inquiry* 42, no. 1 (2017): 100–137.

[10] Linn Hammergren, 'Indices, Indicators and Statistics: A View from the Project Side as to Their Utility and Pitfalls', *Hague Journal on the Rule of Law* 3, no. 2 (2011): 305–316.

[11] William Twining, 'Have Concepts, Will Travel: Analytical Jurisprudence in a Global Context', *International Journal of Law in Context* 1, no. 1 (2005): 5–40.

[12] In development programming related to the rule of law, I look at how development agencies are building projects and programs to support the creation of judicial institutions, administrative procedures, and laws and legislations. See generally Philipp Dann, 'Introduction', in *The Law of Development Cooperation: A Comparative Analysis of the World Bank, the EU and Germany*, 1–32 (Cambridge: Cambridge University Press, 2013).

legal pluralism, this chapter seeks to examine how different political, social and cultural ideologies play out in relation to the concept of the rule of law. The chapter makes the case that one cannot understand the rule of law without confronting the messiness of the everyday resolution of legal disputes and recognizing the multifaceted journeys that people take to resolve their disputes.

This chapter examines six legal indicators projects[13] and discusses the assessments that these indicators make when they rely only on the concept of the rule of law while measuring justice in the context of dispute resolution in plural legal orders. I will look at the concepts and methods in these legal indicators and will explore how these frameworks function if we are to evaluate them considering principles of legal pluralism. These include the varied values and criteria that influence the legitimacy of legal systems, which are informed by different ethical and procedural constructs. In doing so, this chapter seeks to analyse whether the rule of law indicators are cognizant of different legal systems and provide a fair measurement of plurinational and hybrid societies, or whether they continue to perpetuate a state-centric approach to justice in matters of dispute resolution. The chapter will then explore how the rule of law has evolved in international programming and how it must be reframed to reflect the challenges of pluralism. The second section will examine the impact of acknowledging legal pluralism in rule of law promotion in development programming, and will also explore the evolution of the concept of the rule of law. The third section will analyse the existing rule of law indicators and evaluate their efficacy for plural legal orders. The final section reflects on whether it is possible to instead look at access to justice as a more inclusive and expansive concept when developing legal indicators that can be used for evaluating legal systems globally. This chapter not only seeks to examine discussions of legal indicators within work on how the rule of law is promoted globally, but also how these indicators are able to function in contexts where plural legal orders offer different avenues for dispute resolution.

---

[13] The World Justice Project Rule of Law Index, the Democracy Barometer, the World Bank Worldwide Governance Indicators, the United Nations Rule of Law Indicators, the Ibrahim Index on African Governance and the Hague Model of Access to Justice.

A shift to legal pluralism in the promotion of Rule of Law

This section investigates the role that legal pluralism plays in development programming by looking at the ways in which this phenomenon influences how the realities of laws and legal processes emerge, and the implications this has for more statist law. In doing so, it also examines the contours of the rule of law as it is applied and promoted in development programming, and how it applies to the ways in which the law is experienced and encountered by people who use different legal systems.

Unpacking legal pluralism

The concept of legal pluralism accepts that there can be more than one type of legal order and more than one understanding of law within the same social context.[14] It is the recognition that it is not possible to neatly order different legal institutions into one system because in practice, these systems may complement, contradict and overlap with each other.[15] Among legal pluralism scholars, there is a discussion on what is understood by law, with some stating that there is a fundamental or unitary principle but that law emerges through different hierarchies and levels.[16] In addition to this, there is the challenge of knowing when one is describing law and when one is continuing to describe social life.[17] This analytical distinction

---

[14] Chiba has defined legal pluralism as 'the coexisting structure of different legal systems under the identity postulate of a legal culture in which three combinations of official law and unofficial law, indigenous law and transplanted law, and legal rules and legal postulates are conglomerated into a whole by the choice of a socio-legal entity.' Masaji Chiba, 'Other Phases of Legal Pluralism in the Contemporary World', *Ratio Juris* 11, no. 3 (1998): 228–245; John Griffiths, 'What Is Legal Pluralism?', *The Journal of Legal Pluralism and Unofficial Law* 18, no. 24 (1986): 1–55; Ralf Michaels, 'Global Legal Pluralism', *Annual Review of Law and Social Science* 5, no. 1 (2009): 243–262.

[15] Brian Z. Tamanaha, 'Understanding Legal Pluralism: Past to Present, Local to Global', *Sydney Law Review* 30, no. 3 (2008): 375–411. For discussions on typological frameworks for conceptualising legal pluralism, see also Geoffrey Swenson, 'Legal Pluralism in Theory and Practice', *International Studies Review* 20, no. 3 (2018): 438–462.

[16] Baudouin Dupret, 'Legal Pluralism, Plurality of Laws, and Legal Practices', *European Journal of Legal Studies* 1, no. 1 (2007): 1–26, http://cadmus.eui.eu//handle/1814/6852 (accessed 7 December 2017).

[17] Sally Engle Merry, 'Legal Pluralism', *Law and Society Review* 22, no. 5 (1988): 869–896.

is an important one because of the predominance of the idea of legal centralism, where the law and the legal system are viewed from the prism of the state.[18] What is lacking in the discourse is a descriptive idea of law, one that is able to empirically ascertain the nature of the different dispute resolution systems at work and the different degrees of legitimacy and acceptance that these systems have among people.[19] This would allow for a more grounded idea of where the law is and how it manifests, rather than having a framework imposed on what the law should be. It underscores the need to move beyond an essentialist idea of law, in which particular political foundations are entrenched, to one which contains a historical and contextual understanding of how law in a particular society has emerged through dynamic and dialectical processes.[20]

Legal pluralism offers a counter to the idea that the state controls all means of the administration of justice, and suggests that we must not think if something is law or is not law, but rather examine the form a particular law takes.[21] Santos introduces the idea of inter-legality, which, he argues, is the idea that we live in a polycentric world where the state is just one of many different institutions.[22] As a result, there are interpenetrations and transitions between different institutions on account of legalities that are porous and interoperable.[23] In later works, Santos and Garavito look at the impacts of globalization on the making and experiencing of law, and

---

[18] See generally Griffiths, 'What Is Legal Pluralism?'

[19] Siddharth Peter de Souza, 'Non-State Justice Systems', in *Max Planck Encyclopedia of Comparative Constitutional Law*, 2020, https://oxcon.ouplaw.com/view/10.1093/law-mpeccol/law-mpeccol-e650 (accessed 9 April 2020); Franz von Benda-Beckmannn and Keebet von Benda-Beckmannn, 'The Dynamics of Change and Continuity in Plural Legal Orders', *The Journal of Legal Pluralism and Unofficial Law* 38, nos. 53–54 (2006): 1–44.

[20] Sherman Jackson, 'Legal Pluralism between Islam and the Nation-State: Romantic Medievalism or Pragmatic Modernity?', *Fordham International Law Journal* 30, no. 1 (2006): 158–176; Marc Galanter, 'Justice in Many Rooms: Courts, Private Ordering, and Indigenous Law', *The Journal of Legal Pluralism and Unofficial Law* 13, no. 19 (1981): 1–47.

[21] Werner F. Menski, 'Comparative Law and Legal Theory from a Global Perspective', in *Comparative Law in a Global Context: The Legal Systems of Asia and Africa*, 25–81 (Cambridge: Cambridge University Press, 2006).

[22] Boaventura de Sousa Santos, 'Law: A Map of Misreading—Toward a Postmodern Conception of Law', *Journal of Law and Society* 14, no. 3 (Autumn 1987): 279–302.

[23] Ibid.

introduce the need for a new institutional imagination, which accounts for those who are usually marginalized based on gender and class. This is termed a subaltern, cosmopolitan legality,[24] a concept we will come back to in the next chapter in the context of epistemologies of the South.

In this debate about legal pluralism, the role played by institutions needs to be recognized. Douglas North defined institutions as 'the rules of the game in a society' that take the form of constraints, codes and conventions, which are both formal and informal, and are devised by human beings.[25] A detailed analysis of context would show how historical, social, cultural and political factors influence the manner in which interactions take place between formal and informal manifestations of legal institutions. Consequently, different typologies emerge based on whether there is recognition, acceptance or dominance between one institution and another.[26] This understanding of context, and of the continuous state of change in how institutions function, is particularly important because it allows us to evaluate the distinctions between the realities of how institutions function and how they are imagined by ideals of democracy and the rule of law.[27]

An engagement with legal pluralism demands moving beyond the focus on transplantation of legal ideas and procedures, with a preconceived institutional goal in mind, to respecting the knowledge of the conditions

---

[24] Boaventura de Sousa Santos and Cesar A. Rodríguez-Garavito, 'Law, Politics, and the Subaltern in Counter-Hegemonic Globalization', in *Law and Globalization from Below: Towards a Cosmopolitan Legality*, ed. Boaventura de Sousa Santos and Cesar A. Rodríguez-Garavito, 1–26 (Cambridge: Cambridge University Press, 2005).

[25] Douglass C. North, 'Institutions, Ideology, and Economic Performance', *Cato Journal* 11, no. 3 (1991): 477–496.

[26] Miranda Forsyth, 'A Typology of Relationships between State and Non-State Justice Systems', *The Journal of Legal Pluralism and Unofficial Law* 39, no. 56 (2007): 67–112; Brynna Connolly, 'Non-State Justice Systems and the State: Proposals for a Recognition Typology', *Connecticut Law Review* 38, no. 2 (2005): 239–294.

[27] Mareike Schomerus, 'Policy of Government and Policy of Culture, Understanding the Rule of Law in the "Context" Of South Sudan's Western Equatoria State', in *The International Rule of Law Movement: A Crisis of Legitimacy*, ed. David Marshall, 167–190 (Cambridge, MA: Harvard University Press 2014); Mattias Kumm, 'Global Constitutionalism and the Rule of Law', in *Handbook on Global Constitutionalism*, ed. Anthony F. Lang and Antje Wiener, 197–211 (Cheltenham: Edward Elgar Publishing, 2017).

of the society that will receive such reforms and their existing social structures.[28] Engaging with the existence of legal pluralism helps raise questions about the impact of a lack of an overarching system for mediating conflicts and claims between contending subordinate legal and normative orders. It also raises questions about the different political and epistemic systems within which normative orders operate, such that there are different kinds of contending orders from different institutions.[29] Bringing legal pluralism into the matrix of how legal reform works in practice helps establish the notion that law may not be the law.[30] It raises the relevance of 'decentering the law', which implies looking beyond the infrastructures of the state, because the manner in which law is practised and experienced emerges from competing norms and sources of authority.[31]

In one of the earliest studies of NSJS by international organizations, the Department for International Development, United Kingdom (DFID), stated that engaging with NSJS was a core element of its 'pro-poor' approach to security and justice.[32] DFID recognized that to conduct any intervention and prescribe justice reform, it was important that the development agency had a deep understanding of the historical context of how regulatory frameworks shaped the local environment, and the relationship between NSJS and the state. Further, engaging with the values that determine

---

[28] Mark Fathi Massoud, 'Ideals and Practices in the Rule of Law: An Essay on Legal Politics', *Law and Social Inquiry* 41, no. 2 (2016): 489–501; Frank Upham, 'Mythmaking in the Rule of Law Orthodoxy', Carnegie Endowment for International Peace, 2002, https://carnegieendowment.org/2002/09/10/mythmaking-in-rule-of-law-orthodoxy-pub-1063 (accessed 11 April 2020).

[29] Caroline Sage and Michael Woolcock, 'Introduction: Legal Pluralism and Development Policy—Scholars and Practitioners in Dialogue', in *Legal Pluralism and Development: Scholars and Practitioners in Dialogue*, ed. Brian Z. Tamanaha, Caroline Sage and Michael Woolcock, 1–18 (Cambridge: Cambridge University Press 2012).

[30] Daniel Adler and Sokbunthoeun So, 'Towards Equity in Development When the Law Is Not the Law: Reflections on Legal Pluralism in Practice', in *Legal Pluralism and Development: Scholars and Practitioners in Dialogue*, ed. Brian Z. Tamanaha, Caroline Sage and Michael Woolcock, 83–92 (Cambridge: Cambridge University Press 2012).

[31] Eve Darian-Smith, 'Reimagining Legal Geographies', in *Laws and Societies in Global Contexts: Contemporary Approaches*, 167–242 (Cambridge: Cambridge University Press, 2013).

[32] DFID, 'Non-State Justice and Security Systems', DFID Briefing, 2004, http://www.gsdrc.org/docs/open/ssaj101.pdf (accessed 7 May 2020).

the legitimacy of NSJS as well as the incentives and disincentives of key stakeholders to reform were important in order to ensure that the intervention for reform considered both technical and political complexities. The DFID study highlighted the value of an evidence-based approach to reform and presented a checklist to identify how measures should be designed. The checklist included asking if an intervention was needed, whether it would contribute to poverty reduction, whether it should focus on supporting the state or civil society, and whether such action would help the system perform efficiently, fairly, inclusively and accountably. It would examine whether intervention would improve linkages between the state and NSJS, whether the approach would help clarify linkages with the state and allow for political and social change and its effect on the local and national political context. Similarly, the Danish International Development Agency (DANIDA) also adopted a model which emphasized a people-centred and demand-driven approach that aimed to promote local ownership of the reform and a gradual adherence to human rights, and to look for ways that NSJS could complement the state system.[33]

This pluralist lens to legal reform emphasizes the need to diversify the sources of knowledge and institutions that otherwise make up international programming. For the rule of law as a concept, it raises several questions, including whether the concept is inclusive and adaptable enough to introduce different histories, cultures and institutions—issues that we will discuss in the next section.

The concept of the rule of law and the challenges of its promotion and application

'Rule of law' is described by Waldron as an 'essentially contested concept', not only because there is a contestation in terms of the content and requirements of the ideal but also because there is complexity in understanding what the value of the ideal is.[34] This 'essential contestability'

---

[33] DANIDA, 'Informal Justice Systems', 2009, http://um.dk/en/~/media/UM/English-site/Documents/Danida/Activities/Strategic/Human%20rights%20and%20democracy/Human%20rights/Informal%20Justice%20Systems%20final%20print.jpgH (accessed 5 November 2020).

[34] Jeremy Waldron, 'Is the Rule of Law an Essentially Contested Concept (In Florida)?', *Law and Philosophy* 21, no. 2 (2002): 137–164.

is valuable and gives the concept its dynamism, since it permits different political–moral–legal intellectual schools to invest it with different meanings and rival conceptions. In practice, however, it is evident that even the contestability is grounded in particular normative worlds with specific social, political and economic considerations.[35] Among the prominent influences on the framing of the rule of law in development programming are legal philosophers like Fuller, who proposed eight facets, which include that the law should be general, publicly promulgated, prospective, intelligible, consistent, practicable, not frequently changeable and congruent with the behaviour of the officials of the regime, while others such as Raz spoke of the rule of law as a concept that provided standards to 'effectively guide action' and also provide the legal machinery with effective remedies in case of deviation from the standards.[36] In Germany, *Rechtsstaat* is where there is recognition of civil liberties, such as separation of powers, access to courts, freedom of conscience, movement, press, protection of property and equality before law.[37]

These different definitions of the rule of law that have emerged from western contexts have played a predominant role in how the concept is conceived in the work of the United Nations (UN) and other international organizations. In the widely used definition of the UN Secretary General, the rule of law was defined as

---

[35] For a discussion of the rule of law in different contexts, see also Randall Peerenboom, 'Varieties of Rule of Law: An Introduction and Provisional Conclusion', in *Asian Discourses of Rule of Law*, ed. Randall Peerenboom, 1–55 (London: Routledge, 2003). 'The rule of law, in other words, cannot be sensibly detached from the wider normative context of a community's history, politics, morality, ethics and culture', see Iutisone Salevao, 'The Rule of Law: Principles, Issues and Challenges', in *Rule of Law, Legitimate Governance and Development in the Pacific*, 1–35 (Canberra: ANU Press, 2005), 2. See also 'Investigating the rule of law as a set of social and legal practices in context allows scholars to understand the political, social, and economic arrangements coextensive with the pursuit of the rule-of-law ideal' in Massoud, 'Ideals and Practices in the Rule of Law'.

[36] Lon Luvois Fuller, *The Morality of Law* (New Haven: Yale University Press, 1969); Joseph Raz, 'The Rule of Law and Its Virtue', in *The Authority of Law: Essays on Law and Morality*, 210–229 (Oxford: Oxford University Press).

[37] Augusto Zimmermann, 'The Rule of Law as a Culture of Legality: Legal and Extra-Legal Elements for the Realization of the Rule of Law in Society', *eLaw Journal: Murdoch University Electronic Journal of Law* 14, no. 1 (2007): 10–31.

a principle of governance in which all persons, institutions and entities, public and private, including the State itself, are accountable to laws that are publicly promulgated, equally enforced and independently adjudicated, and which are consistent with international human rights norms and standards. It requires, as well, measures to ensure adherence to the principles of supremacy of law, equality before the law, accountability to the law, fairness in the application of the law, separation of powers, participation in decision-making, legal certainty, avoidance of arbitrariness and procedural and legal transparency.[38]

The criteria adopted in this definition are expansive, but if one is to examine the kind of institutions it speaks to and the values it prioritizes, it is clear that such a definition is firmly embedded within epistemologies which require a particular western manifestation of the state and institutions of justice. Considering the plurality of normative and procedural frameworks that order the everyday life of people who utilize justice systems, whether based on religion, custom or tradition, many NSJS clearly do not meet these criteria.[39] Many are not independently adjudicated, publicly promulgated or transparent, and even if they are, the language through which these criteria are evolved and framed deliberately render them outside what is considered basic to the rule of law.[40]

---

[38] Secretary General, 'The Rule of Law and Transitional Justice in Conflict and Post-Conflict Societies', 2004, https://www.un.org/ruleoflaw/blog/document/the-rule -of-law-and-transitional-justice-in-conflict-and-post-conflict-societies-report-of-the -secretary-general/ (accessed 7 May 2020).

[39] Examples include *khap panchayat*s in India, which are based on caste and community, and deal with matters related to marriage and familial relations. See also Bhupendra Yadav, 'Khap Panchayats: Stealing Freedom?', *Economic and Political Weekly* 44, no. 52 (2009): 16–19. They also include religious courts like Federal Sharia Courts in Ethiopia, which apply Islamic law in personal or family matters, or the customary courts in South Africa, which, in matters of family law, allow persons to adjudicate their disputes based on custom and tradition. See also Matthias Kötter, 'Non-State Justice Institutions: A Matter of Fact and a Matter of Legislation', SFB Governance Working Paper Series, 2012, https://www.sfb-governance.de/en/publikationen/sfb-700-working_papers/wp34/index.html (accessed 30 July 2021).

[40] de Souza, 'Non-State Justice Systems'. See the discussion on the colonial organisations of the rule of law in Kalpana Kannabiran, 'The Contexts of Criminology: A Brief Restatement', in *Challenging the Rule(s) of Law: Colonialism, Criminology and Human*

For example, in Timor-Leste, the Maubere tribes are now reviving the old customary law of *tara bandu* to help improve natural resource management and preserve the ocean.[41] *Tara bandu* is a custom that regulates relationships between people, between people and animals, between people and the environment, and maintains peace through public agreement.[42] While this framework is seeing noticeable benefits, as also acknowledged by a report of the Asia Foundation, one of the framing questions of the report is whether *tara bandu* enhances or undermines the rule of law.[43] This is relevant because the rule of law has become a prism through which other compelling world views and concepts are evaluated. What is often not debated is that these systems are conceptualized and ordered differently from the criteria offered by the definition of rule of law, which presupposes a specific kind of legal order.[44] This standardization shows how embedded legal centralism is when one considers the definition of rule of law and its promotion. It also illustrates how, in producing knowledge, the Global North becomes a 'site of production' and the Global South becomes a 'site of reception'.[45] There is a need, therefore, to question whether adopting such a definition

---

Rights in India, ed. Kalpana Kannabiran and Ranbir Singh, 451–476 (New Delhi: SAGE Publications, 2008); Upendra Baxi, '"The State's Emissary": The Place of Law in Subaltern Studies', in *Subaltern Studies VII: Writings on South Asian History and Society*, ed. Partha Chatterjee and Gyanendra Pandey, 247–262 (New Delhi: Oxford University Press, 1992).

[41] Bikash Kumar Bhattacharya, 'Timor-Leste: Maubere Tribes Revive Customary Law to Protect the Ocean', *Mongabay Environmental News*, 26 October 2018, https://news.mongabay.com/2018/10/timor-leste-maubere-tribes-revive-customary-law-to-protect-the-ocean/ (accessed 9 April 2020).

[42] Asia Foundation, 'Tara Bandu: Its Role and Use in Community Conflict Prevention in Timor-Leste', Asia Foundation, 2013, https://asiafoundation.org/publication/tara-bandu-its-role-and-use-in-community-conflict-prevention-in-timor-leste/ (accessed 9 April 2020).

[43] Ibid.

[44] In the report by Asia Foundation, though the report mentions that the communities spoke of the complementarity of the formal justice system and *tara bandu*, it goes on to recommend that regardless of what is done with *tara bandu*, the legal system should be developed with an emphasis on formalising law.

[45] See David Lopez Medina cited in Peer Zumbansen, 'The Rule of Law, Legal Pluralism, and Challenges to a Western-Centric View: Some Very Preliminary Observations', Osgoode Legal Studies Research Paper Series, 2017, https://digitalcommons.osgoode.yorku.ca/olsrps/193; see also Tobias Berger, 'The "Global South" as a Relational

will be problematic, given its lack of acknowledgment of pluralities and contexts, and what an examination of culture would do to this otherwise neat definition of the rule of law.[46]

Carothers argues that in development programming, rule of law promotion offers a menu that contains aspects like rewriting laws, reforming institutions, upgrading the capacity of the legal profession and improving legal access across different programmes and projects.[47] These programmes adopt a more institutional focus, such that they see institutions, whether the judiciary or the police or the laws themselves, not as a means but as ends in themselves.[48] The standardizing and internationalizing of the rule of law is such that it has become a development strategy—one that is central to the vocabulary of economic policies and a concern for international economic institutions.[49] In doing so, not only are these definitions becoming points of reference in larger debates about governance, democracy and freedom,[50] but also, as we will argue later, the standardizing of these definitions results in them becoming tools of exclusion through which a process of 'othering' can take place. For example, a speech by former US President Barack Obama

---

Category: Global Hierarchies in the Production of Law and Legal Pluralism', *Third World Quarterly* 42, no. 9 (2020): 2002–2017.

[46] David Marshall, 'Introduction', in *The International Rule of Law Movement A Crisis of Legitimacy and the Way Forward*, ed. David Marshall, xiii–xxiii (Cambridge, MA: Harvard University Press 2014). See also how the rule of law is translated between international organizations and on the ground in Tobias Berger, 'Linked in Translation: International Donors and Local Fieldworkers as Translators of Global Norms', *Third World Thematics: A TWQ Journal* 2, no. 5 (2017): 606–620.

[47] Thomas Carothers, *Aiding Democracy Abroad: The Learning Curve* (Washington, DC: Carnegie Endowment, 1999).

[48] Rachel Kleinfeld, 'Competing Definitions of the Rule of Law: Implications for Practitioners', Carnegie Endowment for International Peace Washington, DC, 21 January 2005, https://carnegieendowment.org/2005/01/21/competing-definitions-of-rule-of-law-implications-for-practitioners-pub-16405 (accessed 2 August 2018).

[49] Sundhya Pahuja, 'Development and the Rule of (International Law)', in *Decolonising International Law: Development, Economic Growth and the Politics of Universality*, 172–253 (Cambridge: Cambridge University Press, 2011).

[50] Frank Schimmelfennig, 'A Comparison of the Rule of Law Promotion Policies of Major Western Powers', in *Rule of Law Dynamics: In an Era of International and Transnational Governance*, ed. Michael Zürn, André Nollkaemper and Randy Peerenboom, 111–132 (Cambridge: Cambridge University Press 2012); Janse, 'A Turn to Legal Pluralism'.

in Cairo highlights this vision of a standardized rule of law, which is also articulated in USAID documents:

> I do have an unyielding belief that all people yearn for certain things: the ability to speak your mind and have a say in how you are governed; confidence in the rule of law and the equal administration of justice; government that is transparent and doesn't steal from the people; the freedom to live as you choose. These are not just American ideas; they are human rights. And that is why we will support them everywhere. [51]

Without reflecting on the applicability of the transplantation of the rule of law globally, it has been used as a solution to many problems, from helping countries transition into democracies to determining foreign policy debates, to even being held as an essential condition for economic growth by policy makers.[52] The former UN High Commissioner for Human Rights stated that the rule of law 'constitutes the backbone for the legal protection of human rights' and further that 'the rule of law without human rights is only an empty shell'.[53] Many development projects regard the rule of law as a technical project and pay little heed to the political implications that arise through institutional change.[54] Rule of law reform has broadly revolved around the idea that it is essential to the state-building project, where legal institutions are vital to the building of the state.[55] It also reflects a neoclassical economic orthodoxy that places an emphasis on property

---

[51] 'Remarks by the President at Cairo University, 6-04-09', *whitehouse.gov*, 4 June 2009, https://obamawhitehouse.archives.gov/the-press-office/remarks-president-cairo-university-6-04-09 (accessed 10 April 2020). See also USAID, 'Democracy, Human Rights and Governance Strategy', 7 May 2019, https://www.usaid.gov/democracy/democracy-human-rights-and-governance-strategy (accessed 22 February 2022).

[52] Thomas Carothers, 'The Rule of Law Revival', *Foreign Affairs*, 1998, https://www.foreignaffairs.com/articles/1998-03-01/rule-law-revival (accessed 13 August 2018).

[53] 'Statement by the UN High Commissioner for Human Rights, Navi Pillay to the Security Council Open Debate on Maintenance of International Peace and Security', https://www.ohchr.org/EN/NewsEvents/Pages/DisplayNews.aspx?NewsID=14958&LangID=E (accessed 7 May 2020).

[54] Faundez, 'The Rule of Law Enterprise'.

[55] Julio Faundez, 'Legal Pluralism and International Development Agencies: State Building or Legal Reform?', *Hague Journal on the Rule of Law* 3, no. 1 (2011): 18–38.

rights and contract enforcement.[56] These dominant paradigms determine the manner in which the rule of law is promoted. As Desai et al. argue, a state-centrism that grounds reform work around institutions of the state, because these are seen as critical to achieving economic, political and social development, produces an 'organizational isomorphism' where inputs, incentives and information deemed successful by experts are presumed to function across contexts, and are justified under the rubric of 'best practices'.[57] As a consequence, there are unwarranted expectations on rule of law projects, where impact is expected in very short time frames that are largely unrealistic.[58] There are also expectations that things improve by following a linear trajectory. It is often the case, however, that the situation is more dynamic. As a result, donors have developed programmes with particular 'end-states' in mind, and emphasize the creation of standards and institutions that are at odds with local contexts.[59]

The problem is not that rule of law principles are not important and cannot be applied to plural legal contexts, but that there is a lack of understanding of how institutional change works, and that legal systems actually involve negotiations between different interest groups, such that many interventions within justice reform, seen mainly as technical assistance and capacity building, are in practice essentially political decisions.[60] Sage et al. argue that this approach to justice programming, by focussing on 'best practices' according to international norms, has privileged

---

[56] Simon Deakin, David Gindis, Geoffrey M. Hodgson, Kainan Huang and Katharina Pistor, 'Legal Institutionalism: Capitalism and the Constitutive Role of Law', *Journal of Comparative Economics* 45, no. 1 (2017): 188–200, http://uhra.herts.ac.uk/handle/2299/17715 (accessed 13 August 2018).

[57] Deval Desai, Deborah Isser and Michael Woolcock, 'Rethinking Justice Reform in Fragile and Conflict-Affected States: Lessons for Enhancing the Capacity of Development Agencies', *Hague Journal on the Rule of Law* 4, no. 1 (2012): 54–75.

[58] Ibid.

[59] Peter Albrecht and Helena Maria Kyed, 'Introduction: Non-State and Customary Actor in Developing Programs', in *Perspectives on Involving Non-State and Customary Actors in Justice and Security Reform*, ed. Peter Albrecht, Helene Maria Kyed, Deborah Isser and Erica Harper, 3–22 (Rome: IDLO and DIIS, 2011).

[60] Caroline Sage, Nicholas Menzies and Michael Woolcock, 'Taking the Rules of the Game Seriously: Mainstreaming Justice in Development—The World Bank's Justice for the Poor Program', Justice and Development Working Paper Series no. 7, 51845, The World Bank, 2009, http://documents.worldbank.org/curated/en/431161468331052929/

certain approaches over others, based on ideas of what institutions should exist and how they should function, resulting in lip-service being paid to realities that construct the local environment.[61] They further argue that the focus on justice-related institutions of the state such as the judiciary, police and executive ignore that the rule of (state) law is only a small component of the overall institutional framework and is unlikely to yield favourable results, and by focussing on state institutions, a lack of justice is promoted for cross sections of the population that do not constitute the elite, urban and educated, and those positioned to influence the state.[62] Such an approach is not only exclusionary but would also have limited impact.

A common trend in rule of law reform has been a market-driven approach, where a premium is placed on reducing dependence on an overburdened criminal justice system by prioritizing efficiency over human rights outcomes.[63] For example, cases can sometimes be sent to alternative dispute resolution forums in order to unburden an overburdened legal system, as in the case of *lok adalats* (people's courts) in India. In these cases, while priority is placed on reducing caseload, the quality of substantive procedures in these other forums is not investigated.[64] This narrow focus on quantity rather than quality of reform also limits the impact on enhancement of access to justice.[65] These factors illuminate the myopic approach that statist rule of law reform has taken, especially when operating in plural legal contexts. It can be seen in the workings of development agencies, which place more importance on making wholesale rather than incremental

---

Taking-the-rules-of-the-game-seriously-mainstreaming-justice-in-development-the-World-Banks-justice-for-the-poor-program (accessed 7 May 2020).

[61] Ibid., 17.

[62] Ibid., 3.

[63] International Council on Human Rights Policy, *When Legal Worlds Overlap: Human Rights, State and Non-State Law* (Geneva: International Council on Human Rights Policy, 2009).

[64] This question of efficiency in the types of data that is collected by legal indicators is dealt with in detail in Chapter 4 of the book. See also Siddharth Peter de Souza, 'India's Parallel Justice Systems: Engaging with Lok Adalats, Gram Nyayalayas, Nari Adalats and Khap Panchayats through Human Rights', in *Human Rights in India*, ed. Satvinder Juss, 80–101 (London: Routledge, 2019); Marc Galanter and Jayanth K. Krishnan, 'Bread for the Poor: Access to Justice and the Rights of the Needy in India', *Hastings Law Journal* 55 (2004): 789–834.

[65] International Council on Human Rights Policy, *When Legal Worlds Overlap*.

changes to the legal system, thereby exhibiting a lack of ownership and insufficient knowledge of the local realities that inform such work.[66] This has also led Carothers to remark that the lack of coherence in various rule of law projects results in a sense of not knowing what interventions would work.[67]

These reforms, which focussed on technocratic approaches such as altering laws and institutions, building infrastructure, power structures and capacity, have been called first generation reforms. They have now made way for second generation reforms, which acknowledge that it is necessary for the local power structures and culture to engage with the rule of law.[68] There is an acceptance that if this is not done, the institutions and laws will not function efficiently.[69]

More international organizations have started to build more reflexive and context-specific rule of law programmes. For instance, the International Development Law Organization (IDLO) has attempted to operationalize this new approach, which aims at balancing knowledge of the rule of law with a grounded approach that is fulfilled through an engagement with civil society.[70] In a recent project called DREAMS (Determined, Resilient, Empowered, AIDS-free, Mentored and Safe), a project in Tanzania which is related to HIV-related legal advice, the IDLO examines the utility of

---

[66] Golub, 'Beyond Rule of Law Orthodoxy'; Franz von Benda-Beckmann, 'The Multiple Edges of Law: Dealing with Legal Pluralism in Development Practice', in *The World Bank Legal Review: Law, Equity and Development*, ed. Caroline Mary Sage and Michael Woolcock, vol. 2, 51–86 (Washington, DC: The World Bank, 2006); Julio Faundez, 'Should Justice Reform Projects Take Non-State Justice Systems Seriously? Perspectives from Latin America', in *The World Bank Legal Review: Law, Equity and Development*, ed. Caroline Mary Sage and Michael Woolcock, vol. 2, 113–139 (Washington, DC: The World Bank 2006).

[67] Thomas Carothers, 'The Problem of Knowledge', in *Promoting the Rule of Law Abroad: The Problem of Knowledge*, ed. Thomas Carothers, 15–30 (Washington, DC: Carnegie Endowment, 2006).

[68] Rachel Kleinfeld, 'How to Advance the Rule of Law Abroad', Carnegie Endowment for International Peace, 2013 https://carnegieendowment.org/files/how_to_advance_ROL.pdf (accessed 24 December 2020).

[69] Ibid.

[70] IDLO, 'The 2nd Generation of Rule of Law Reform', International Development Law Organization, https://www.idlo.int/news/events/2nd-generation-rule-law-reform (accessed 6 April 2020).

such services by looking at all drivers of injustice—social, economic and cultural—and aims to not only strengthen justice institutions but also people's capacities to claim rights through empowerment and awareness initiatives.[71]

In another example, the World Bank's 'Justice for the Poor' (J4P) project argues for a grounded approach to reform, which is to understand

> 'real rules of the game'—that is, how law, social norms, power and authority work in practice (as opposed to how they 'should' work)— has meant engaging with a broad set of institutions and authorities and appreciating the challenges as well as capabilities they bring to the process.[72]

It seeks to build legal empowerment with a commitment to local realities where there is a need to examine diverse voices who can participate in the reordering of a society. Such reform should not be seen as something that is a one-off, but instead should be viewed as an iterative and dynamic process, which is responsive to change depending on the evolving contextual realities.[73] In order to achieve responsiveness, J4P advances building local research capacity in order to drive context-driven reform while also employing diverse sources of empirical evidence.[74] A deeper engagement with local contexts has resulted in projects that examine 'what is' the situation on the ground rather than making assumptions on 'what should be' the situation to prevent importing idealized solutions in all areas of development and not just the legal sector.[75]

Similarly, in Germany, the Federal Ministry for Economic Development and Cooperation has articulated the need for more a grounded approach by stating that

---

[71] IDLO, 'HIV-Related Legal Services for Adolescent Girls, Young Women', International Development Law Organization, 20 December 2016, https://www.idlo.int/news/highlights/hiv-related-legal-services-adolescent-girls-and-young-women (accessed 6 April 2020).

[72] World Bank, 'Justice for the Poor', https://www.worldbank.org/en/topic/governance/brief/justice-for-the-poor, (accessed 7 May 2020).

[73] Sage, Menzies and Woolcock, 'Taking the Rules of the Game Seriously', 15.

[74] Ibid.

[75] Ibid., 18.

[t]he German government believes that the principles of the rule of law, democracy, the welfare state and human rights are interdependent, and frames its development policy accordingly. However, there is no one-size-fits-all strategy for establishing structures based on the rule of law since every country has its own particular history and constitutional traditions. It would not do simply to transplant the German legal system to other countries. Rather, in its cooperation with developing countries and emerging economies, Germany always seeks to analyse the existing structures in each country and come up with solutions and support measures suited to that country.[76]

In addition to adopting new methods for justice reform, there have also been steps to improve the method and efficiency of distributing foreign aid in order to better reflect a participatory, coordinated and locally owned framework. In 2005, the Paris Declaration was endorsed by over 100 countries to improve the quality and effectiveness of aid.[77] The principles adopted in this agreement state that developing countries would take ownership for their own strategies for poverty reduction and that donor countries would align their objectives accordingly; that donor countries would co-ordinate and share results to avoid duplication; and finally that results would be measured and mutual accountability enforced on all parties.[78] The Accra Agenda for Action in 2008 with over 80 developing countries, all OECD countries and 3,000 civil society organizations, meant to strengthen the implementation of the Paris Declaration, emphasized a model of participative inclusive ownership, wherein aid-recipient countries had more say in their development processes, and donors, foundations, and civil society coordinated with each other on aid delivery.[79] This is relevant to the discussion because it points to a more grounded approach to development programming.

---

[76] BMZ, 'Rule of Law: Protecting Citizens from Arbitrary Rule by the State', Federal Ministry for Economic Cooperation and Development,http://www.bmz.de/en/issues/rule_of_law/hintergrund/index.html (accessed 10 April 2020).

[77] OECD, 'Paris Declaration on Aid Affectiveness and Accra Agenda for Action', https://www.oecd.org/dac/effectiveness/parisdeclarationandaccraagendaforaction.htm (accessed 7 May 2020).

[78] Ibid.

[79] Ibid.

These developments point to a shift in terms of how rule of law programming is taking place. It is important to document how the rule of law is now developing with local partnerships and keeping in mind the institutional and people needs for why projects are being introduced and employed. The reason for reflecting on this shift is to examine how the concept is moving beyond a statist conception to one that can be reimagined for plural legal contexts. In the next section, I explore the interconnections between the rule of law and legal pluralism before examining its applicability in legal indicators. In the fourth section, I study how the rule of law can be reframed and made less technical and included in an access to justice framework to make it suitable for plural legal contexts.

Rule of law and legal pluralism and the search for interconnections

Reframing the rule of law must begin with an understanding of the limitations in how it is framed. One way of doing this is to acknowledge that if we are to use the ideal of the rule of law, then it must be developed and nurtured as much by local communities as it is in international courts for a more meaningful approach and, as Baxi argues, to make it a 'participative enterprise of myriad of subaltern voices'.[80] This also reflects on the need to factor in how the history of ideas, grassroots movements, constitutional

---

[80] Baxi argues,

> The authentic quest for renaissance of the Rule of Law has just begun its world historic career. ROL epistemic communities have choices to make. Our ways of ROL talk may either wholly abort or aid to a full birth some new ROL conceptions now struggling to find a voice through multitudinous spaces of people's struggles against global capitalism that presage alternatives to it. We need after all, I believe, to place ourselves all over again under the tutelage of Michael Oakeshott. He reminds us, preciously, that far from being a 'finished product' of humankind history, the Rule of Law discourse 'remains an individual composition, a unity of particularity and generality, in which each component is what it is in virtue of what it contributes to the delineation of the whole'. That virtue of the 'whole' may not any longer legitimate Euro American narratology. Rather the task remains re-privileging other ways of telling ROL stories as a form of participative enterprise of myriad "subaltern" voices.

traditions and domestic and international institutions can play a role in the emergence of the concept of the rule of law.[81] Doing so will allow for a more dynamic and inclusive idea of the rule of law.

Reflecting on this need to incorporate diversity, a UN General Assembly resolution in 2006 on 'Human Rights and Cultural Diversity' urged that state political and legal systems incorporate the diversity that is constituent in their societies. [82] In a background paper on the rule of law and the post-2015 development agenda, the United Nations Development Programme (UNDP) highlighted the importance of multiple realities and diversities, and described the rule of law as

> (a) a social and political reality that exists according to different values, norms and institutional forms; (b) a system of rules, values and organisations that underpins governance; and (c) a set of processes, enabling conditions and outcomes that operates at multiple levels and cuts across sectors to affect sustainable human development.[83]

In Upendra Baxi, 'The Rule of Law in India', *Sur – Revista Internacional De Direitos Humanos* 6 (2007): 7–27 http://socialsciences.scielo.org/scielo.php?script=sci_abstract &pid=S1806-64452007000100001&lng=en&nrm=iso&tlng=en (accessed 2 June 2021). For how the rule of law should be seen as work in progress, see also James A. Goldston, 'New Rules for the Rule of Law', in *The International Rule of Law Movement: A Crisis of Legitimacy and the Way Forward*, ed. David Marshall, 1–42 (Cambridge, MA: Harvard Law School 2014).

[81] For the discussion on human rights, see generally Philip Alston, 'Does the Past Matter? On the Origins of Human Rights', *Harvard Law Review* 126, no. 7 (2013): 2043–2081, 2077. See also Narasappa who speaks of the impetus of socio-economic rights in thinking about the rule of law in India in Harish Narasappa, 'India's Rule of Law: A Theoretical Analysis', in *Rule of Law in India: A Quest for Reason*, 37–62 (New Delhi: Oxford University Press, 2019).

[82] United Nations General Assembly, 'Human Rights and Cultural Diversity A/Res/60/167', 27 February 2000, https://digitallibrary.un.org/record/404848?ln=en (accessed 30 July 2021).

[83] Louis-Alexandre Berg and Deval Desai, 'Background Paper: Overview on the Rule of Law and Sustainable Development for the Global Dialogue on Rule of Law and the Post-2015 Development Agenda', UNDP, 2013, https://tijpublicforum.org/wp-content/uploads/2018/06/4-20130801-READING_Global-Dialogue-Background-Paper-Rule-of-Law-and-Sustainable-Developme....pdf (accessed 22 February 2022).

The Secretary General's *Report on the Rule of Law and Transitional Justice in Conflict and Post-Conflict Societies* is also relevant here because it acknowledges that

> due regard must be given to indigenous and informal traditions for administering justice or settling disputes, to help them to continue their often vital role and to do so in conformity with both international standards and local tradition. Where these are ignored or overridden, the result can be the exclusion of large sectors of society from accessible justice.[84]

This strengthens the argument that the role of NSJS as forums for promoting the rule of law is essential. Tamanaha argues that while NSJS do not meet all the requirements of the rule of law, such as the rules being publicly promulgated or stable, 'they can satisfy several rule-of-law functions by supplying some of the benefits that make the rule of law valuable'.[85] While the approach to the rule of law initially focussed on state institutions like judiciaries, establishing business-friendly regimes, and promoting government-based institutions, [86] the global debate is slowly making way for approaches that are less technocratic and more context dependent. While this is a starting point, more needs to be done to problematize these requirements of the rule of law and why these requirements should be challenged when thinking through a pluralist lens.[87]

In 1989, the International Labour Organization Convention, concerning Indigenous and Tribal Peoples in Independent Countries (No. 169), also emphasized that there must be recognition of the forums that people use to

---

[84] Secretary General, 'The Rule of Law and Transitional Justice in Conflict and Post-Conflict Societies', 12.

[85] Brian Z. Tamanaha, 'Introduction: A Bifurcated Theory of Law in Hybrid Societies', in *Non-State Justice Institutions and the Law: Decision-Making at the Interface of Tradition, Religion and the State*, ed. M. Kötter, Tilmann J. Röder, Gunnar Folke Schuppert and Rüdiger Wolfrum, 1–21 (London: Springer, 2015), 17.

[86] Golub, 'Beyond Rule of Law Orthodoxy'.

[87] Faundez, 'Should Justice Reform Projects Take Non-State Justice Systems Seriously?'; Deborah H. Isser, 'The Problem with Problematizing Legal Pluralism', in *Legal Pluralism and Development: Scholars and Practitioners in Dialogue*, ed. Brian Z. Tamanaha, Caroline Sage and Michael Woolcock, 237–248 (Cambridge: Cambridge University Press, 2012).

adjudicate their disputes as long as these did not contravene with a universal conception of human rights.[88] In General Comment No. 32 to Article 14 of the International Covenant on Civil and Political Rights (ICCPR), the Human Rights Committee, acknowledging legal plurality, stated, 'Article 14 is also relevant where a State, in its legal order, recognizes courts based on customary law, or religious courts, to carry out or entrusts them with judicial tasks'.[89] In 2007, the UN Declaration on the Rights of Indigenous People acknowledged the resilience of plural legal orders.[90] Article 4 provides for the 'right to maintain and strengthen their distinct political, legal, economic, social and cultural institutions' while also continuing to be able to participate fully in the life of the state.[91] The importance of continuing to cultivate different forums finds support in Article 34, which speaks of a right to 'promote, develop, maintain their institutional structures and their distinctive customs, spirituality, traditions, procedures, practices and, in the cases where they exist, juridical systems in accordance with international human rights'.[92] However, the declaration also reiterated that using such forums does not mean that users cannot use other systems of the state for a fair resolution of their cases. In 2013, UNDP, UNICEF (United Nations Children Fund) and UN Women released a comprehensive report suggesting a human rights engagement with informal justice systems, arguing that it was imperative because of the sheer scale and entrenchment of these systems across the world.[93]

These developments with regard to engaging at a systemic level with plurality in legal systems are scattered and uncoordinated and have resulted in gaps and lack of clarity on aspects of indigenous and minority-rights,

---

[88] International Labour Organization, 'Indigenous and Tribal Peoples Convention (No. 169)', 1989, https://www.ilo.org/dyn/normlex/en/f?p=NORMLEXPUB:12100:0::NO::P12100_ILO_CODE:C169 (accessed 7 May 2020).

[89] United Nations Human Rights Committee, 'General Comment No. 32, Article 14: Right to Equality before Courts and Tribunals and to a Fair Trial', 2007, http://hrlibrary.umn.edu/gencomm/hrcom32.html (accessed 7 May 2020).

[90] United Nations General Assembly, 'United Nations Declaration on Rights of Indigenous Peoples 61/295', 13 September 2007, https://www.un.org/esa/socdev/unpfii/documents/DRIPS_en.pdf (accessed 7 May 2020).

[91] Ibid.

[92] Ibid.

[93] Danish Institute for Human Rights, 'Informal Justice Systems'.

gender equality and the right to culture.[94] These are the sites where contestations, rival meanings and alternative conceptions, including what constitutes the rule of law, are most apparent. The complexity and reluctance of engaging with plurality is also reflected in empirical approaches to evaluating the rule of law. In one of the few indicators that even considers legal pluralism, the Rule of Law Index of the World Justice Project (WJP), a factor as part of its indicator framework for 'informal justice' (traditional, tribal, religious and community) is included for the important role when formal institutions are seen as ineffective.[95] However, in evaluation, the difficulty of reconciling NSJS with statist rule of law is evidenced when the WJP states that despite this factor being included in the framework of 'Rule of Law', which also includes 'constraints on government powers, absence of corruption, open government, fundamental rights, order and security, regulatory enforcement, civil justice, criminal justice', it has been excluded from 'aggregated scores and rankings in order to provide meaningful cross-country comparisons'.[96] It is important to ask whether such an approach fosters more meaningful comparison when it limits the frame through which to evaluate the rule of law. If it is more meaningful, then who is it meaningful for? How does one distinguish meaningfulness from a donor perspective, a recipient perspective, a North perspective or a South perspective? Are other factors more amenable to cross-country comparison? Kötter makes the important distinction that when NSJS are evaluated with respect to access to justice, they must take into account both their 'functional capability' and their 'normative legitimacy'.[97] This is missing in the existing debate as often the search for something 'meaningful' is limited to outcomes that are palatable to a state-building project, which has been a feature of rule of law reform and also symptomatic of its failings. [98]

---

[94] International Council on Human Rights Policy, *When Legal Worlds Overlap*.

[95] World Justice Project, *WJP Rule of Law Index 2020* (2020), https://worldjusticeproject. org/our-work/research-and-data/wjp-rule-law-index-2020 (accessed 22 April 2020).

[96] Ibid, 163.

[97] Matthias Kötter, 'Better Access to Justice by Public Recognition of Non-State Justice Systems?', Social Science Research Network, SSRN Scholarly Paper ID 2613408, 2015, https://papers.ssrn.com/abstract=2613408 (accessed 7 May 2020).

[98] Janse, 'A Turn to Legal Pluralism'; Tamanaha, 'The Rule of Law and Legal Pluralism in Development'. See generally Brian Z. Tamanaha, Caroline Sage and Michael Woolcock (eds.), *Legal Pluralism and Development: Scholars and Practitioners in Dialogue* (Cambridge: Cambridge University Press 2012).

While still fragmented, engaging with legal plurality has gained increasing acceptance in international organizations, policy work and donor engagement in justice reform. This recognition of the interaction between multiple forums for dispute resolution is a positive change from earlier programmes that were rooted in legal centralism, perpetuating a particular form of legal and normative ordering. In this context, in the next section, I explore how the discussions on legal pluralism percolate to discussions on legal indicators, and how these shifts in recognizing institutional plurality and diversity in communities and people are reflected (or not) in the development and conceptualization of tools that are used to measure how justice systems function. I will return to the discussion of whether it is possible to have a more grounded concept that can complement a statist rule of law that is embedded in people's experiences and realities.

Legal Indicators and Rule of Law

This section begins with a description of the concepts and methods that are used to describe the rule of law in six legal indicator projects. It outlines the key variables that are used as well as the ways in which data are generated. The indicator frameworks are analysed and evaluated in terms of how they capture contexts in the Global South and plural legal contexts. Thereafter, the indicators are evaluated in terms of how they are developed, how they engage with and contribute to discourses around them and how they are sustained.

The concept and method to describe the rule of law in legal indicators

The chapter has so far focussed on rule of law programming in general. In this section, I extend the discussion to how indicators play an important role in describing the contours of the rule of law and influence how it manifests as a concept.[99] As Merkel demonstrates in his analysis of different

---

[99] The definition of indicators used in Chapter 2 is provided here for reference. Davis et al. have defined indicators as 'a named collection of rank-ordered data that purports to represent the past or projected performance of different units generated through a process that simplifies raw data about a complex social phenomenon' in Davis,

legal indicators,[100] there are different conceptions of the rule of law in legal indicators that can be seen on a continuum: from a narrow minimalist construction of law and order, to an intermediate form that examines issues of separation of powers and checks and balances, to a more maximalist order grounded in human rights.[101] Legal indicators are used to assess and evaluate the state of governance, the functioning of a democracy and the management of political and judicial institutions across the world.[102] They are designed to provide analysis about the state of the world, and through that their concepts and methods illustrate the particular choices of what constitutes the rule of law.

This section will examine six indicator projects. These are the WJP Rule of Law Index, the Democracy Barometer, the World Bank Worldwide Governance Indicators, the United Nations Rule of Law Indicators, the Ibrahim Index on African Governance, and the Hague Model of Access to Justice; the projects aim to measure how justice systems function. These six indicator projects have been selected because each of them offers a specific and explicit formulation of the idea of the rule of law.[103] Some are frameworks dedicated entirely to the rule of law, like the WJP and the UN Rule of Law indices, while others include the rule of law as a subset of a larger concept such as governance or democracy. The Hague Model of

---

Kingsbury and Merry, 'Introduction', 6. The term indicator is used in the description of the six projects to identify the key elements of the framework. They will also have sub-dimensions and criterion that make up the composite indicator.

[100] Wolfgang Merkel, 'Measuring the Quality of Rule of Law', in *Rule of Law Dynamics: In an Era of International and Transnational Governance*, ed. Michael Zürn, André Nollkaemper and Randy Peerenboom, 21–47 (Cambridge: Cambridge University Press, 2012).

[101] Ibid. See also Svend-Erik Skaaning, 'Measuring the Rule of Law', *Political Research Quarterly* 63, no. 2 (2010): 449–460; Jørgen Møller and Svend-Erik Skaaning, 'Evaluating Extant Rule of Law Measures', in *The Rule of Law: Definitions, Measures, Patterns and Causes*, ed. Jørgen Møller and Svend-Erik Skaaning, 41–61 (London: Palgrave Macmillan, 2014).

[102] Such as the World Bank Worldwide Governance Indicators, The Rule of Law Index of the World Justice project and the Democracy Barometer.

[103] In contrast, The Ease of Doing Business Index does not have a specific indicator set on the rule of law, as compared to the World Governance Indicator by the Work Bank. Sustainable Development Goal 16, which uses the framework of access to justice over the rule of law, is also discussed later in this chapter.

Access to Justice presents a contrast to how measuring access to justice can offer a different approach to focussing on the rule of law.

Each of the six indicator projects is described on two grounds. The first outlines the concept of the rule of law, which is a component of these indicator frameworks, and the second elaborates on the method used to collect data to populate these indicators. These two aspects assume importance in understanding legal indicators because they give a sense of the kinds of values, institutions and ideals that the frameworks seek to measure, as well as the priorities they have in their data collection methods.

a. The World Justice Project

The Rule of Law Index of the World Justice Project (WJP)[104] was developed to provide a comprehensive measure to understand how the rule of law is experienced in everyday life. It conducts an analysis in 128 countries around the globe and produces an index annually that adopts four universal principles in its methodological framework. These are

> (1) the government and its officials and agents are accountable under the law; (2) the laws are clear, publicized, stable, and fair, and protect fundamental rights, including the security of persons and property; (3) the process by which the laws are enacted, administered, and enforced is accessible, fair, and efficient; and (4) access to justice is provided by competent, independent, and ethical adjudicators, attorneys or representatives, and judicial officers who are of sufficient number, have adequate resources, and reflect the makeup of the communities they serve.[105]

---

[104] The World Justice Project is described as an independent multidisciplinary organization that aims to advance the rule of law internationally and is headquartered in the United States. World Justice Project, 'Advancing the Rule of Law Worldwide', https://worldjusticeproject.org/ (accessed 6 November 2020).

[105] Mark David Agrast, Juan Carlos Botero and Alejandro Ponce, *The World Justice Project: Rule of Law Index* (Washington, DC: World Justice Project, 2010), https://worldjusticeproject.org/sites/default/files/WJP_Rule_of_Law_Index_2010_Report.pdf (accessed 5 July 2020).

Based on these four principles, the index is organized around nine themes: constraints on government powers, absence of corruption, open government, fundamental rights, order and security, regulatory enforcement, civil justice, criminal justice and informal justice. [106] The first theme of *limited government* examines the checks and balances that address the principle of whether the government in power is subject to legal (constitutional and institutional) constraints such that it is accountable and there are no unbridled excesses. The second theme of *absence of corruption* measures how public power is used for private gain, in particular through three forms: bribery, improper influence by the public or private interests, and misappropriation of public funds. The third theme of *order and security* examines how security of persons and property are guaranteed by society. The fourth theme measures the protection of *fundamental rights* and draws largely from core human rights guaranteed under international law. The fifth theme of *open government* looks at how access, participation and collaboration play a crucial role in transparency and accountability. The sixth theme examines issues of *fairness and effectiveness* in enforcing government regulations. The seventh theme looks at *access to civil justice* and measures whether users can resolve their civil disputes peacefully. The eighth theme constitutes an examination of how the *criminal justice system* redresses grievances and brings actions against individuals for offences against society. The ninth theme on *informal justice* examines whether such systems are impartial and effective and whether they respect and protect fundamental rights.

The formulation of the rule of law adopted in this index presents a wide range of factors. Their criterion of open government examines both the quality of the law as well as transparency. The emphasis on absence of corruption is also seen as an effort to ensure accountability. Factors such as civil, criminal, informal justice and regulatory enforcement look at the management of justice delivery in different spheres. It also examines plurality through its focus on informal justice, and personal rights through the component on fundamental rights. Finally, through limited government, it examines the separation of powers.

The WJP attempts to provide a focus on rule of law outcomes and not on institutional means. As a result, it attempts to position itself as end oriented, such that it is a measurement not of how law is written but how

---

[106] World Justice Project, *WJP Rule of Law Index 2020*.

it plays out in practice.[107] The data is based on over 130,000 households and 4,000 legal expert surveys worldwide. There are two original data sources that are used, a general population poll (GPP) and a series of qualified respondent questionnaires (QRQ). The GPP surveys enable an analysis of the experiences and perceptions of ordinary people through an analysis of their interactions and dealings with the justice system. The QRQ, in addition, are meant to complement the GPP with inputs and assessments from those who have expertise in different aspects of justice delivery. These sources are equally weighted in the sense that the data from each source is given the same importance.[108] Further, while the factor on informal justice is included in the framework, it is excluded from aggregated scores and rankings because, as the methodology argues, this makes it simpler to engage in cross-country comparisons.[109]

b. The Democracy Barometer

The Democracy Barometer was conceptualized to measure the quality of democracy in a country based on three main factors: freedom, control and equality.[110] Each of these three factors has three further components. 'Freedom' comprises individual liberty, rule of law and the public sphere; 'control' includes competition, mutual constraints and governmental capability; and 'equality' includes transparency, participation and representation.[111]

---

[107] Juan Carlos Botero and Alejandro Ponce, 'Measuring the Rule of Law', Social Science Research Network, SSRN Scholarly Paper ID 1966257, 2011, https://papers.ssrn.com/abstract=1966257 (accessed 7 May 2020).

[108] World Justice Project, *WJP Rule of Law Index 2020*.

[109] Ibid.

[110] This project was supported by the Swiss National Centre of Competence in Research (NCCR) and was a joint project between the Berlin Social Science Centre (WZB) and the Centre for Democracy Studies Aarau (ZDA). It is now run by the ZDA and the Department of Political Science at the University of Zurich. Democracy Barometer, 'Democracy Barometer Project Background', 9 September 2020, https://democracybarometer.org/team/ (accessed 6 November 2020); WZB, 'Democracy Barometer: Project Description', https://www.wzb.eu/en/node/4858/subpage/7494 (accessed 6 November 2020).

[111] Marc Bühlmann, Wolfgang Merkel, Lisa Müller and Bernhard Weßels, 'The Democracy Barometer: A New Instrument to Measure the Quality of Democracy and Its Potential for Comparative Research', *European Political Science* 11 (2012): 519–536.

The component on the rule of law has been defined through two broad factors: equality before law and the quality of the legal system. The factor concerning equality before law includes the existence of constitutional provisions that provide for impartial courts, an independent and effective judiciary, and an impartial and effective legal system. The quality of the legal system is determined by the existence of constitutional provisions for judicial professionalism as well as the existence of confidence in the justice system and the police.[112]

The conceptualization of the rule of law dimensions of the Democracy Barometer is a much thinner formulation compared to the WJP, primarily because it is seen as one element in the study of the quality of democracy. In this form of measurement, the features are limited to those of separation of powers through an emphasis on the independence of the judiciary and the impartiality of the legal system, and accountability in ensuring judicial professionalism and confidence, which could also be related to the aspect of maintenance of law and order.

In the Democracy Barometer approach, a total of 105 indicators were selected from an overall initial umbrella group of 300 indicators. These indicators were chosen based on the aforementioned theoretical framework as well as empirical considerations. In order to ensure the reliability of the measurement, different kinds of data are used, including aggregated survey data and expert inputs from a broad set of sources. These are seen as essential to reduce the variability and randomness of survey results.

c. The Worldwide Governance Indicators

The World Bank in its Worldwide Governance Indicators (WGI) sought to develop cross-country indicators for measuring governance. The WGI consists of six composite indicators, including voice and accountability, political stability and absence of violence and terrorism, government effectiveness, regulatory quality, the rule of law and control of corruption.[113] Governance is defined as

---

[112] Ibid.

[113] Daniel Kaufmann, Aart Kraay and Massimo Mastruzzi, 'The Worldwide Governance Indicators: Methodology and Analytical Issues', *Hague Journal on the Rule of Law* 3 (2011): 220–246.

The traditions and institutions by which authority in a country is exercised. This includes (a) the process by which governments are selected, monitored and replaced; (b) the capacity of the government to effectively formulate and implement sound policies; and (c) the respect of citizens and the state for the institutions that govern economic and social interactions among them.[114]

The rule of law is defined as 'the extent to which agents have confidence in, and abide by, the rules of society, including quality of contract enforcement and property rights, the police and the courts, as well as the likelihood of crime and violence'.[115] This definition looks at three characteristics: the obedience of the law, the manner of enforcement by different institutions, and the existence of violence. The conceptualization of the WGI is narrow, and the rule of law is seen as only one component of a wider concept of governance, where indicators are interrelated. It thus focuses on the rule of law in terms of rules that govern its functioning.

The WGI gets its data from diverse perception-based governance data sources. These include surveys of households and firms, as well as assessments from business, non-governmental and multilateral organization information providers.[116] Among the surveys is the World Economic Forum's *Global Competitiveness Report*. Among the public sector data sources, major country reports of multilateral organizations like the World Bank and Asian Development Bank were analysed, and non-governmental organizations like Freedom House were included. Finally, for commercial business providers, the Economic Intelligence Unit was used as a source of information. In 2009, of the 31 data sources used, 5 were commercial business providers, 9 were from surveys or data from non-governmental organizations and the remaining 8 from public sector providers.[117]

---

[114] Ibid., 222.

[115] In this case, where citizens, officials and the state have respect for the institutions. Ibid., 223.

[116] For more on the WGI data sources and documentation, please refer to World Bank, 'WGI 2020 Interactive: Documentation', https://info.worldbank.org/governance/wgi/Home/Documents#wgiDataSources (accessed 24 December 2020).

[117] World Bank, 'World Governance Indicators 2019', https://info.worldbank.org/governance/wgi/ (accessed 7 May 2020).

d. The UN Rule of Law Indicators

In the UN Rule of Law Indicators, the rule of law is taken as a principle of governance, one that is fundamental to peace building and establishing effective state institutions. The scope of this set of indicators is limited to the functioning of criminal justice institutions. The three main institutional heads that are covered by this framework are the police and other law enforcement agencies, the judiciary and prisons.

The framework consists of 135 indicators grouped under the three institutions: the police, the judicial system and the prison. The institutions are measured in terms of the following dimensions:

Performance: Institutions provide efficient and effective services that are accessible and responsive to the needs of the people

Integrity, transparency and accountability: Institutions operate transparently and with integrity, and are held accountable to rules and standards of conduct.

Treatment of members of vulnerable groups: How criminal justice institutions treat minorities, victims, children in need of protection or in conflict with the law, and internally displaced persons, asylum-seekers, refugees, returnees, stateless and mentally ill individual

Capacity: Institutions have the human and material resources necessary to perform their functions, and the administrative and management capacity to de-ploy these resources effectively[118]

There are four different sources of data for this framework. This includes administrative data, which are data from criminal justice institutions, international organizations, civil society organizations and sometimes even NSJS; survey data from experts, which is confidential information from persons with specialized knowledge; a public survey of a representative sample of the general population; field data available to UN organizations; and document review of constitutions, procedure codes, ruling and

---

[118] United Nations, *The United Nations Rule of Law Indicators: Implementation Guide and Project Tools* (2011), https://reliefweb.int/sites/reliefweb.int/files/resources/Full_Report_1653.pdf (accessed 22 February 2022), 3.

decisions from courts and tribunals.[119] The purpose of this variety of sources is to suggest a multiplicity of perspectives when evaluating the functioning of the justice institutions, and also for them to be complementary such that they compensate for sources that may be weaker.[120] In doing so, the indicators aspire to be flexible and customisable, such that they can be adaptable to different settings.

e. Ibrahim Index of African Governance

When measuring overall governance, this index[121] takes into account several factors that can be broadly organized in four main aspects: safety and rule of law, participation and human rights, sustainable economic opportunity, and human development. Each of these factors has sub-components and, for the purpose of our measurement of rule of law, the first one assumes importance. Under safety and rule of law, there are four further dimensions: rule of law, transparency, accountability, personal safety and national security. The rule of law includes six indicators, namely the independence of the judiciary, the independence and transparency of the judicial process, access to justice, property rights, mechanisms for orderly transfers of power, and absence of multilateral sanctions. In this framework, while there is overlap with many of the other framings of the rule of law, the aspects of an orderly transfer of power and the absence of sanctions stems from experiences that are unique to the thirty-three countries in Africa that are being measured.

In terms of data collection, this is populated by relying on external sources such as the Bertelsmann Stiftung Bertelsmann Transformation Index, data from the Economist Intelligence Unit, the World Economic Forum's *World Competitiveness Report* and the Varieties of Democracy Project.[122]

f. The Hague Model of Access to Justice

This approach to measuring justice has been developed by the Tilburg Institute for Interdisciplinary Studies of Civil Law and Conflict Resolution

---

[119] Ibid., 24.

[120] Ibid., 3.

[121] Mo Ibrahim Foundation, 'Ibrahim Index of African Governance (IIAG)', http://mo.ibrahim.foundation/iiag (accessed 7 May 2020).

[122] Ibid.

Systems and the Hague Institute for Internationalization of the Law (now called the Hague Institute for Innovation of Law). It aims at exploring the functioning of a justice system by embarking on a study of the urgent legal needs of people. The methodology consists of three critical elements that need to be addressed when a user embarks upon a path to justice, which include the cost involved in people using particular procedure, the quality of the procedure, and the quality of the outcome.[123] The methodology can be applied to a whole legal system, specific legal systems or parts of the system, and seeks to ask the following questions: 'How does the particular legal system meet the demand for justice? Are the paths to justice performing consistently, or are there significant variations? What are the gaps? Which practices are better suited to study in greater detail?'[124]

Each of the three elements considers several sub-elements. The *cost of procedure* includes out-of-pocket expenses, time spent on dealing with procedure, the opportunity cost due to length of proceedings and other intangible costs including emotional and social effects of prolonged litigation. The *quality of procedure* consists of factors including procedural justice related to perceptions of fairness from the user, restorative justice concerned with the need for reparation, interpersonal justice concerned with politeness, respect and propriety, and informational justice related to decision-making processes. *Quality of outcomes* are measured by distributive justice in allocating resources between competing claims; corrective justice, which requires the injurer to make the harmed party whole; restorative justice, which looks at the best means for reparation of harm; retributive justice, which looks at proportional pain to achieve justice, informational justice as the foundation for all decision processes; transformative justice, which is related to finding ways to live together in reconciliation; and legal pragmatism, which is concerned with facts and consequences and formal justice.

This framework offers three options, which differ in terms of the depth of the data collected through questionnaires: an Instant Scan, a

---

[123] Tilburg Institute for Interdisciplinary Studies of Civil Law and Conflict Resolution Systems (TISCO), Martin Gramatikov, Maurits Barendrecht, Malini Laxminarayan, Jin Ho Verdonschot, Laura Klaming and Corry van Zeeland, *A Handbook for Measuring the Costs and Quality of Access to Justice* (Apeldoorn, Antwerpen and Portland: Maklu Publishers, 2010).

[124] Ibid., 16.

Quick Scan and a Thorough Scan.[125] For the most thorough investigation, called the Thorough Scan, a detailed questionnaire is prepared for a cross-sectional survey in combination with a focus group and diary study. The aim of combining methods is to ensure validity and reliability of the results.[126]

This section has examined the concepts and methods used by leading measurement frameworks and has sought to unpack what issues are amplified and examined by these frameworks. In the following section, I will examine the limitations and constraints of indicators, particularly in the light of legal pluralism.

Plurality, power structures, and the Global South: Factors to evaluate legal indicators

In the study of legal indicators in a plural legal context, a number of questions assume importance. Are the indicators viewed as part of a global project that suggests that different countries should reflect on their own processes to meet an idealized standard for the rule of law? Are these tools to suggest reform or tools to build similar legal systems globally? Do these indicators reflect values only of the Global North or are there influences from the Global South? Are these indicators adaptable for different contexts?

In order to address these questions and uncover some of the existing power structures when discussing the creation of global law projects, it is important to look at the kinds of structures that give rise to such indicator projects. Do these systems have the potential to create hegemonic structures that attempt to establish universally acceptable norms, and does this dilute the diverse cultures of the world?[127]

---

[125] Ibid., 17.

[126] Ibid., 81.

[127] See Darian-Smith for discussions on questions of knowledge production in indicators. Eve Darian-Smith, 'Mismeasuring Humanity: Examining Indicators through a Critical Global Studies Perspective', *New Global Studies* 10, no. 1 (2016): 73–99. For discussions on thinking critically about plural normative orders, see also Luis Eslava and Sundhya Pahuja, 'Beyond the (Post)Colonial: TWAIL and the Everyday Life of International Law', *Verfassung Und Recht In Übersee / Law and Politics in Africa, Asia and Latin America* 45, no. 2 (2012): 195–221.

In order to do this, I argue for three criteria of analysis: (*a*) the construction of the indicator, which examines the antecedents of how the rule of law is conceptualized and how data is gathered on its functioning; (*b*) how the indicator reflects and responds to the context and complexities of the lives it seeks to evaluate; and (*c*) the projected impact that is seen as an expected outcome from the indicator.

On the criteria of construction, I examine whether the use of indicators advances a particular notion of what a well-functioning legal system is by attempting to synchronize different conceptualizations of justice such that they are applicable across various contexts. This connects to an argument made by Frydman and Twining, who ask the question of 'how to regulate issues arising from the emerging global society in the midst of a multiplicity of legal systems and fragmented legal regimes'.[128] They go on to ask whether it requires an ordered pluralism that posits the harmonizing of legal regimes and relationships, or a radical pluralism that looks more closely at the perspectives of the actors involved?[129] In the context of fragmented regimes and concepts of justice, radical pluralism engages in the multiplicity of norms that arise from the varied contexts, and, as we will discuss in the next chapter, this becomes a very important bridge to being able to articulate and amplify the different ways in which challenges to access to justice are realized. It is important to examine the historicization and socialization of the rule of law that considers different sources, values, experiences and institutions that make up the delivery of justice.[130] In doing so, I would like to examine whether the framework of the rule of law, espoused in legal indicators, reflects divergent narratives or if it

---

128 Benoît Frydman and William Twining, 'A Symposium on Global Law, Legal Pluralism and Legal Indicators', *The Journal of Legal Pluralism and Unofficial Law* 47, no. 1 (2015): 1–8, DOI: 10.1080/07329113.2015.1030210.

129 Ibid.

130 Martin Krygier, 'Four Puzzles about the Rule of Law: Why, What, Where and Who Cares?', *Nomos* 50 (2011): 64–104; Marc Hertogh, 'A Sociology of the Rule of Law: Why, What, Where? And Who Cares?', Social Science Research Network, SSRN Scholarly Paper ID 2285996, 2013, https://papers.ssrn.com/abstract=2285996 (accessed 6 November 2020). See generally Mattias Kumm, 'The Rule of Law, Legitimate Authority and Constitutionalism', in *Legal Positivism, Institutionalism and Globalization: Vienna Lectures on Legal Philosophy*, ed. Christoph Bezemek, Michael Potacs and Alexander Somek, vol. 1, 113–126 (Oxford: Hart Publishing, 2018).

instead takes recourse to certain generalizations grounded in Eurocentric principles.[131]

A critical question on construction is whether indicators promote 'a rule of law orthodoxy', where the concepts and strategies are geared towards goals like economic growth, poverty alleviation and good governance[132] that reflect a 'technocratic' understanding of the administration of justice, but pay little credence to the specificity of the space in which the systems were being transplanted.[133] This is because they are often developed from the perspective of the donor and therefore operate at too high a level of abstraction from reforms that are required at a local level.[134] While narrowing the scope of the concept into a minimum set of variables can help validate measurements in terms of making the concept comparable, it may compromise the potential to evaluate the range of challenges that affect the user of justice because it will be difficult to capture the diversity of its use and effects.[135] Therefore, in using these criteria of construction to evaluate the legal indicator projects mentioned earlier, I will examine whether the rule of law may be contested, and if there is a scope for it to be seen as a plural concept or whether it must be seen as an unambiguous standard that has intuitive appeal and use.

In interaction and engagement, the second criterion of analysis, a central question is whether the contexts and values of the Global South are captured and reflected in the methods that seek to measure the functioning of the rule of law. The question of interaction and engagement must consider whether

---

[131] Marc Hertogh, 'Your Rule of Law Is Not Mine: Rethinking Empirical Approaches to EU Rule of Law Promotion', *Asia Europe Journal* 14 (2016): 43–59.

[132] Golub, 'Beyond Rule of Law Orthodoxy'; Upham, 'Mythmaking in the Rule of Law Orthodoxy'; David M. Trubek, 'The "Rule of Law" in Development Assistance: Past, Present, and Future', in *The New Law and Economic Development: A Critical Appraisal*, ed. David M. Trubek and Alvaro Santos, 74–94 (Cambridge: Cambridge University Press 2006).

[133] Stephen Golub, 'Make Justice the Organizing Principle of the Rule of Law Field', *Hague Journal on the Rule of Law* 1, no. 1 (2009): 61–66.

[134] Hammergren, 'Indices, Indicators and Statistics'.

[135] Merkel, 'Measuring the Quality of Rule of Law'; Randall Peerenboom, Michael Zürn and André Nollkaemper, 'Conclusion: From Rule of Law Promotion to Rule of Law Dynamics', in *Rule of Law Dynamics: In an Era of International and Transnational Governance*, ed. Michael Zürn, André Nollkaemper and Randy Peerenboom, 305–324 (Cambridge University Press 2012).

the rule of law indicator frameworks are reflexive enough to capture the lives of people, given the institutional, social, political, economic and other constraints that limit their choices. In countries that have plural legal systems, it is important to investigate and engage with other legal systems that function in those contexts and understand what role they play in dispute resolution.

Here, I investigate whether indicators adopt a rule of law framework to accurately reflect decision-making frameworks where there exist pluralities of institutions that offer dispute-resolution solutions.[136] Faundez has argued that when studying forums outside the state, there is a need to move away from conceptual understandings to more empirical understandings, otherwise the understanding is more influenced by ideology rather than a sense of how communities resolve matters of governance and disputes.[137] Sen argues that it is necessary to distinguish between an 'arrangement focussed view of justice', where the focus is on getting institutions right, and a 'realization focussed view of justice', where the focus is on the kind of lives that people can live, given the rules, institutions and other influences.[138] The realization-focussed view of justice assumes significance in evaluating the lived experiences of justice seekers and their encounters with everyday justice. The latter approach accounts for the practical manifestations for how the justice systems work and the negotiations that people need to make to have the rule of law in practice.[139]

With regard to the question of impact, the third criterion, it is critical to evaluate whether the purpose of the indicator is to offer prescriptions

---

[136] Martin Krygier, 'The Rule of Law: Legality, Teleology, Sociology', in *Relocating the Rule of Law*, ed. Gianluigi Palombella and Neil Walker, 45–70 (London: Hart Publishing, 2008). Cheesman argues for a rule of law ethnography for three reasons as a 'counterhegemonic practice, in response to counterintuitive observations, and as a means to do constitutive theorizing' in Nick Cheesman, 'Rule-of-Law Ethnography', *Annual Review of Law and Social Science* 14, no. 1 (2018): 167–184.

[137] Julio Faundez, 'Non-State Justice Systems in Latin America Case Studies: Peru and Colombia' (DFID, 2003).

[138] See generally Amartya Sen, *The Idea of Justice* (Cambridge, MA: Harvard University Press, 2011).

[139] Kalypso Nicolaidis and Rachel Kleinfeld, 'Rethinking Europe's Rule of Law and Enlargement Agenda: The Fundamental Dilemma', SIGMA Papers, no. 49, OECD Publishing, Paris, 2012, https://www.oecd-ilibrary.org/governance/rethinking-europe-s-rule-of-law-and-enlargement-agenda_5k4c42jmn5zp-en (accessed 6 November 2020).

for reform or a re-engineering of local institutions for a foreign alternative, or does it instead result in an evaluation of the needs and requirements of individuals who engage with the justice system in a particular jurisdiction.[140] In this regard, it is critical to examine whether such evaluation, based on the concept of the rule of law, takes place through a top-down approach or a bottom-up analysis of the needs and challenges of the particular context.[141] It is pertinent to explore whether indicators in plural legal systems adopt a 'supply side' analysis of justice delivery.[142] This implies that they examine the delivery of justice in terms of outputs geared towards strengthening the administrative capacity of the judiciary, the training of judges, the response to institutional challenges such as the backlog of cases, corruption, costs and alienating procedures. At the other end is the question of whether these indicators focus on the 'demand side', where it would be important to understand how the use of courts, community mechanisms, language and public awareness can enable the poor and marginalized to overcome barriers and challenges to access a justice delivery system.[143] This alternative is also critical because it reflects on the need to examine the perspectives of the stakeholders involved and how these different experiences and stories are integrated in the indicator. In considering impact, a key aspect is the backgrounds of those who are building the indicators (international organizations, donor agencies, country missions), their purposes of measurement and whether for these groups the rule of law is conceived as part of a larger framework for measuring and evaluating different systems. These questions are important from an impact standpoint because they provide a perspective of the priorities and agendas of indicator frameworks.

In many ways, each of the three criteria used here—construction, interaction and engagement with the complexity of people's lives, and projected impacts—are interrelated, in that they emerge from trying to evaluate the indicators for their ability to be responsive to the plural contexts in which they are required to operate, being cognizant of the

---

[140] Ibid.

[141] Benjamin van Rooij, 'Bringing Justice to the Poor, Bottom-up Legal Development Cooperation', *Hague Journal on the Rule of Law* 4, no. 2 (2012): 286–318.

[142] See also Yash Ghai and Jill Cottrell, 'The Rule of Law and Access to Justice', in *Marginalized Communities and Access to Justice*, ed. Yash Ghai and Jill Cottrell, 1–22 (London: Routledge, 2009).

[143] Ibid.

distinctive experiences that determine engagements with law and their impact on the public discourse on the delivery of justice. Thinking of the construction, interaction and engagement is more conducive to a pluralist understanding of law, as compared to a formalist approach, because the sources, vocabularies, usages and resistances in the manifestation and life of law come from a varied set of experiences and practices.

Evaluating rule of law indicators for plural legal systems

Having identified key features upon which these indicators have been conceptualized, this section conducts a further inquiry into the aforementioned indicators, particularly in terms of how their construction, interactions and impact fit within plural legal systems. In discussing the spread of global indicators and the challenges of an aspirational global law model, it becomes critical to examine whether indicators today are being used as a tool to perpetuate, under a mask of universality, a regime of domination and subordination, and a narrative of how justice systems should function rather than how they actually function. The three criteria identified previously of construction, interaction and engagement, and impact will guide this assessment.

In the Rule of Law Index of the WJP, an attempt was made to provide a comprehensive articulation of various aspects of the rule of law. It pays attention to not only the functioning of different procedural branches of the legal system (civil, criminal and informal) but also substantive aspects of different institutions and principles critical to the framework of the rule of law. In its construction, however, a rather technocratic understanding was adopted through the presumption of institutional limits, efficient functioning of dispute systems, enforcement of government regulations, and maintenance of standards of transparency and accountability. These properties that make up the Rule of Law Index presume that across contexts countries have legal regimes with similar institutional dynamics and mechanisms. Eighty per cent of the top ten countries are European in the 2020 iteration of the index, and South Asia and Sub-Saharan Africa ended up with lowest average scores among the regions.[144] Additionally, while informal justice is considered a criterion in the construction and conceptual

---

[144] World Justice Project, *WJP Rule of Law Index 2020*. See also Rajah who speaks of the epistemic limitations of the indicator in Jothie Rajah, "'Rule of Law' as Transnational

framework of the index, it is not included in the aggregation because the WJP argues they need to engage in cross-country comparisons, and this would be difficult were they to include informal justice. However, this argument could also be used for the other factors, such as transparency and accountability in public procurement, which do not have a similar contextual basis for their measurements in countries in the Global South, as evidenced by the ranking disparities.

On the second point of interaction and engagement, while the index attempts to balance both institutional and user-centred experiences,[145] it is more organization focussed rather than realization focussed. This is evidenced by the fact that factors evaluating the civil justice and criminal justice system are primarily framed in terms of the institution's 'effectiveness', 'affordability', 'timeliness', and only look partially at the individual's ability to access these institutions. Thus, the nature of the measurement is based on a supply side dynamic by looking at how the providers of justice create an enabling or disenabling environment for individuals. As mentioned previously, this will result in a de-emphasis on the resistances, experiences and interaction of persons whose engagement with the justice system may be outside the institutions being covered, or whose experiences become subsumed under technocratic merits of a justice system.

On the third criterion of impact, it is clear that the rule of law should be measured in a comparative frame, and by doing so the index constructs areas that can be identified to have poor adherence to the rule of law. While this is useful in understanding how some countries do with respect to others, it also becomes problematic when particular countries dominate the rankings year after year. Does this imply that they have a better functioning

---

Legal Order', in *Transnational Legal Orders*, ed. Terence C. Halliday and Gregory Shaffer, 340–373 (Cambridge: Cambridge University Press, 2015).

[145] In their paper, Versteeg and Ginsburg disaggregated data by population and experts in the WJP indicator and found

> the WJP's expert-based scores tend to have substantially higher correlations with the other RoL indicators than do the WJP's population-based scores. The exercise thus suggests that it is the expert-based scores that are driving the convergence between the RoL indicators. It also suggests that the population-based assessments ultimately play a small part in the construction of the overall WJP RoL indicator. (Versteeg and Ginsburg, 'Measuring the Rule of Law')

system, or that the criteria being used are more suitable to evaluate their functioning?

I analyse the Democracy Barometer and the World Bank Worldwide Governance Indicators together because in these approaches the rule of law is seen as part of a larger project, democracy and governance respectively, and I would like to explore how the rule of law works as a subset of a larger framework. In both these frameworks, for the criterion of construction, the rule of law assumes a very narrow formulation. It is technocratic in construction seen in the fact that it examines justice through the administration of institutions. While in the Democracy Barometer, this is through the quality of the judiciary and the legal system, in the World Bank Governance Indicators, it is through the police and courts. These indices also look at the confidence of users. Their responses are, however, qualified in terms of institutions, such as professionalism of judges and independence of the judiciary, and not in terms of the lives that the individuals themselves lead when they access these justice institutions. The responses may provide a sense of how the institutions function but not of how justice users function within these justice processes. As a result, there is once again a predominance of the organizational aspect of justice as compared to the realization-focussed aspect of justice.

In terms of the question of impact, the Democracy Barometer was designed to measure established democracies, and has made a clear calculus to focus initially on 30 countries that were largely in Europe and North America due to challenges of missing data.[146] If it were to study democracies in transition, or go beyond western democracies, the question remains whether its conception of the rule of law and the other criteria would change. One of the potential questions that could arise is if the framework places too much emphasis on procedural aspects of the rule of law. In terms of the impact that the World Bank Worldwide Governance Indicators have, a key issue here is that the composition of the rule of law in these indicators is different to the conception used in its other projects, such as the Justice for the Poor, which I will discuss later. As Santos argues, the World Bank adopts a 'hodge podge' approach towards conceptualizing the rule of law, but the internal dynamics of the group allow it to continue to sustain such a

---

[146] Bühlmann et al., 'The Democracy Barometer'.

practice, even though many conceptions are contradictory.[147] This divergent approach across different projects reduces the efficacy and impact of such a rule of law formulation.

The UN Rule of Law indicators construct the rule of law in a manner that they themselves outline is limited in scope. The purpose of this framework is to look at how institutions of the police, courts and prisons conform with the idea of the rule of law, which is likened to a principle of governance.[148] The challenge of such a construction is that while the framework clearly states that it is focussed on criminal law, it also uses the concept of the rule of law, and further suggests the ambiguity and contested nature of this concept. By focussing solely on a formal institutional approach, and its relationship with the rule of law, the indicators fail to capture the lived experiences of those who engage with customary and informal justice mechanisms in a plural justice system, which the framework outlines is important to understand context in those regions.[149] This raises an important question of whether priority is given to integrating informal and plural legal systems within what is conceived of as the rule of law. This is despite there being a long tradition of reports detailing the criticality of these forums to how people engage with the law.[150] As with the World Bank, this shows a fragmented approach to understanding legal needs, and the functioning of legal systems, because rather than a cohesive understanding of rule of law, and how people use legal systems, there are many parallel narratives being encouraged.

In the case of the Ibrahim Index of African Governance, in terms of construction, while the framing of the rule of law continues to reflect a rule of law orthodoxy in that it continues to measure institutions and

---

[147] Alvaro Santos, 'The World Bank's Uses of the "Rule of Law" Promise in Economic Development', in *The New Law and Economic Development*, ed. David M. Trubek and Alvaro Santos, 253–300 (Cambridge: Cambridge University Press, 2006).

[148] United Nations, 'Introduction', in *The United Nations Rule of Law Indicators: Implementation Guide and Project Tools*, v–vi (2011), https://reliefweb.int/sites/reliefweb.int/files/resources/Full_Report_1653.pdf (accessed 22 February 2022).

[149] Ibid., 20.

[150] Danish Institute for Human Rights, 'Informal Justice Systems'; International Council on Human Rights Policy, *When Legal Worlds Overlap*; Ewa Wojkowska, *Doing Justice: How Informal Justice Systems Can Contribute* (UNDP, 2006), https://www.un.org/ruleoflaw/blog/document/doing-justice-how-informal-justice-systems-can-contribute/ (accessed 3 February 2018).

organizations, what is distinct about this framework is that it focuses on the perception of the country, through the analysis of sanctions imposed on the country, and places emphasis on transition, which is meant to measure the robustness of democratic traditions as part of the rule of law. However, if we look at the kind of data being used in the interaction and engagement with these issues, many of the data sources include those emerging from international organizations. These include think tanks such as the World Economic Forum and the Economist Intelligence Unit, which also suggest that when we speak of the presence of data, or lack thereof, there is a need to acknowledge where the data is being produced. It raises the question of whether, along with the frameworks being developed with particular agendas, the data used also comes from producers that replicate the same politics. Even though the Ibrahim African Governance Index is focussed on Africa, its use of data indicates that it cannot break free from the intellectual hegemony of the North since, in a supposedly objective resource such as data, it has to rely on western sources to make its case.

In terms of its focus on Africa, the index has a regional focus, which enables it to be more context-specific for the nations it looks at. It, however, still adopts a global perspective in its approach in terms of the choices of criterion and priorities,[151] which raises the question of impact and whether it accounts for pluralism in the ways governance and rule of law are experienced in Africa (regionally and locally), or presents a set of global standards that are developed by international institutions and then used as a basis to create a framework for targets that need to be achieved. These data sources, as we have discussed, are not value-neutral, and lack a situated knowledge of the place, which can only come from being contextually developed.[152]

---

[151] Rachel M. Gisselquist, 'Developing and Evaluating Governance Indexes: 10 Questions', *Policy Studies* 35, no. 5 (2014): 513–531.

[152] See also the idea of situated knowledge and the development of categories:

> Situated knowledge recognizes time, place, and circumstance, and assumes that individuals and their capacities are marked by them. It proceeds from specificities and works upward to comparative generalizations, rather than downward from a priori assumptions. Theory construction for situated knowledge takes into account local knowledge and practice—how denizens perceive and interpret their world. Theory constructed from below produces different futures than theory constructed

In examining the Hague Model of Access to Justice, the approach taken by this framework is markedly different from those discussed previously.[153] It focuses on the legal needs and problems of users, and traces their experiences through a path to justice. The index is constructed not from the perspective of an institution, such as the judiciary or the police, but from the perspective of the individual user, and adopts a demand-oriented approach that focuses upon the citizen's experience. Through the key indicators of cost, quality of procedures and quality of outcomes, the framework highlights a diverse set of factors that capture the struggles that a user faces in terms of costs, respect, equality and compensation. By adopting a method that studies how people use legal institutions and their experiences with them, the framework adopts a broad approach to the role that different institutions perform in the delivery of legal services. In this regard, this framework goes further to be able to capture the different ways in which people resolve their disputes as well as the different paths and journeys that they are required to take for justice to be realized. In the next chapters, I introduce a complementary measurement framework to this model that, while focussing on a demand-oriented approach to justice, also offers a realization approach to access to justice, which, through the capability approach, focuses not just on needs but also on how legal needs are realised.

Although global indicators are constructed with the purpose of meeting transferable standards, often the struggles of the Global South are subsumed by issues of practicality and universalism, which results in secondary importance being paid to approaching law beyond its technocratic constructs. There is, therefore, a need for an outlook that is anti-hierarchical—a counter-hegemonic approach that allows for a plurality of discourses on matters of law and governance.[154] There is a need for a global historicization rather than a western-dominated narrative, such that there is a focus on how the law is experienced and constituted in the Global South in order to offer a compelling counterpoint on aspects that

---

from above. (Susanne Hoeber Rudolph, 'The Imperialism of Categories: Situating Knowledge in a Globalizing World', *Perspectives on Politics* 3, no. 1 [2005]: 5–14, 12)

[153] TISCO et al., *Measuring the Costs and Quality of Access to Justice*.
[154] Makau Mutua, 'What Is TWAIL?', *Proceedings of the ASIL Annual Meeting* 94 (2000): 31–38.

otherwise dictate an international legal imagination.[155] The reason for engaging with such counter-narratives is to challenge discourses around how the law ought to be regulated, which can then be perceived as natural and established practice.[156] In order to do this, the vocabulary and language used, including by the law, plays a central role in defining the parameters through which global problems are constructed and advanced. Chimni further states that the use of international law, understandings of good governance, development and debates about rights are given a particular outlook that in turn legitimizes the dominant view of world order of statist law.[157] It is worth asking whether the narratives of poor performance that these legal indicator frameworks suggest for countries of the Global South exist because there is little input or recognition of values, procedures and practices intrinsic to their understanding of the rule of law.

Access to Justice and the measurement of justice delivery in plural legal systems

The identification of the challenges in the development of legal indicators is meant to open up indicators to the scrutiny of whether they reflect the complexity that exists empirically in legal systems around the world. It helps to unpack whether indicators are the means to understand existing narratives or are instead ways to construct narratives themselves. The former is where indicators play the role of an accounting or monitoring device whereas, in the latter, they are descriptors and become the framework around which concepts are structured.

In this section, reflecting on the issues regarding indicators presented earlier, I advance whether it is possible to build a more inclusive concept when measuring justice in plural legal systems. I argue that the concept of 'access to justice' allows for this by building a more grounded notion of how the law is experienced and realized. It is a concept that is broad enough

---

155 Obiora Okafor, 'Critical Third World Approaches to International Law (TWAIL): Theory, Methodology, or Both?', *International Community Law Review* 10, no. 4 (2008): 371–378.

156 B. S. Chimni, 'Third World Approaches to International Law: A Manifesto', *International Community Law Review* 8, no. 1 (2006): 3–27.

157 Ibid.

to include the statist conceptions of the rule of law and also include other plural manifestation of institutions as they play out in people's lives. This section explores the responsiveness of access to justice in its potential use for development programming and will, thereafter, elaborate on certain features that make up this concept.

Exploring the responsiveness of the concept of access to justice

The development of global standards of measurement presupposes the existence of a universal legal system, the existence of global rules and the establishment of global constitutional values. However, such a conception is at odds with a society where there are a plurality of norms and regimes competing within the same space. Due to the challenges of a mismatch between context, institutions and how justice reform can work in development programmes, there is a need to examine alternative approaches to promoting rule of law reform. Adopting a realization-focussed view of justice enables greater flexibility to capture the plurality and complexities of experiences with justice delivery, which may not be possible if a strict understanding of normative standards is used to evaluate the rule of law.[158]

An important way to understand a realization-focussed view of justice is to examine the legal empowerment of the poor, which includes 'the process of systemic change through which the poor are protected and enabled to use the law to advance their rights and their interests as citizens and economic actors' such that 'every individual must have access to justice, including due process, justice and remedies and that action must be taken to eliminate discrimination'.[159] Legal empowerment has been posited as

---

[158] Michael Zürn, André Nollkaemper and Randall Peerenboom, 'Introduction: Rule of Law Dynamics in an Era of International and Transnational Governance', in *Rule of Law Dynamics: In an Era of International and Transnational Governance*, ed. Michael Zürn, André Nollkaemper and Randy Peerenboom, 1–18 (Cambridge: Cambridge University Press, 2012).

[159] Secretary General, 'Report of the Secretary-General on Legal Empowerment of the Poor and Eradication of Poverty (A/64/133)', 2009, https://www.un.org/ruleoflaw/blog/document/report-of-the-secretary-general-on-legal-empowerment-of-the-poor-and-eradication-of-poverty-a64133/ (accessed 7 May 2020), p. 2.

enabling 'the use of legal services and related development activities to increase disadvantaged populations control over their lives'.[160] The purpose behind this approach is to focus more on community-driven, rights-based development.[161] It enables those disadvantaged to also participate in the development process and in setting priorities and agendas. [162]

Another departure from the statist approach to justice programming is to suggest experimentalism in policy and reform.[163] In this approach, architects of rule of law programmes monitor interventions in real time, use new information to refine project design through learning and adaptation, and seek to establish through constant evaluation what the best fit to context is.[164] The three components of such experimentalism include practitioners testing operational alternatives against one another and counterfactuals, engaging in systematic data collection before, during and after an intervention, and incorporating an iterative design process by learning from experience.[165] The Problem-Driven Iterative Adaption framework suggests that there must be institutional experimentation in building state capability.[166] The key principles in this approach include: placing importance on solving problems, not selling solutions, and thus

---

[160] Golub, 'Beyond Rule of Law Orthodoxy', 3. See also Robert B. Porter, 'Measurement of Legal Empowerment through the Subjective Perceptions of Individuals', *Impact Assessment and Project Appraisal* 32, no. 3 (2014): 213–221; Stephen Golub, 'Legal Empowerment: Impact and Implications for the Development Community and the World Bank', in *The World Bank Legal Review: Law, Equity and Development*, ed. Caroline Mary Sage and Michael Woolcock, vol. 2, 167–184 (Washington, DC: The World Bank, 2006).

[161] Vivek Maru, 'Between Law and Society: Paralegals and the Provision of Justice Services in Sierra Leone and Worldwide', *Yale Journal of International Law* 31 (2006): 427–476 .

[162] Golub, 'Beyond Rule of Law Orthodoxy'; Laura Goodwin and Vivek Maru, 'What Do We Know about Legal Empowerment? Mapping the Evidence', *Hague Journal on the Rule of Law* 9 (2017): 157–194.

[163] Margaux Hall, Nicholas Menzies and Michael Woolcock, 'From HiPPOs to "Best Fit" in Justice Reform: Experimentalism in Sierra Leone', in *The International Rule of Law Movement: A Crisis of Legitimacy and the Way Forward*, ed. David Marshall, 243–266 (Cambridge, MA: Harvard Law School 2014).

[164] Ibid.

[165] Ibid.

[166] Matt Andrews, Lant Pritchett and Michael Woolcock, 'Escaping Capability Traps through Problem-Driven Iterative Adaptation (PDIA)', working paper 299, CGDEV,

framing the question as 'what is the problem' rather than 'what solution should we adopt'; creating an environment that allows for experimentation and positive deviance; ensuring that the process is iterative and facilitates continuous learning; and engaging a broad set of stakeholders to ensure that reforms are viable, legitimate and relevant.[167]

Berg et al. recognize a need to move away from a technical approach to the rule of law and propose that an attempt be made to instead study how issues of conflict arise, what the perceptions of justice according to the user are, and what the associated barriers to development are.[168] They have proposed looking at issues of justice reform by asking about the nature of the justice problem, which would involve looking beyond particular institutions of justice and instead examining the outcome of sociopolitical and economic contests mediated by a multiplicity of state and non-state actors.[169] Such an approach would examine how the justice problem is being governed, using political, organizational and normative lenses, and the role external assistance plays, particularly with respect to how to make such intervention not purely technical but also political.[170]

---

22 June 2012, https://www.cgdev.org/publication/escaping-capability-traps-through -problem-driven-iterative-adaptation-pdia-working-paper (accessed 7 May 2020).

[167] Ibid., 7. Further, I have also previously developed how the concept of design thinking can be used for rule of law promotion. Here I proposed a framework that takes into account user needs (in this case the recipient of the rule of law programme), immerses itself in their contexts, and only then frames the problem and the iterative solution. I argue that 'the ambition of rule of law promotion must be to arrive at locally owned and context-specific solutions that above all do meet the needs of their users, and not the donor's (political) ambitions' in Siddharth Peter de Souza, 'Beyond Best Practices: How to Use Design Thinking in Rule of Law Promotion', Peace Lab Blog, 13 March 2019, https://peacelab.blog/2019/03/beyond-best-practices-how-to-use-design-thinking (accessed 28 August 2019). See also RSF Hub, 'User-Centred Law: What Law, Which Rights Do People in Fragile Contexts Need?' Impulse Paper No. 2, November 2018, https://www.fu-berlin.de/sites/rsf-hub/_medien/RSF_Hub_IP02.pdf (accessed 30 July 2021).

[168] Louis-Alexandre Berg, Deborah Isser and Doug Porter, 'Beyond Deficit and Dysfunction: Three Questions toward Just Development in Fragile and Conflict-Affected Settings', in *The International Rule of Law Movement: A Crisis of Legitimacy and the Way Forward*, ed. David Marshall, 267–296 (Cambridge, MA: Harvard Law School 2014).

[169] Ibid.

[170] Ibid.

When we think of legal indicators, however, much of this reflexive thinking is still absent from the frameworks discussed, and part of the problem is the rigidity in the use of the concept of the rule of law. Can we incorporate a more grounded approach when conceptualizing the rule of law in legal indicators? In analysing the different legal indicators, it is clear that the concept of the rule of law as it is currently designed, focussing on formal institutions, is not enough, and there is a need to engage empirically and sociologically with the rule of law, while also examining how the law materializes on the ground through local institutions and practices.[171]

Thinking in a more grounded manner will allow for the examination of who the local providers of justice are, how they are linked to each other, what justice and security mechanisms are available, how such alternatives are experienced by different local users, and what local users see as legitimate forms of justice and security.[172] This would result in a more flexible and iterative engagement with justice reform, which adapts and responds to challenges to making an impact in the legal reform and justice sector.[173]

A recent debate on the development of the Sustainable Development Goals (SDGs) presents a good example of the limitation of a statist understanding of the rule of law. In the discussions on SDGs, there was opposition by several member states to the inclusion of the rule of law in Agenda 2030. This was for reasons including that there was no one-size-fits-all policy on what the rule of law was, that rule of law did not have a universal definition, and that having a statist version of the rule of law would impinge on state sovereignty to allow for other institutional practices

---

[171] See the work of Krygier and Hertogh on examining rule of law sociologically. Krygier, 'The Rule of Law: Legality, Teleology, Sociology'; Krygier, 'Four Puzzles about the Rule of Law'; Hertogh, 'Your Rule of Law Is Not Mine'.

[172] Albrecht and Kyed, 'Introduction'. See also reflections on the work of Krygier that think about the rule of law critically, without mythologizing it or seeing is as a technocratic solution. Gianluigi Palombella, 'Two Threats to the Rule of Law: Legal and Epistemic (Between Technocracy and Populism)', *Hague Journal on the Rule of Law* 11 (2019): 383–388; Veronica L. Taylor, 'The Mythology of (Rule of) Law', *Hague Journal on the Rule of Law* 11 (2019): 331–339; Christopher May, 'The Rule of Law and Technocratisation', *Hague Journal on the Rule of Law* 11 (2019): 321–326.

[173] Deval Desai and Michael Woolcock, 'Experimental Justice Reform: Lessons from the World Bank and Beyond', *Annual Review of Law and Social Science* 11, no. 1 (2015): 155–174.

to emerge.[174] The concept of the rule of law included in the access to justice was seen as more acceptable and inclusive.

In many discussions around the goals, it is argued that access to justice is a watering down of the rule of law, and that the rule of law is a broader concept. However, these discussions also show that the rule of law, as a concept, is one that is divisive and antagonistic because it contains particularities that may not be suited everywhere.[175] If such debates had considered the deeply embedded nature of pluralism in countries that objected to the rule of law, it is clear that accepting a rule of law framework, which also implies accepting a governance framework, an economic architecture and a social system, would be tantamount to developing a new order at the behest of external agencies and influences.[176] Access to justice, meanwhile, has the capacity to draw from the ideals of 'empowerment' and 'experimentation' to present a framework to analyse how people's needs and aspirations can be addressed to contribute to justice reform. However, in the current framing of Agenda 2030, access to justice as a concept has been limited to a relationship between an individual and a state as regards criminal matters.[177] Satterthwaite and Sukti advance that indicators should measure a broader concept of access to justice, and this would entail 'the collection of data about the kind of "justiciable problems" people experience, the full range of rights guaranteed under human rights law, the formal and informal institutions that exist to handle barriers to achieving those rights, and the quality of needed assistance in obtaining justice'.[178]

---

[174] Noora Johanna Arajärvi, 'The Rule of Law in the 2030 Agenda', KFG Working Paper Series, No. 9, Berlin Potsdam Research Group, 'The International Rule of Law—Rise or Decline?', 2017, https://www.ssrn.com/abstract=2992016 (accessed 10 April 2020).

[175] Ibid. See also the work by Mattei and Nader that argues for how the rule of law is used to legitimize the imposition of institutions from the west upon other societies. Ugo Mattei and Laura Nader, 'Plunder and the Rule of Law', in *Plunder: When the Rule of Law Is Illegal*, 10–34 (Oxford: John Wiley & Sons, 2008). See also Baxi, 'The Rule of Law in India'.

[176] Erbeznik, 'Money Can't Buy You Law'; Marshall, 'Introduction'; Ugo Mattei and Marco de Morpurgo, 'Global Law and Plunder: The Dark Side of the Rule of Law', IUC Research Commons 1–10, International University College of Turin, 2010, https://ideas.repec.org/p/iuc/rpaper/1-10.html (accessed 9 April 2020).

[177] Margaret L. Satterthwaite and Sukti Dhital, 'Measuring Access to Justice: Transformation and Technicality in SDG 16.3', *Global Policy* 10, no. 1 (2019): 96–109.

[178] Ibid., 103.

In their practice note, UNDP defines access to justice as the 'ability of people to seek and obtain a remedy through formal or informal institutions of justice, and in conformity with human rights standards.'[179] The American Bar Association states that, 'for access to justice, citizens must be able to use justice institutions to obtain solutions to their common justice problems. For access to justice to exist, justice institutions must function effectively to provide fair solutions to citizens' justice problems'.[180] The definitions focus on a demand perspective where access to justice is understood in terms of the needs and requirements of the justice user to participate in the legal process and the decisions, negotiations and challenges involved in utilizing a particular forum.[181] This is in contradistinction to a supply side approach (discussed earlier) that focuses on formal institutions and the manner in which these bodies respond to legal needs and aspirations.[182]

When discussing access to justice as a theoretical approach, Capelletti argues that in addition to criticizing doctrine and formalism, it is also a framework that seeks to engage with the complexity of people.[183] He argues that while the normative aspects of law are important, they are but one component. For him, 'people, with all their cultural, economic and psychological features' assume primary importance.[184] In terms of how access to justice has developed as a concept to make rights effective,

---

[179] UNDP, *Programming for Justice: Access for All—A Practitioner's Guide to a Human Rights-Based Approach to Access to Justice* (Bangkok: UNDP, 2005), https://www.un.org/ruleoflaw/blog/document/programming-for-justice-access-for-all-a-practitioners-guide-to-a-human-rights-based-approach-to-access-to-justice/ (accessed 31 December 2020).

[180] American Bar Association, *Access to Justice Assessment Tool: A Guide to Analyzing Access to Justice for Civil Society Organizations* (Washington, DC: ABA, 2012), https://www.americanbar.org/content/dam/aba/directories/roli/misc/aba_roli_access_to_justice_assessment_manual_2012.authcheckdam.pdf (accessed 19 April 2020), 1.

[181] Ghai and Cottrell, 'The Rule of Law and Access to Justice'. See also Vivek Maru, 'Access to Justice and Legal Empowerment: A Review of World Bank Practice', *Hague Journal on the Rule of Law* 2, no. 2 (2010): 259–281.

[182] Ghai and Cottrell, 'The Rule of Law and Access to Justice'; Maru, 'Access to Justice and Legal Empowerment'.

[183] Mauro Cappelletti, 'Alternative Dispute Resolution Processes within the Framework of the World-Wide Access-to-Justice Movement', *The Modern Law Review* 56, no. 3 (May 1993): 282–296.

[184] Ibid.

Capelletti and Garth speak of three waves: the first is the question of having access to representation, which includes access to legal aid, which is a more economic and financial aspect; the second is the question of diffuse and collective interest and the ability to represent collective rights; and the third is the emergence of alternative dispute resolution forums and relates to procedure.[185] Barendrecht adds two further waves, which are the opening up of legal market to services as well as regulation of the legal profession.[186]

In the next section, I build upon three key attributes of access to justice to better examine how such a concept could work for legal indicators. These include exploring the networks of relationships between different actors in a justice system, systems and processes between different elements of a justice system, and abilities that individuals have to access and use justice systems.

Access to justice: Networks, processes and a user focus

In a dispute around a justice problem, relations of access are complex and distinct. This is because in understanding the nature of the relationships, it is relevant to ask who the access is meant for, what kind of resources are required, and what kind of institutions or procedures are needed to ensure its delivery.[187] These lead to an engagement with parties, values, institutions and cultures, all of which determine the evolution of access.[188] The purpose of examining disputes as a fundamental organizing frame is to understand access to justice as it is realized.

In thinking about a measurement framework for access to justice, it is critical to maintain a distinction between *access* to justice and access to

---

[185] Bryant Garth and Mauro Cappelletti, 'Access to Justice: The Newest Wave in the Worldwide Movement to Make Rights Effective', *Buffalo Law Review* 27, no. 2 (1978): 181–292; Mauro Cappelletti and Bryant Garth, 'Access to Justice as a Focus of Research Foreword', *Windsor Yearbook of Access to Justice* 1 (1981): ix–xxv.

[186] Maurits Barendrecht, 'Understanding the Market for Justice', Tilburg University Legal Studies Working Paper No. 009/2009, 2009, http://www.ssrn.com/abstract=1416841 (accessed 10 October 2019).

[187] Upendra Baxi, 'Access, Development and Distributive Justice: Access Problems of the "Rural" Population', *Journal of the Indian Law Institute*, 18, no. 3 (1976): 375–430, 375.

[188] Ibid.

justice.[189] I focus on elements that constitute limitations on 'access' while treating 'justice' as an ideal. In doing so, I explore different elements of how access can be construed, before reflecting on what justice can mean in plural legal systems. Baxi, in discussing notions of access, introduces the concepts of representation, democracy, participation and pluralism in the discourse and highlights the expansive nature of access to justice, which is often denied through spatial, temporal, linguistic, social or symbolic barriers. Access to justice encompasses the recognition that everyone is entitled to protection and redressal by the law and justice systems, and that rights are meaningless unless they are enforced and guaranteed.[190] It implies protecting people and ensuring they have the capability and agency to solve their problems in a proactive manner.[191] This is an important epistemic shift.

Take, for example, the case of a violent crime where a woman has been raped. According to a rule of law approach, which focuses largely on supply side aspects of justice, the following would be of note: whether the case has been registered, the police have taken statements, investigations have begun, the court has been notified, and the judge has started to hear the case. If so, we can infer that the standards of the rule of law have been met. Framing the case instead in terms of access to justice would mean asking if the woman was comfortable when interviewed by the police, whether she was made to feel safe, whether she was taken through the different aspects of the dispute resolution process, whether she had the agency to participate, be it in court or at the police station. Envisaging access to justice as a network allows for an investigation into the relationships that emerge in resolving a dispute. Are these relationships linear between user and institution? Are they dynamic and evolving, based on context? The centrality of the network is to place emphasis on what people, procedures and practices matter when the negotiation and navigation of different decisions is taking place.

If we are to study access to justice in terms of networks that manifest in different disputes, then it allows for the possibility of including different

---

[189] Pratiksha Baxi, 'Access to Justice and Rule of (Good) Law: The Cunning of Judicial Reform in India', *Indian Journal of Human Development* 2, no. 2 (2008): 279–302.

[190] See generally S. Muralidhar, *Law, Poverty, and Legal Aid: Access to Criminal Justice* (New Delhi: LexisNexis Butterworth, 2004); Francesco Francioni, *Access to Justice as a Human Right* (Oxford: Oxford University Press, 2007).

[191] Daniel M. Brinks, 'Access to What? Legal Agency and Access to Justice for Indigenous Peoples in Latin America', *Journal of Development Studies* 55, no. 3 (2019): 348–365.

narratives, examining different stages, and also moving away from seeing the delivery of law purely from a formal institutional standpoint, making the exercise less ethnocentric to certain kinds of traditions than others.[192] Characterizing the role that a network of relations plays in a study of access to justice is to suggest that in addition to looking at institutional influences other factors such as symbolism, finance, information also determine whether the individual has access to justice.[193]

The second attribute of access to justice I examine is the different stages that make up the journey towards access to justice. Sarat and Miller in their study show that several disputes are in fact not litigated. They construct a dispute pyramid to show that many disputes remain 'unperceived injurious experiences'.[194] Even when these were recognized, only some of them were constructed in a manner that held the other person liable. Very few disputes were constructed such that the injured party sought a remedy.[195] The concept of a 'dispute' therefore takes on a series of acts as a social construct. These can be attributed to stages of naming, blaming and claiming, where when the nature of the injury is recognized, someone is held accountable and a remedy is sought.[196]

However, as instances of legal pluralism attest, there are multiple avenues for the resolution of disputes, with competing standards of legitimacy. Many disputes are solved in community forums, among neighbours, in families, at religious courts, and thus the singular idea of a court is substituted by

---

[192] Francis G. Snyder, 'Anthropology, Dispute Processes and Law: A Critical Introduction', *British Journal of Law and Society* 8, no. 2 (1981): 141–180.

[193] 'Legality is not sustained solely by the formal law of the Constitution, legislative statutes court decisions, or explicit demonstrations of state power such as state power. Rather legality is enduring because it relies on and invokes common place scheme of everyday life' in Patricia Ewick and Susan S. Silbey, *The Common Place of Law: Stories from Everyday Life* (Chicago: University of Chicago Press, 1998), 17.

[194] Richard E. Miller and Austin Sarat, 'Grievances, Claims, and Disputes: Assessing the Adversary Culture, Special Issue on Dispute Processing and Civil Litigation: Part Two – The Civil Litigation Research Project: A Dispute-Focused Approach: Surveying Disputes', *Law and Society Review* 15, no. 3/4 (1980): 525–566.

[195] Ibid.

[196] William L. F. Felstiner, Richard L. Abel and Austin Sarat, 'The Emergence and Transformation of Disputes: Naming, Blaming, Claiming ...', *Law and Society Review* 15, no. 3/4 (1980): 631–654.

several other options.[197] Albiston et al. argue that the dispute pyramid is not a sufficient metaphor because it presents a 'single linear path through which a dispute progresses' and 'undertheorizes a substantial proportion of the ways in which people respond to injuries'.[198] They instead propose the metaphor of a tree to suggest not just the multiplicity of options to resolve a dispute but also to acknowledge the living nature of the dispute.[199]

In outlining its definition of 'access to justice', UNDP also highlighted that this concept involves a series of stages, including legal protection, legal awareness, legal aid and counsel, adjudication, and enforcement and monitoring.[200] This idea of examining access to justice through various instances in the life of a user is akin to the approach of 'justiciable events' advocated by Hazel Genn, who examined legal problems and justice needs of users, and whether civil justice reforms actually responded to public experiences and expectations.[201]

This user-centred approach has been further developed in the approach of the Hague Model of Access to Justice, which evaluates justice systems based on the users' *paths to justice*, which are defined as 'a commonly applied process which users address in order to cope with their legal problem'.[202] The process of dispute resolution requires multiple points of decision-making before a conflict is resolved. Barendrecht identifies elements of

---

[197] TISCO et al., *Measuring the Costs and Quality of Access to Justice*; HiiL, 'HiiL Justice Dashboard: Justice Data at Your Fingertips'; Maurits Barendrecht, Peter Kamminga and Jin Ho Verdonschot, 'Priorities for the Justice System: Responding to the Most Urgent Legal Problems of Individuals', TISCO Working Paper, 2008, https://papers.ssrn.com/abstract=1090885 (accessed 7 August 2019).

[198] Catherine R. Albiston, Lauren B. Edelman and Joy Milligan, 'The Dispute Tree and the Legal Forest', *Annual Review of Law and Social Science* 10, no. 1 (2014): 105–131.

[199] Ibid., 106.

[200] UNDP, 'Access to Justice Practice Note', 2004, http://www.undp.org/content/undp/en/home/librarypage/democratic-governance/access_to_justiceandruleoflaw/access-to-justice-practice-note.html (accessed 21 January 2018). See also Vivek Maru for a review of World Bank Practice. Maru, 'Access to Justice and Legal Empowerment'.

[201] Hazel Genn, 'The Landscape of Justiciable Problems', in *Paths to Justice: What People Do and Think about Going to Law*, 21–66 (Oxford: Hart Publishing, 1999).

[202] TISCO et al., *Measuring the Costs and Quality of Access to Justice*, 24. See also Martin Gramatikov, Maurits Barendrecht and Jin Ho Verdonschot, 'Measuring the Costs and Quality of Paths to Justice: Contours of a Methodology', *Hague Journal on the Rule of Law* 3 (2011): 349–379.

this process to include where the parties *meet* and try and present their sides of the dispute, *talk* about the various challenges before them, *share* the expectations of the process, *decide* about potential compromises and finally *stabilize* the relationship in determining possible outcomes.[203] Understanding these different elements makes it clear how multifaceted adjudicating a dispute really is. This analogy of a 'dispute tree' is useful for the purpose of constructing the concept of access to justice because, as with the idea of a network of relations, the plurality of processes and paths that a user will encounter when a dispute is sought to be resolved is filled with competing and sometimes equally persuasive options.

The third attribute that is valuable for an access to justice framework focuses on the ability of the user to demand and achieve valuable outcomes from the dispute resolution experience.[204] In focussing on how the individual uses access or is able to achieve particular outcomes through the access, emphasis is laid on the nature of the interactions that an individual is required to face in the context of resolving a dispute. Coming back to the idea of legal empowerment, which seeks to move away from a rule of law orthodoxy (a more technical formulation of institutions providing governance) to a focus on how people can use the opportunities available to them to have more control over their lives and over the decisions they make to resolve disputes, we explore the importance of agency and ability that people have.[205]

The concept of legal empowerment is relevant to understanding the ability of people to engage in the stages that make up a dispute resolution process.[206] In their study of empowerment, Alsop et al. argue that

---

[203] Maurits Barendrecht, 'In Search of Microjustice: Five Basic Elements of a Dispute System', Tilburg University Legal Studies Working Paper No. 02/2009, 2009, http://www.ssrn.com/abstract=1334644 (accessed 2 September 2019).

[204] Goodwin and Maru, 'What Do We Know about Legal Empowerment'; Maike de Langen and Maurits Barendrecht, 'Legal Empowerment of the Poor: Innovating Access to Justice', in *The State of Access: Success and Failure of Democracies to Create Equal Opportunities*, ed. Jorrit de Jong and Gowher Rizvi, 250–271 (Washington, DC: Brookings Institution Press, 2009).

[205] Golub, 'Beyond Rule of Law Orthodoxy'; Golub, 'Make Justice the Organizing Principle of the Rule of Law Field'; Golub, 'Legal Empowerment'.

[206] Golub, 'Beyond Rule of Law Orthodoxy'; Goodwin and Maru, 'What Do We Know about Legal Empowerment'; de Souza, 'Evaluating "Access to Justice" in Informal Justice Systems'.

empowerment involves the ability to make choices such that those choices can then become particular actions and outcomes.[207] They introduce two key aspects of empowerment: one is agency-centric, defined as 'the ability to make choices', the other is opportunity structure-centric, which is the institutional setting to 'transform agency into action'.[208]

Gramatikov and Porter introduce the idea of self-belief, and argue that legal empowerment is a subjective and psychological state, which involves investigating how individuals or groups can find solutions to their legal problems.[209] The purpose of focussing on legal empowerment is to strengthen the agency of the individual to act by supporting increased legal knowledge, enhancing capacities to obtain remedies and facilitating participation in the decision-making process.[210] However, this focus on ability and agency cannot just be seen in terms of individual action, but also how these aspects of agency connect to communities within which individuals live.[211] In this sense it locates the individual ability in the networks and processes that also play a role in determining access to justice, and looks at ways in which voice and accountability can be offered to users who are otherwise marginalized by legal processes.[212]

In describing the attributes of the concept of access to justice, the focus has been on the networks that emerge around a dispute, the processes that need to be navigated and the ability of the individual to achieve valuable outcomes. A linked question that emerges is how does one conceive of 'justice' in such a framework? Can one ascribe a particular quality to justice

---

[207] Ruth Alsop, Mette Frost Bertelsen and Jeremy Holland, 'Empowerment: An Analytic Framework', in *Empowerment in Practice: From Analysis to Implementation*, 9–28 (Washington, DC: The World Bank, 2006), 10.

[208] Ibid.

[209] Martin Gramatikov and Robert B. Porter, 'Yes, I Can: Subjective Legal Empowerment—Tisco Working Paper Series on Civil Law and Conflict Resolution Systems', *Georgetown Journal on Poverty Law and Policy* 18, no. 2 (Spring 2010): 169–200.

[210] Goodwin and Maru, 'What Do We Know about Legal Empowerment'.

[211] Lars Waldorf, 'Legal Empowerment and Horizontal Inequalities after Conflict', *The Journal of Development Studies* 55, no. 3 (2019): 437–455.

[212] Stephen Golub, 'What Is Legal Empowerment? An Introduction', in *Legal Empowerment: Practitioners' Perspectives*, ed. Stephen Golub, 9–12 (Rome: IDLO, 2010); Secretary General, 'Report of the Secretary-General on Legal Empowerment', Lars Waldorf, 'Introduction: Legal Empowerment in Transitions', *The International Journal of Human Rights* 19, no. 3 (2015): 229–241.

in situations where claims, processes and values are plural and distinct? Does justice have an institutional grounding? Is it a constant?

In relation to the realization-focussed view of justice, which entails that in addition to the roles that institutions, rules and organizations play in the delivery of justice, an emphasis needs to be placed on how the world actually emerges from practice. Sen uses the example of *niti* and *nyaaya*, two concepts which both mean 'justice' in Sanskrit, to illustrate the difference.[213] Whereas the former is concerned with the organizational aspects of justice, the latter is concerned with how it materializes in the everyday lives of people.[214] Focussing on the realization aspects of justice means adopting a bottom-up approach that is rooted in considering people's experiences and resistances. Baxi has argued that to take human rights seriously, one needs to take suffering seriously.[215] He elucidates how human rights must give voice to human suffering, make it visible, and that its value arises when it serves as a protection against deprivation, powerlessness and degradation.[216] This focus on suffering draws attention to the violence and silence that people face when using the law and legal systems, and focuses particularly on those who are most marginalized and disenfranchised.[217] It is also important to think of the different ways in which such suffering can manifest. Doing so will help us explore how disadvantages and inequalities emerge at two levels: a distributional level in terms of wealth, standard

---

[213] Amartya Sen, 'Introduction: An Approach to Justice', in *The Idea of Justice*, 1–27 (Cambridge, MA: Harvard University Press, 2009), 20.

[214] Ibid.

[215] Upendra Baxi, 'Voices of Suffering and the Future of Human Rights', *Transnational Law and Contemporary Problems* 8 (Fall 1998): 125–169.

[216] Ibid.; Sam Adelman and Abdul Paliwala, 'Voicing Suffering and Commitment of the Intellectual', *Jindal Global Law Review* 9 (2018): 315–325.

[217] Oishik Sircar, 'Professor of Pathos: Upendra Baxi's Minor Jurisprudence', *Jindal Global Law Review* 9, no. 2 (2018): 203–222. See also Debolina Dutta, 'Another Story of the Open Letter: An Inheritance of Relationship-Making', *Jindal Global Law Review* 9, no. 2 (2018): 181–201. Baxi and three other law professors, Vasudha Dhagamwar, Raghunath Kelkar and Lotika Sarkar, had written an open letter to the Chief Justice regarding a matter concerning the decision of the Supreme Court in *Tukuram v State of Maharashtra* where the accused were let off because the court said the victim had not resisted or shouted for help. Baxi and others conveyed their outrage at this decision-making of the court and showcased an illustration of the importance of considering suffering when thinking about the procedural and abstract aspects of the law and justice.

of living and so on, as well as at a relational level in thinking of power hierarchies, oppressions, dominations, and so on, offering an insight into the plural ways in which people experience and engage with issues.[218]

In the fifth chapter, I will draw on these aspects of how the law materializes and is realized in people's lives to construct an access to justice framework for plural systems.

Conclusion

I have explored the connections of legal indicators to plural legal contexts. In doing so, several challenges of measurement were raised, including how indicators are constructed, realized and used. Through an examination of the conceptualization of the rule of law, as well as the manner in which it is applied through leading indicators, this chapter highlighted the changes required in order to apply the rule of law to a plural context.

At the outset, three ideas assume importance when looking at the use of indicators for measuring the rule of law in the context of plural legal orders. The first is whether the rule of law is conceived with a maximalist, minimalist or pluralist interpretation when determining what factors influence the quality of the justice system. The second is whether these indicators make certain assumptions regarding the role of the state and state institutions, regardless of the context in which these frameworks are applied. And third is whether the indicators examine factors central to the rule of law, constructed around the experiences of an individual or an institution.

I then examined how the challenges of the rule of law reform begin with the limitations of the concept of the rule of law. In its current form, it is a concept that is limited in its way of seeing the world, hegemonic in terms of the standards it demands, and rigid in terms of its ability to engage with the complexity of a plural legal world. It is therefore crucial to acknowledge that while attempts at legal empowerment and experimentalism are telling us that there are new ways of doing rule of law reform, we need to go one step further and push for broader concepts that can include the rule of law, but also other plural legal concepts.

---

[218] See also Jonathan Wolff and Avner De-Shalit, 'Introduction', in *Disadvantage*, 1–15 (Oxford: Oxford University Press, 2007).

I argue thereafter that if we are to use a concept that considers the plurality of legal systems, it may be more useful to embrace the concept of access to justice, because it has the capacity to look beyond an institutional approach to also tap into the networks, processes and abilities that expand or constrain how people resolve challenges that emerge when the law manifests in everyday life. In being more expansive, it has the potential to cover justiciable problems of a plural legal world.

4

Epistemic Diversity and Voices from the Global South

Countering the Managerial Implications of Measuring Justice

The development of legal indicators is a function of many decisions that in turn contribute to the epistemological power of these quantification tools. These decisions include the choices of theoretical concepts and methodologies employed in order to develop indicators, the locations from where the knowledge is constructed and from where it is extracted, the purposes for which the indicators are developed and the desired impact they are meant to achieve. These decisions influence the development of indicators and impact how they function. Through these different choices and decisions, indicators are built with a particular point of view and, as a result, while they can tell stories and convey a particular reading of the world, they also simplify and reduce complexity, create silences and engineer absences in understanding the world.

This chapter is concerned with offering a framework to embed an epistemic plurality and diversity into how we can build and develop legal indicators. It does so by engaging with epistemologies of the Global South and with embedding the realities of legal pluralism in the making of indicator frameworks. It explores how indicator frameworks can pay attention to the way in which concepts and values are represented while also engaging with different experiences and realizations of justice as they materialize in people's lives.

An important starting point for this chapter is an acknowledgment of the ubiquity of quantification. In the next section, I provide an overview of how we live in a quantified society and that legal indicators, like other indicators, have become pervasive in their use in public discourse, government functioning, international business and development cooperation.[1] Acknowledging the pervasiveness of quantification, however, does not mean that the practice of quantification cannot be done differently. In the ensuing section, I will introduce the idea of 'persistence' as a strategy to address some of the challenges posed by the critiques and argue that through persistence, steps can be taken to make the process of development and construction of indicators more open and transparent. The aim of this chapter is to address some of the critiques of legal indicators by offering an epistemological perspective, particularly by drawing from legal pluralism and through concepts from the South. It is an attempt to directly address the silences and absences in the current framing of legal indicators.

This chapter discusses the key aspects that would be critical to building a bottom-up and grounded legal indicator. It does so by addressing three interrelated issues. First, why, given the challenges of quantification addressed in previous chapters, should we engage with legal indicators at all? Is it possible to build a contextual approach to legal indicators? What does such an exercise entail? Second, what is the nature of the legal indicator, and can it move beyond being merely a technical and managerial device? And third, is it possible to construct a legal indicator that considers the voices of those who are marginalized by engaging actively with their political and social conditions?

The second section of the chapter introduces the idea of 'persistence', and how this can be an effective strategy to problematize and influence the development of legal indicators from the Global South. The third section will look beyond the managerial role of indicators and the rule by experts to instead reconstruct legal geographies by embracing the messiness of law in action. I will also draw on the analysis of how justice data is collected and evaluated in India to demonstrate this point. The final section will provide and reflect on the key choices for building a legal indicator that is grounded in the phenomenon of legal pluralism.

---

[1] 'The quantified society describes the widespread collection of information—or big data—about individuals, groups, and even whole societies, and the use of that information by public and private actors to make inferences and decisions about many aspects of our lives.' See this discussion in Julie Angwin, 'Life in a Quantified Society', *Open Society Foundations*, May 2019, https://www.opensocietyfoundations. org/explainers/life-quantified-society (accessed 30 July 2021).

Persisting with quantification

In Chapter 2, I examined criticisms of quantification and the development of indicators as not being neutral, for privileging particular imaginations and political leanings, and for portraying an abstract way of seeing the world divorced from its context.[2] In this section I argue why, despite this critique, it has become important to engage with legal indicators and bring in a Global South perspective to the thinking on, and framing of, these tools. I will argue that for a global legal indicator to be truly global, it needs to bring a more comprehensive and plural approach that pulls together voices and thinking from both the North and the South. In the course of this section, I first look at the ways in which quantification has permeated the society we live in, examining its pervasiveness, before arguing for how some of the standard narratives on legal indicators can be reclaimed and pluralized.

The pervasiveness of data and the need to pluralize its narratives

Quantification as a phenomenon is deeply embedded into different spheres of everyday life. At a general level, this takes place in numerous ways: from the ways in which we use our phones, and contribute to the creation of Big Data,[3] or in our engagement with social media platforms for making choices and decision.[4] Taking a slight detour from legal indicators to explore some other examples is necessary to showcase how ubiquitous numbers are in everyday life. Take, for example, The Data Detox Kit developed by Tactical Tech, a civil society organization in Berlin that works at the interface of

---

[2] For more details on this critique, please refer to Chapter 2 of this book where I discuss how indicators are developed to convey particular meanings, how they have the ability to evoke trust and further, how they are able to influence different policies and practices through the power of their narratives.

[3] Big Data is distinguished by the volume of the data, the variety of the data in terms of the heterogeneity of the data set and the velocity or speed with which data is generated. See Amir Gandomi and Murtaza Haider, 'Beyond the Hype: Big Data Concepts, Methods, and Analytics', *International Journal of Information Management* 35, no. 2 (2015): 137–144.

[4] Norjihan Binti Abdul Ghani, Suraya Binti Hamid, Ibrahim Abaker Targio Hashem and Ejaz Ahmed, 'Social Media Big Data Analytics: A Survey', *Computers in Human Behavior* 101 (2019): 417–428.

technology and society. It is an experiment to encourage users through an eight-day programme to engage more healthily with data. The Kit asks several questions which include 'Who are you online to others?', 'How well does Google know you?', and 'Who is your phone talking to?'[5] Each of these questions reveal how unknown and entangled our digital footprints are, but also help us piece together how these different interactions, when put together, contribute to the generation of data with more macro consequences. As this data detox project showcases, the challenge isn't with answering individual questions but rather how these different pieces of information create footprints that come together to offer a narrative that reveals patterns of connecting preferences, choices, interests, and so on.[6]

This illustration is to put forward the idea that we live in a society where there is widespread collection of information that is then used by different kinds of actors, both public and private, to make decisions that materially affect our everyday life.[7] This collection and use of data can have real-life consequences such as access to housing, credit and even jobs.[8] In an exhibition curated at the Haus der Kulturen der Welt by Tactical Tech called 'Nervous Systems', the curators, by looking at different materials, objects and visuals, show how new data economies are being created and how users become part of large networked infrastructures which are controlled by the market, corporations and finance.[9] One particular exhibit was the example of 'data brokers', who are part of an industry that buys and sells data to create an analysis for a wide range of activities based on the user's digital footprint.[10] Kosinski et al. showed how, by analysing the digital behaviours of people by using Facebook likes, it was possible to understand a wide range of preferences of people, including their religious and political views,

---

[5] Tactical Tech, 'The Data Detox Kit: An 8 Day Data Detox', https://theglassroomnyc. org/files/2016/12/DataDetoxKit_optimized_01.pdf (accessed 30 July 2021).

[6] Ibid.

[7] Sheila Jasanoff, 'Virtual, Visible, and Actionable: Data Assemblages and the Sightlines of Justice', *Big Data and Society* 4 (December 2017), doi:10.1177/2053951717724477; Linnet Taylor, 'What Is Data Justice? The Case for Connecting Digital Rights and Freedoms Globally', *Big Data and Society* 4 (December 2017), doi:10.1177/2053951717736335.

[8] Angwin, 'Life in a Quantified Society'; Taylor, 'What Is Data Justice'.

[9] Haus der Kulturen der Welt, 'Nervous Systems', 11 February 2016, https://www.hkw. de/en/programm/projekte/2016/nervoese_systeme/nervoese_systeme_mehr.php (accessed 5 February 2019).

[10] Ibid.

their sexual orientation, age and gender.[11] This psychological profiling was the basis for the use of methods such as data mining and analysis, along with targeted communication that was used by Cambridge Analytica to influence voters in the United States presidential election in 2016 and, in the same year, during the Brexit referendum in the United Kingdom to leave the European Union.[12]

These examples are important to showcase how different data points have emerged and have permeated institutions, policies, corporations and people's daily lives.[13] Living in a quantified society results in different ways in which people produce, contribute, consume and mine data, and are nudged to act in different ways by data.[14] However, within societies that rely on different forms of quantification, it is important to realize that there are different ways in which data is used and consumed. In this sense, there is no digital universalism in the ways in which data permeates the lives of people, and there is a need to deconstruct western approaches to data and think about diversities from the South.[15]

---

[11] Michal Kosinski, David Stillwell and Thore Graepel, 'Private Traits and Attributes Are Predictable from Digital Records of Human Behavior', *Proceedings of the National Academy of Sciences of the United States of America* 110, no. 15 (April 2013): 5802–5805, DOI: 10.1073/pnas.1218772110.

[12] Edmund L. Andrews, 'The Science Behind Cambridge Analytica: Does Psychological Profiling Work?', Stanford Graduate School of Business, 12 April 2018, https://www.gsb.stanford.edu/insights/science-behind-cambridge-analytica-does-psychological-profiling-work (accessed 13 September 2019); Issie Lapowsky, 'The Man Who Saw the Dangers of Cambridge Analytica Years Ago', *Wired*, 19 June 2010, https://www.wired.com/story/the-man-who-saw-the-dangers-of-cambridge-analytica/ (accessed 13 September 2019); Mike Butcher, '"The Great Hack": Netflix Doc Unpacks Cambridge Analytica, Trump, Brexit and Democracy's Death', *TechCrunch*, 24 July 2019, http://social.techcrunch.com/2019/07/23/the-great-hack-netflix-doc-unpacks-cambridge-analytica-trump-brexit-and-democracys-death/ (accessed 13 September 2019).

[13] Jasanoff, 'Virtual, Visible, and Actionable'.

[14] See also the work of Steffen Mau who argues how the fact that numbers are being used to track and monitor behaviour so widely from GDP to credit ratings to grades in school implies that without such data the modern world would not function. Steffen Mau, *The Metric Society: On the Quantification of the Social* (Cambridge: John Wiley & Sons, 2019).

[15] In her work, Anita Chen showcases how digital cultures can flourish in more ways than one, and that in different locations, there are different ways in which data is imagined and experienced. Similarly, Payal Arora also speaks of how the use of the

Locating the question of legal indicators within this discussion of a quantified society is extremely important because it highlights the need to acknowledge the pervasiveness of numbers in everyday life, and how indicators as specific as those concerning questions of law and justice contribute to the culture of evaluating phenomena from the vantage point of numerical evaluation.

At the level of legal indicators, the different kinds of quantification tools, whether for sustainable development,[16] corruption,[17] business,[18] freedom,[19] or democracy,[20] reveal certain underlying trends that give us a picture of how different institutions function and the impact that this has on people's lives. For example, in Venezuela, there is an ongoing debate about the brutality of the police forces, the methods of counting being employed to determine how many persons have been killed, and the lack of transparency about the data, where the state is trying to manipulate indicators to push a more favourable agenda.[21] Similarly, the Government of India, earlier

---

internet in the Global South is very different from the North, whether in approaches to privacy or in terms of work or leisure. In this regard, it is important to think of the plurality of the ways in which data is collected and used and examine how such lessons can hold relevance when evaluating legal systems. See Anita Chan, *Networking Peripheries: Technological Futures and the Myth of Digital Universalism* (Cambridge, MA: MIT Press, 2013); Payal Arora, *The Next Billion Users: Digital Life beyond the West* (Cambridge, MA: Harvard University Press, 2019).

[16] Jeffrey Sachs, Guido Schmidt-Traub, Christian Kroll, Guillaume Lafortune and Grayson Fuller, *Sustainable Development Report 2019: Transformations to Achieve the Sustainable Development Goals* (New York: Bertelsmann Stiftung and Sustainable Development Solutions Network [SDSN]), https://www.sustainabledevelopment. report (accessed 13 September 2019).

[17] Transparency International, 'Corruption Perception Index: Overview', https://www. transparency.org/research/cpi/overview (accessed 13 September 2019).

[18] World Bank, 'Doing Business Rankings', https://www.doingbusiness.org/en/rankings (accessed 13 September 2019).

[19] Freedom House, *Freedom in the World 2019: Democracy in Retreat*, 3 January 2019, https://freedomhouse.org/report/freedom-world/freedom-world-2019 (accessed 13 September 2019).

[20] Marc Bühlmann, Wolfgang Merkel, Lisa Müller and Bernhard Weßels, 'The Democracy Barometer: A New Instrument to Measure the Quality of Democracy and Its Potential for Comparative Research', *European Political Science* 11 (2012): 519–536.

[21] Keymer Avila, 'Use of Lethal Force in Latin America: A Sinister Political Priority', *openDemocracy*, 9 September 2019, https://www.opendemocracy.net/en/

in 2019, withheld unemployment data which showed alarming rates of joblessness in India, and it was argued that they did this because of an upcoming general election.[22] In both instances, massaging or withholding the data is because of the power and meanings that data are able to convey and communicate, and the value they hold in a society that increasingly explores different phenomena through metrics.[23]

A key factor in the life cycle of legal indicators is the role that different stakeholders and institutions play which contributes to their sustenance, use and growth. The ways in which indicators are framed are a function of the institutional architectures of the organizations that produce such frameworks. These institutions play a key role in ensuring the permanence and longevity of the indicators because, for many, the data is also central to ensuring their relevance and importance.[24] Institutions such as the World Bank, Transparency International and Freedom House all generate copious amounts of narratives around the data and the indicators that they produce, and therefore their influence is also dependent on these indicators.[25] The audiences for such data are also diverse. Some are funders, which include large donor countries who rely on these assessments for their own programs and policies, others are recipient countries, who are required to meet conditions stipulated by the indicator frameworks in order to have access to aid packages, and some include researchers, who contribute to the knowledge economy around the rankings given.[26]

---

democraciaabierta/uso-de-la-fuerza-letal-en-am%C3%A9rica-latina-una-siniestra prioridad-pol%C3%ADtica-en/ (accessed 13 September 2019).

[22] Kaushik Basu, 'India Can Hide Unemployment Data, but Not the Truth', *New York Times*, 1 February 2019, https://www.nytimes.com/2019/02/01/opinion/india-unemployment-jobs-blackout.html (accessed 13 September 2019).

[23] Reference to the power of data and indicators can also be seen in the example used in chapter 2 of the Doing Business rankings, where governments in both India and Chile used the information to influence political decisions and outcomes.

[24] Sally Engle Merry, 'Measuring the World: Indicators, Human Rights, and Global Governance', *Current Anthropology* 52 (2011): S83–S95.

[25] Kevin E. Davis, Benedict Kingsbury and Sally Engle Merry, 'Indicators as a Technology of Global Governance', *Law and Society Review* 46 (2012): 71–104.

[26] Kevin E. Davis, Benedict Kingsbury and Sally Engle Merry, 'Introduction: The Local-Global Life of Indicators: Law, Power, and Resistance', in *The Quiet Power of Indicators: Measuring Governance, Corruption, and Rule of Law*, ed. Sally Engle Merry, Kevin E. Davis and Benedict Kingsbury, 1–24 (Cambridge: Cambridge University Press, 2015);

In all of this, an ecosystem emerges around the creation, spread and further analysis of these indicators and we need to ask, for whom are these indicators produced? What kind of approach do they take? How do they conceptualize different components? What kind of philosophies do they prescribe? It is imperative to ask whose normativity are we analysing when we support, use or subscribe to these indicators.

If these are global indicators, is the Global South present in the conception of such legal indicators? Do the philosophies, values and histories of the Global South remain passive recipients to the generation of indicator frameworks but not contributors? Are international institutions that develop global indicators incorporating epistemic diversity in their development of these tools? It is important to ask these questions because there is an absence of epistemologies of the South in global legal indicators. And as Boaventura de Sousa Santos eloquently says:

> The epistemologies of the South concern the knowledges that emerge from social and political struggles and cannot be separated from such struggles. They are not, therefore, epistemologies in the conventional sense of the word. Their aim is not to study knowledge or justified belief as such, let alone the social and historical context in which they both emerge (social epistemology is a controversial concept as well). Their aim, rather, is to identify and valorize that which often does not even appear as knowledge in the light of the dominant epistemologies, that which emerges instead as part of the struggles of resistance against oppression and against the knowledge that legitimates such oppression. Many such ways of knowing are not thought knowledges but rather lived knowledges. The epistemologies of the South occupy the concept of epistemology in order to resignify it as an instrument for interrupting the dominant politics of knowledge. They are experiential epistemologies.[27]

Sally Engle Merry, Kevin E. Davis and Benedict Kingsbury (eds.), *The Quiet Power of Indicators: Measuring Governance, Corruption, and Rule of Law* (Cambridge: Cambridge University Press, 2015).

[27] Boaventura de Sousa Santos, 'Introduction: Why the Epistemologies of the South? Artisanal Paths for Artisanal Futures', in *The End of the Cognitive Empire: The Coming of Age of Epistemologies of the South*, 1–35 (Durham: Duke University Press, 2018), 2.

These ideas of lived experiences, of identifying knowledge ecologies, which are otherwise ignored, of speaking from experience and empirically, are concepts and issues that I will engage with in the next section. In doing so, I would like to propose not just an appreciation of different knowledge ecosystems and values, but a cognitive justice that goes beyond merely tolerating diversity to one that actively recognizes and implements it as a way of life.[28]

How to engage with legal indicators from the Global South

Legal indicators use a particular set of terms such as 'rule of law', 'democracy', 'rights', 'separation of powers', 'freedoms', and so on that are located in the legal geography of the Global North.[29] While these terms undoubtedly hold

---

[28] Shiv Visvanathan, 'The Search for Cognitive Justice', *Seminar Magazine* 597 (May 2009), https://www.india-seminar.com/2009/597/597_shiv_visvanathan.htm (accessed 30 September 2020).

[29] In their work on Big Data, Milan and Treré speak of the need to bring in non-western experiences in understanding how data are created and consumed. This is central to building evaluative frameworks that measure diverse contexts. See Stefania Milan and Emiliano Treré, 'Big Data from the South: The Beginning of a Conversation We Must Have', *DATACTIVE*, 16 October 2017, https://data-activism.net/2017/10/ bigdatasur/ (accessed 15 April 2020). Further in the work of Ashish Kothari, Wolfgang Sachs, and others there is a call to examine key concepts of development with a more plural approach.

> In this respect, the development discourse is an outcome of the post-war era of fossil-fuel-based triumphalism, undergirded by colonial perceptions and the legacy of Western rationalism. Cleansing the mind from development certainties, however, requires a conscious effort; therefore, the authors of this book have ventured to expose those key concepts that make up much of the mental furniture of 'development'. As it emerges, just to name some examples in the book, 'poverty' incorporates a materialistic prejudice, 'equality' is transmogrified into sameness, 'standard of living' reduces the diversity of happiness, 'needs' make the dependency trap snap, 'production' brings forth disvalue next to value, and 'population' is nothing but a statistical artefact. Exposing the epoch-specific nature of key concepts liberates the mind and prompts it to find a language that is equal to tomorrow's challenges. The Development Dictionary is meant to help in this endeavour. (Wolfgang Sachs, 'Preface', in *The Development Dictionary*, ed. Wolfgang Sachs, vi–vii [New York: ZED Books, 2009], xii)

value, and in many regards have applications across geographies of the North and South, from a legal standpoint, they are enmeshed in a legal formalism that is not represented globally.[30] The result of this focus on formalism is based on the need to compare from the vantage point of the familiar (using concepts that are familiar) rather than exploring what concepts and realities would be required in order to perform a meaningful comparison. This distinction is important because the choice of some concepts and the exclusion of others based on what is considered to be familiar underlies the location and context of who is developing the tools for comparison and who has the power to direct and generate the terms of evaluation.[31] It also points to the fact that there is a process of otherization of anything that makes doing comparison messy.[32] This kind of limited language and grammar constrains the political and legal imaginations with which to ask questions and give answers, and also the concepts with which we engage.[33]

See also Ashish Kothari, Ariel Salleh, Arturo Escobar, Federico Demaria, and Alberto Acosta (eds.), *Pluriverse: A Post-Development Dictionary* (New Delhi: Tulika Books, 2019). These arguments point to the need to pluralize the concepts, vocabularies and ideas that under-grid the development of legal indicators.

[30] John Griffiths, 'What Is Legal Pluralism?', *The Journal of Legal Pluralism and Unofficial Law* 18, no. 24 (1986): 1–55; Franz von Benda-Beckmann, 'Who's Afraid of Legal Pluralism?', *The Journal of Legal Pluralism and Unofficial Law* 34, no. 47 (2002): 37–82.

[31] Menski, in the context of his work on comparative law, argues for the need to problematize the universal acceptance of concepts and a need to engage with manifold pluralities that allow for different meanings and experiences with law. Werner F. Menski, 'Comparative Law and Legal Theory from a Global Perspective', in *Comparative Law in a Global Context: The Legal Systems of Asia and Africa*, 25–81 (Cambridge: Cambridge University Press, 2006).

[32] Comparative law requires an engagement with cultural complexities, such that it does meaningful comparison and does not resort to reductionism. It requires an epistemological reflection on how certain approaches can result in the creation of the other. See generally Emma Patrignani, *Otherness, Pluralism and Context: Underground Issues in Comparative Legal Studies* (Rovaniemi: Lapland University Press, 2017). See also Philipp Dann and Arun K. Thiruvengadam, 'Comparing Constitutional Democracy in the European Union and India: An Introduction', in *Democratic Constitutionalism in India and the European Union: Comparing the Law of Democracy in Continental Polities*, ed. Philipp Dann and Arun K. Thiruvengadam, 1–41 (Cheltenham: Edward Elgar Publishing, 2021).

[33] See generally Daniel Bonilla Maldonado, 'Introduction: Toward a Constitutionalism of the Global South', in *Constitutionalism of the Global South: The Activist Tribunals of*

Attempting to include Southern perspectives in building legal indicators can be developed in a variety of ways. The reason for outlining the different ways of doing so is to pre-empt the tired criticism that scholars in the South do not offer alternatives but just critiques.[34] It is also to demonstrate that an alternative canon is not always necessary when being critical but rather that there are several options that can be fruitful for such academic exercises.[35] To engage with legal indicators by drawing perspectives from the Global South, I develop three different approaches, namely reproduction, transformation and co-production.

The first approach is of *reproduction*. This process entails reproducing the legal indicators that are being developed either in institutions located in the North, or with a focus on values from the North and applying them to the Global South. This would involve using the frameworks already provided and populating them with data from contexts in the South. Reproducing these standards would not involve challenging the manner in which these frameworks have been developed but include adopting the frameworks and using them to understand local contexts. It is akin to how legal transplantation was seen as an important component in modern law

---

India, South Africa, and Colombia, ed. Daniel Bonilla Maldonado, 1–38 (Cambridge: Cambridge University Press, 2013). See also Eve Darian-Smith, 'Mismeasuring Humanity: Examining Indicators through a Critical Global Studies Perspective', *New Global Studies* 10, no. 1 (2016): 73–99

[34] See discussions on the importance of thinking critically about international law as a way to uncover power and knowledge hierarchies that constitute the field in B. S. Chimni, 'Third World Approaches to International Law: A Manifesto', *International Community Law Review* 8, no. 1 (2006): 3–27; Sébastien Jodoin and Katherine Lofts, 'What's Critical about Critical International Law? Reflections on the Emancipatory Potential of International Legal Scholarship', in *Critical International Law: Postrealism, Postcolonialism and Transnationalism*, ed. Prabhakar Singh and Benoit Mayer, 326–345 (New Delhi: Oxford University Press, 2014); Jochen von Bernstorff and Philipp Dann, 'The Battle for International Law: An Introduction', in *The Battle for International Law: South-North Perspectives on the Decolonization Era*, ed. Jochen von Bernstorff and Philipp Dann, 1–31 (Oxford: Oxford University Press, 2019).

[35] Prabhakar Singh and Benoit Mayer, 'Introduction: Thinking International Law Critically One Attitude, Three Perspectives', in *Critical International Law: Postrealism, Postcolonialsm, and Transnationalism*, ed. Prabhakar Singh and Benoit Mayer, 1–26 (New Delhi: Oxford University Press 2014).

making, [36] and also a strategy in the promotion of the rule of law, where ideas and values were implemented by international organizations regardless of their contextual relevance.[37] This is a common occurrence with many global legal indicators, where countries do not have a say in the methodology of constructing the indicator, nor are their histories, politics, cultures given importance, yet they are held accountable to the narratives that emerge from these indicators.[38] In this regard, the method of reproduction is the form of engagement with the Global South that is the most passive, since it accepts certain preconceived dimensions without offering different concepts and narratives. For example, if we look back at the framing of the rule of law discussed in the previous chapter, the formalism that underpins it shows that there is little scope for models of legal pluralism to be incorporated in the framing of those indicators. Rather, a legal centralism–influenced indicator is promoted as being one that can be used to evaluate legal systems all over the world.

---

[36] In this approach of transplantation, laws and legal institutions were borrowed from one country to another, but oftentimes without considering the cultural specificities of the transfer. See Jaakko Husa, 'Developing Legal System, Legal Transplants, and Path Dependence: Reflections on the Rule of Law', *The Chinese Journal of Comparative Law* 6, no. 2 (December 2018): 129–150.

[37] Please refer to the discussion on the promotion of the rule of law as discussed in Chapter 3. See also Thomas Carothers, 'The Rule of Law Revival', *Foreign Affairs*, 1998, https://www.foreignaffairs.com/articles/1998-03-01/rule-law-revival (accessed 13 August 2018).

[38] The knowledge generated from the indicator results in a range of different impacts, such as through international pressure to comply with certain standards imposed by the indicator or through pressure and control exerted by donor countries to meet particular goals. Refer to the discussion in Chapter 2 on how indicators influence reactivity through their evaluation and measurements of institutional performance. See also the works by Musaraj and Serban that explore indicators as technologies of power. Smoki Musaraj, 'Indicators, Global Expertise, and a Local Political Drama: Producing and Deploying Corruption Perception Data in Post-Socialist Albania', in *The Quiet Power of Indicators: Measuring Governance, Corruption, and Rule of Law*, ed. Sally Engle Merry, Kevin E. Davis and Benedict Kingsbury, 222–247 (Cambridge: Cambridge University Press, 2015); Mihaela Serban, 'Rule of Law Indicators as a Technology of Power in Romania', in *The Quiet Power of Indicators: Measuring Governance, Corruption, and Rule of Law*, ed. Sally Engle Merry, Kevin E. Davis and Benedict Kingsbury, 199–221 (Cambridge: Cambridge University Press, 2015).

In the second approach of *transformation*, the legal indicators are not merely accepted but are re-examined and reimagined in order to make them suitable for a local context. The process of transformation is a critical process and one that requires an engagement with the production and construction of the indicator, and an inquiry into whether its existing framing works for a particular context. The process requires a change in approach from the normative to the empirical. Whereas a normative approach would involve asking what ought to work and creating indicators based on that premise, the empirical would ask what works and contexualizing the indicator to respond to specificities on the ground. This is where the idea of translation is important in the process of transformation, so that concepts are adapted to a local context, but more than that, through the use of inspirations from the vernacular, these global ideas of rule of law and justice are understood in concepts that are familiar and relatable.[39] The process of transformation may lead to several outcomes. It could be in the form of a hybrid set of indicators, which blend different forms of influence. It could also be a more localized set of indicators, which through the process of translation seek to move away from the normative consideration to the more descriptive and empirical aspects.[40] An example of this form of transformation could be

---

[39] Sally Engle Merry, *Human Rights and Gender Violence: Translating International Law into Local Justice* (Chicago: University of Chicago Press, 2009); Daniel M. Goldstein, 'Whose Vernacular? Translating Human Rights in Local Contexts', in *Human Rights at the Crossroads*, ed. Mark Goodale, 111–121 (Oxford: Oxford University Press, 2014); Maya Unnithan and Carolyn Heitmeyer, 'Challenges In "Translating" Human Rights: Perceptions and Practices of Civil Society Actors in Western India', *Development and Change* 45 (2014): 1361–1384.

[40] Sally Engle Merry, 'Transnational Human Rights and Local Activism: Mapping the Middle', *American Anthropologist* 108, no. 1 (2006): 38–51. See also the following extract which speaks to the tension that emerges between universal concepts in different cultural settings:

> During the public presentation of the report in New York City by Fiji's Assistant Minister for Women, the nuances of *bulubulu* as a sociolegal practice in postcolonial Fiji were obscured within what quickly became complicated layers of political miscommunication, the imperatives of a surging Fijian nationalism, and, as always, the politicization of culture. On the one hand, the CEDAW committee, though staffed by members from a range of different countries, was required by its UN mandate to fulfil a fairly simple task: to decide whether individual countries were taking the requirements of CEDAW seriously, as measured by national

seen in the approaches taken by the Justice Needs studies, by the Hague Model of Access to Justice of the Hague Institute for Innovation of Law. They aim to listen to people's needs, and understand their challenges in access to justice, while each study and survey is adjusted to the country's context and experiences.[41]

The idea of *co-production* emerges from theories of empowerment and collaboration when thinking of its impact in public policy.[42] In this approach the research impetus is very much to focus on the voices, preferences and

---

self-assessments of violence against women and official responses to this violence. But, on the other hand, because CEDAW expresses both the conceptual and practical constraints of universal human rights discourse, the UN committee was prevented from considering the social contexts within which *bulubulu* functions in Fiji. To open up the possibility that CEDAW's requirements for defining, preventing, and redressing violence against women were contingent upon their correspondence with circumstance, tradition, or instrumental efficacy would be to deracinate CEDAW, to destroy its potential as one key component in a still-emergent international human rights system. (Mark Goodale, 'Introduction: Locating Rights, Envisioning Law between the Global and the Local', in *The Practice of Human Rights: Tracking Law between the Global and the Local*, ed. Mark Goodale and Sally Engle Merry, 1–38 [Cambridge: Cambridge University Press, 2007], 1)

[41] HiiL, *Understanding Justice Needs: The Elephant in the Courtroom* (The Hague: HiiL, 2018), https://www.hiil.org/wp-content/uploads/2018/11/HiiL-Understanding-Justice-Needs-The-Elephant-in-the-Courtroom.pdf (accessed 9 December 2020); Tilburg Institute for Interdisciplinary Studies of Civil Law and Conflict Resolution Systems (TISCO), Martin Gramatikov, Maurits Barendrecht, Malini Laxminarayan, Jin Ho Verdonschot, Laura Klaming and Corry van Zeeland, *A Handbook for Measuring the Costs and Quality of Access to Justice* (Apeldoorn, Antwerpen and Portland: Maklu Publishers, 2010).

[42] Taco Brandsen and Marlies Honingh, 'Distinguishing Different Types of Coproduction: A Conceptual Analysis Based on the Classical Definitions', *Public Administration Review* 76 (2016): 427–435; Catherine Durose, Yasminah Beebeejaun, James Rees, Jo Richardson and Liz Richardson, 'Towards Co-Production in Research with Communities', Arts and Humanities Research Council Connected Communities Programme, 2011, https://ahrc.ukri.org/documents/project-reports-and-reviews/connected-communities/towards-co-production-in-research-with-communities/ (accessed 15 September 2019); Yasminah Beebeejaun, Catherine Durose, James Rees, Joanna Richardson and Liz Richardson, '"Beyond Text": Exploring Ethos and Method in Co-Producing Research with Communities', *Community Development Journal* 49, no. 1 (January 2014): 37–53.

knowledge of the people themselves, and giving them voice so as to build people-centred approaches. It is a conscious disentangling with expert knowledge and focuses more on drawing from the context and the societal milieu to produce knowledge in a deliberative and reflexive manner.[43] Co-production is an exercise in a more interactive type of knowledge production.[44] This entails that the nature in which the information is gathered, selected, distilled and finalized involves greater participation, iteration and input from the community.[45] It is a mechanism where different normative universes are integrated and where there is an emphasis on engagement with experiences and realizations of justice. In this sense, co-production challenges knowledge hierarchies and attempts to equalize the field by drawing from numerous sources to create more grounded outputs.[46] In the case of indicators, co-production involves moving away from a technical discourse to instead draw from a plurality of different sources of values and ideas.

What these three approaches demonstrate is that engaging with a mainstream approach does not have to be by offering an alternative canon, but that distinctions in the ways in which concepts are framed and used can

---

[43] See also the idea of 'slow comparison', which speaks of a need for a more deliberate and epistemologically aware approach in Dann and Thiruvengadam, 'Comparing Constitutional Democracy'.

[44] Christian Pohl, Stephan Rist, Anne Zimmermann, Patricia Fry, Ghana S Gurung, Flurina Schneider, Chinwe Ifejika Speranza, Boniface Kiteme, Sébastian Boillat, Elvira Serrano, Gertrude Hirsch Hadorn and Urs Wiesmann, 'Researchers' Roles in Knowledge Co-Production: Experience from Sustainability Research in Kenya, Switzerland, Bolivia and Nepal', *Science and Public Policy* 37, no. 4 (May 2010): 267–281.

[45] Elinor Ostrom, 'Crossing the Great Divide: Coproduction, Synergy, and Development', *World Development* 24, no. 6 (1996): 1073–1087.

[46] Jasanoff outlines co-production as follows: 'Briefly stated, co-production is shorthand for the proposition that the ways in which we know and represent the world (both nature and society) are inseparable from the ways in which we choose to live in it. Knowledge and its material embodiments are at once products of social work and constitutive of forms of social life; society cannot function without knowledge any more than knowledge can exist without appropriate social supports. Scientific knowledge, in particular, is not a transcendent mirror of reality. It both embeds and is embedded in social practices, identities, norms, conventions, discourses, instruments and institutions—in short, in all the building blocks of what we term the social.' In Sheila Jasanoff, 'The Idiom of Co-Production', in *States of Knowledge: The Co-Production of Science and the Social Order*, ed. Sheila Jasanoff, 1–12 (London: Routledge, 2004), 2–3.

also be ways of engaging critically. This study will develop further ways to build a co-produced indicator framework, one where concepts are chosen and methodologies are employed by engaging with a plurality of sources with which to understand and evaluate legal systems. The objective is to be able to build an indicator framework that is grounded in the concept of legal pluralism.

Persistence with indicators is political

Though this book has critiqued indicator frameworks and the ways in which they reduce complexity and plurality in favour of finding comparable and universal methods of evaluation, I still argue that it is important to persist with indicators. I argue that the exercise of building and using indicators is not a compromise of principles despite the critique but a deeply political decision of persistence. Persistence is a method and strategy that requires challenging the status quo for why indicators are problematic, arguing for why reproduction of transplanted indicators does not work and for why it is imperative that beyond translating and transforming standards for a Southern audience, the South must be a part of the development process of the legal indicators. The question of bringing in voices, diverse histories and cultures is critical in order to pluralize the discourse and make comparisons more meaningful and persisting with legal indicators through the method of co-production would entail a more grounded and reflexive framework that is more inclusive.

I see persistence as a methodology because it involves asking uncomfortable questions about silences that emerge when knowledge is produced and demanding that these absences be confronted and not forgotten.[47] It involves questioning the status quo by infiltrating it with different ecologies of knowledge and in a sense 'researching back', which, as Tuhiwai Smith argues, is about challenging underlying codes and regulations that dominate scientific disciplines and paradigms.[48] In this regard, I term persistence research as research that is grounded

---

[47] See the idea of sociology of absences by de Souza Santos as ways to highlight knowledge and epistemologies that are otherwise side lined or marginalized. Santos, 'Introduction: Why the Epistemologies of the South?', 2.

[48] Linda Tuhiwai Smith, 'Introduction', in *Decolonizing Methodologies: Research and Indigenous Peoples*, 1–41 (New York: ZED Books, 2012), 7.

in the knowledge that there are ingrained power differentials in the manner in which knowledge is generated and it is important to build a framework to both acknowledge these power differentials and find ways to respond to it. Being persistent is a form of resistance against dominant methods of knowledge production and I unpack what persistence means methodologically because these facets allow me to think about ways to build indicators that have a global focus yet are cognizant of epistemic diversity. I will argue that persistence enables us to *remember* the absences, to *infiltrate* the status quo and to *pluralize* the discourse when it comes to developing legal indicator frameworks.

The process of remembering is where there is a historical and contextual examination of otherwise unjust and structural discriminations that exist in the creation of knowledge.[49] Remembering is a technique that can be used to raise questions about the silences of certain bodies of knowledge or cultural contexts that are not included when frameworks are developed. Through this, we can investigate why these situations came about, what allowed them to flourish and who gave them currency. In the case of legal indicators, it is a signalling exercise that locates the sites where selection and development of standards are taking place, who is funding it and what kind of agendas they come with. It provides insights into the epistemologies of knowledge that are privileged and those that are side lined.

The second aspect of the method of persistence is that it allows for a fight back against hegemonizing tendencies. One way of doing this is through infiltrating the vocabularies that dominate the arena of legal indicators with new textures and layers. Why is it that words such as 'democracy' have such obvious currency whereas 'swaraj' are less universal?[50] There is a need to ensure that there are different ways in which vocabularies can be expanded to include new ways of seeing and describing concepts—infiltrating is also about ensuring that structures that exist are being

---

[49] Linda Tuhiwai Smith, 'Twenty-Five Indigenous Projects', in *Decolonizing Methodologies: Research and Indigenous Peoples*, 142–162 (New York: ZED Books, 2012), 146

[50] For discussions on *swaraj* as a form of self-governance and self-regulation see Rudolf C. Heredia, 'Interpreting Gandhi's Hind Swaraj', *Economic and Political Weekly* 34, no. 24 (12 June 1999): 1497–1502.

challenged.[51] Legal indicators are currently deeply embedded in a legal formalism.[52] There are only different versions of the rule of law, which may be narrow or expansive but are different reproductions of the same root concept.[53] The problem with this is that despite the challenges of the transfer of rule of law standards and institutions as we discussed in the last chapter, it remains a normative standard but without opportunity to allow for other normativity that are descriptive of the contexts in other parts of the world to flourish.

At present, indicators tell a story that is already largely known—that rule of law will be higher in countries that are closely connected culturally with similar institutions and values to those imagined in the indicators; it is a futile exercise to create such rankings. This is why infiltration at a conceptual level is important, because it demands that more concepts, values and histories are part of the conversation, and will enable a more inclusive concept that builds on the rule of law to be arrived at. One of the reasons access to justice is a preferred concept is not because it is less demanding than the rule of law, but rather that it is more flexible, contextual and capable of being infiltrated. It is a concept that is able to articulate the sufferings and injustices of those who are marginalized, and to find ways to amplify these experiences, while at the same time maintaining elements of the rule of law.[54]

---

[51] Peter Ronald de Souza, 'Epilogue', in *Keywords for India: A Conceptual Lexicon for the 21st Century*, ed. Rukmini Bhaya Nair and Peter Ronald de Souza, 415–419 (London: Bloomsbury Academic, 2020).

[52] Baxi has argued for a need to rethink categories when making comparisons in comparative law by examining views from the subaltern. See Upendra Baxi, 'Constitutionalism as a Site of State Formative Practices', *Cardozo Law Review* 21 (1999): 1183–1210.

[53] Wolfgang Merkel, 'Measuring the Quality of Rule of Law', in *Rule of Law Dynamics: In an Era of International and Transnational Governance*, ed. Michael Zürn, André Nollkaemper and Randy Peerenboom, 21–47 (Cambridge: Cambridge University Press, 2012). For a history on global constitutionalism, see generally Mattias Kumm, 'On the History and Theory of Global Constitutionalism', in *Global Constitutionalism from European and East Asian Perspectives*, ed. Takao, Suami, Anne Peters, Dimitri Vanoverbeke and Mattias Kumm, 168–200 (Cambridge: Cambridge University Press, 2018).

[54] Upendra Baxi, 'From Human Rights to the Right to Be Human: Some Heresies', *India International Centre Quarterly* 13, no. 3/4 (December 1986): 185–200. See also the

The third aspect of persistence is to build on the act of infiltration. Whereas infiltration is a challenge to the status quo, the process of pluralizing the discourse is one that requires us to institutionalize the idea that plurality is not a myth, but one that is enmeshed in the everyday practice of law and legal institutions.[55] Through this, ensuring representation becomes important because not only does it acknowledge silences and infiltrate the status quo, but it also builds on this by introducing a new set of concepts, and values to the existing frameworks.[56] Ensuring representation and being representative are distinct concepts. While it is likely that there will still be silences because persistence is an ongoing process, it requires epistemic reflection both in terms of combating the dominant narrative and in articulating new ways of seeing, and deliberating on what questions are being asked.[57] What is essential is that the ways of thinking about representation do not become a post facto decision but are an intrinsic part of the development of legal indicators. Pluralizing the discourse with respect to indicators is a difficult process and will be examined in detail in the final section of this chapter.

This section has sought to demonstrate why persisting with indicators beyond critique is important because it acknowledges that quantification is deeply embedded in our everyday life and knowledge systems. It recognizes that persisting is a political action and aims to provide a method for how to embed different experiences and realities. This section exhorts why legal indicators cannot just be created by some institutions or countries and used

discussions on access to justice in Chapter 3.

[55] Boaventura de Sousa Santos, 'Law: A Map of Misreading—Toward a Postmodern Conception of Law', 4 *Journal of Law and Society* 14 (Autumn 1987): 279–302; Sally Engle Merry, 'Legal Pluralism', *Law and Society Review* 22, no. 5 (1988): 869–896; Baudouin Dupret, 'Legal Pluralism, Plurality of Laws, and Legal Practices', *European Journal of Legal Studies* 1, no. 1 (2007): 1–26, http://cadmus.eui.eu//handle/1814/6852 (accessed 7 December 2017).

[56] See generally Santos, 'Introduction: Why the Epistemologies of the South?'; Boaventura de Sousa Santos, *Toward a New Legal Common Sense: Law, Globalization, and Emancipation* (Cambridge: Cambridge University Press 2002).

[57] See also the idea of 'epistemic reflexivity' for Comparative Constitutional Law, which speaks of rethinking the questions, categories and voices that are heard in Philipp Dann, Michael Riegner and Maxim Bönnemann, 'The Southern Turn in Comparative Constitutional Law: An Introduction', SSRN Electronic Journal, 2020, https://www.ssrn.com/abstract=3553852 (accessed 16 April 2020).

to evaluate other countries that have no input in its design. It argues that in the making of indicators, the engagement of the Global South must involve including their inputs and experiences in the creation of new ideas and concepts.

The managerial role of measuring justice: why the social matters

How can indicators be built to ensure that they represent more than just technocracy and matters of performance and effectiveness, and also convey the social realities of people's lives? In this section, I look at the concept of managerialism and how it affects the ways in which data on justice systems is collected. As an illustration, I look deeply at how justice is measured in the Indian context and how data is collected and presented. Thereafter, I also examine the kind of narratives that have emerged from this and the absences that result.

Managerialism and its role in justice data

The ubiquity of metrics in a quantified society has resulted in the production and consumption of data that evaluates behaviours and performances of institutions and individuals. Legal indicators, among such kinds of metrics, adopt devices such as benchmarking and auditing, which in turn enable a specific managerial mindset to understand and make sense of matters for adjudication and law making.[58] With managerialism and its particular ways of evaluating comes the expectation that specific actors like judges, lawyers and court managers each play a role to ensure that targets are determined, data gathered and standards adhered to, to meet particular outcomes.[59]

---

[58] David Restrepo Amariles, 'Supping with the Devil? Indicators and the Rise of Managerial Rationality in Law', *International Journal of Law in Context* 13, no. 4 (2017): 465–484; Michael Power, *The Audit Explosion* (Oxford: Oxford University Press, 1999).

[59] Kevin E. Davis, Benedict Kingsbury and Sally Engle Merry, 'Introduction: Global Governance by Indicators', in *Governance by Indicators: Global Power through Quantification and Rankings*, ed. Kevin E. Davis, Angelina Fisher, Benedict Kingsbury and Sally Engle Merry, 3–28 (Oxford: Oxford University Press, 2012).

Managerialism involves adopting mindsets and languages that are technical, complex and developed by experts in the field.[60] Experts are able to engage with the manner in which knowledge is produced and how it is applied, and by doing so help to examine particular contexts and prepare agendas for how to engage with them.[61] Legal indicator frameworks are synonymous with expertise. They are seen as normative instruments that attempt to showcase how things ought to work. Amariles argues that the impact of legal indicators is that they encourage performance-based and managerial modes of governance.[62] This results in two main consequences: first, that law is not only defined by a set of rules but also in terms of measurable outcomes that can be capable of improvement and, second, that law becomes a part of a managerial process which enables an engagement with thinking about aspects of creation and enforcement of norms as well as benchmarking, auditing and data gathering.[63]

While expertise produces technical knowledge, it also raises critical questions of equality in terms of who is creating knowledge and how democratic the process is, and accountability in ascertaining who is responsible for the development of the outputs from such expertise.[64] Additionally, knowledge produced by experts is not of the kind that is neutral in nature, but is very much ideological.[65] As Jasanoff argues, experts themselves are aware that expertise is a hybrid between scientific knowledge and other forms of knowledge deeply embedded in the political and social worlds, and is very much a function of factors that are not all objective.[66]

---

[60] Thomas Klikauer, 'What Is Managerialism?', *Critical Sociology* 41, nos. 7–8 (2015): 1103–1119.

[61] Reiner Grundmann, 'The Problem of Expertise in Knowledge Societies', *Minerva* 55 (2017): 25–48.

[62] David Restrepo Amariles, 'Legal Indicators, Global Law and Legal Pluralism: An Introduction', *The Journal of Legal Pluralism and Unofficial Law* 47, no. 1 (2015): 9–21.

[63] Ibid. See also Ann Janette Rosga and Margaret L. Satterthwaie, 'The Trust in Indicators: Measuring Human Rights', *Berkeley Journal of International Law* 27, no. 2 (2009): 253–315.

[64] Stephen Turner, 'What Is the Problem with Experts?', *Social Studies of Science* 31, no. 1 (2001): 123–149.

[65] Ibid.

[66] See generally Sheila Jasanoff, *The Fifth Branch: Science Advisors as Policy Makers* (Cambridge, MA: Harvard University Press, 1998).

Whereas expertise is a key factor of managerialism, the other underlying element is the role of the market. With this outlook, 'society' is viewed as a space for competing interests, rather than one with a common goal, and what drives these managerial frameworks is not the welfare of society but rather which result has the most value.[67] A language of the market also results in demands of efficiency and of achieving targets and outcomes. In the case of legal indicators, this managerialism translates into, for example, managing the performance of the judiciary. This could mean that factors in the indicator frameworks would include determining the number of cases that a judge adjudicates, ascertaining the ways in which finances are spent, and giving precedence to the economics of justice over the substantive aspects of justice delivery.[68]

A case study conducted at the Brazilian National Council of Justice showed how institutions internalize the vocabulary of indicators.[69] There is now greater awareness of aspects of managerial efficiency by officials who manage administrative systems and about the importance of paying attention to measurable outcomes such as length of trial, procedural bottlenecks, number of sentences, and so on. This has caused internal competition between judges and also facilitated adherence to new standards of efficiency based on these measures. This illustration shows how the delivery of justice in legal systems is being reconceived in a vocabulary of outcomes and outputs over aspects of ideology.[70]

As I will demonstrate in the next section with data from India, a focus on efficiency can come at the cost of measuring other substantive aspects of justice delivery. This will include whether the language of managerialism, and the market, have resulted in the user, who engages with the legal system, to become peripheral to how performance and standards of justice

---

[67] Ming-sum Tsui and Fernando C. H. Cheung, 'Gone with the Wind: The Impacts of Managerialism on Human Services', *The British Journal of Social Work* 34, no. 3 (2004): 437–442.

[68] See generally Marcia Neave, 'Law Reform in the Age of Managerialism', speech delivered at the Australian Law Reform Agencies Conference, Darwin, 20 June 2002, https://www.lawreform.vic.gov.au/publications-and-media/speeches/law-reform-age-managerialism (accessed 24 February 2019).

[69] Pedro Rubim Borges Fortes, 'How Legal Indicators Influence a Justice System and Judicial Behavior: The Brazilian National Council of Justice and "Justice in Numbers"', *The Journal of Legal Pluralism and Unofficial Law* 47, no. 1 (2015): 39–55.

[70] Ibid.

are measured. To build on these arguments, in the following section I take a detailed look at how data that has been collected to measure justice in India provides narratives that place an emphasis on managerialism.

Measuring justice in India: Examining what is measured

India presents an interesting case study for analysing how justice systems are measured for several reasons. First, it is increasingly witnessing initiatives that are designed to build judicial statistics and assessments to measure the justice needs of people.[71] Second, it has a large court and formal justice system infrastructure that operates across the country with different degrees of capacity, scope and legitimacy.[72] And third, it also has parallel legal systems based on custom, tradition and religion, which continue to have authority in large parts of the country. The existence of legal pluralism with competing forms of legality offers an opportunity to understand how people embark on paths to justice, and what they find as hurdles and barriers to justice.

This section will seek to highlight the motivations and politics of the data being collected that plays a role in assembling an image of justice delivery in India. It is important from an indicator perspective because it provides an insight into the kind of data that is available and the kind of priorities for data collection that exist, which can then be used to develop a measurement framework. This section will inductively develop an understanding of what it means to measure justice in India by delving into the kind of narratives that emerge when one critically reflects on the impacts and consequences of the data, how it is represented, how the data is structured and what functions data serves through its performance.[73] I aim to locate where the data is emerging

---

[71] I will look at case studies of government bodies collecting data like the National Judicial Data Grid, Law Commission reports as well as Civil Society projects that were engaged in collecting data.

[72] I will look at sources that measure how the formal court system (the Supreme Court, High Courts and district courts) are measured as well as non-state systems like *lok adalats*, which are designed to enable speedy resolution of disputes as alternative dispute resolution forums.

[73] Erin Sahlstein Parcell and Benjamin M. A. Baker, 'Narrative Analysis', in *The SAGE Encyclopedia of Communication Research Methods*, ed. Mike Allen, 1069–1072 (Thousand Oaks, CA: SAGE Publications Inc, 2018), http://methods.sagepub.com/reference/the-sage-encyclopedia-of-communication-research-methods/i9374.xml (accessed 28

from, what its purpose is and what kind of story data tells us about the challenges, experiences and needs of people as they encounter and resolve their common justice problems.[74] In this section, the different projects that collect data are organized according to matters concerning government sources, commissions and non-governmental sources.[75]

A major source for data on the Indian judiciary is through the National Judicial Data Grid (NJDG), which was established by the Supreme Court of India in 2015 to provide information on the number of cases pending and disposed of in courts across the country.[76] It was an initiative of the E-Courts project, which similarly provides data largely connected with judicial administration.[77] The data on the NJDG can also be sub-organized into civil cases and criminal cases, including whether under each category the cases are pending for 0 to 1 year, 1 to 3 years, 3 to 5 years, 5 to 10 years, 10 to 20 years, 20 to 30 years and more than 30 years.[78] The cases are organized according to the 'type of the case', for example, whether it is at an original jurisdiction or an appellate jurisdiction, and also according to 'stage of the case', for example, if an appearance has been made or a stay has been issued. It also helps sort cases depending on whether women or senior citizens have filed them.

August 2019); David Michael Boje, 'Narrative Analysis', in *Encyclopedia of Case Study Research*, ed. Albert Mills, Gabrielle Durepos and Elden Wiebe, 591–594 (Thousand Oaks, CA: SAGE Publications Inc, 2012), http://methods.sagepub.com/reference/encyc-of-case-study-research/n220.xml (accessed 19 February 2022).

[74] David Michael Boje and Grace Ann Rosile, 'Storytelling', in *Encyclopedia of Case Study Research*, ed. Albert Mills, Gabrielle Durepos and Elden Wiebe, 899–901 (Thousand Oaks, CA: SAGE Publications, Inc 2012), http://methods.sagepub.com/reference/encyc-of-case-study-research/n331.xml (accessed 28 August 2019).

[75] A survey of publicly listed data sources has been provided. See Aparna Chandra and Rishabh Sharma, 'The Indian Judicial System by Numbers (Part I)', *Daksh*, 30 August 2016, http://dakshindia.org/indian-judicial-system-numbers-part/ (accessed 12 August 2019); Aparna Chandra and Rishabh Sharma, 'The Indian Judicial System by Numbers (Part II)', *Daksh*, 8 September 2016, http://dakshindia.org/indian-judicial-system-numbers-part-ii/ (accessed 12 August 2019).

[76] 'NJDG – National Judicial Data Grid', https://njdg.ecourts.gov.in/njdgnew/index.php (accessed 12 August 2019).

[77] 'Home – ECourt India Services', ECourt Services, https://ecourts.gov.in/ecourts_home/ (accessed 12 August 2019).

[78] 'NJDG – National Judicial Data Grid'.

In addition to the NJDG, the Supreme Court *Annual Reports* and the *Annual Reports* from High Courts across India also provide data in relation to the institution, the disposal and the pendency of cases. As of 2018 (January–October), the *Annual Report* of the Supreme Court showed that 33,743 cases were instituted, 33,011 were disposed of and 56,320 cases were pending.[79] For data on criminal matters, the National Crime Records Bureau (NCRB) produces three annual publications. The first is *Crime in India*, which contains information on the cases registered and their disposal along with information regarding persons who have been arrested and their disposal.[80] The report has data on cognizable crimes reported from police stations for that year. The NCRB also publishes a report on prison statistics that contains data on the number of prisons, prisoners, information on the prison infrastructure, how long persons have been detained and the age and sex of detainees.[81] The National Legal Services Authority (NALSA) also provides data for the national *lok adalats* (people's courts), which are organized to settle cases—by offering data on the settlements arrived at, the values of the settlements, and whether the matter was pre litigation or pending.[82] To illustrate, the national *lok adalat* held on 8 December 2018 across the country in India took up 5,113,821 cases and settled 1,193,598 for a value of INR 40,020,841,561.[83]

Another source of data on justice systems in India is the Law Commission of India. Under the chairmanship of Justice Khanna, the

---

[79] Supreme Court of India, *Indian Judiciary: Annual Report 2017–2018* (New Delhi: Supreme Court of India, 2018), https://ncrb.gov.in/en/crime-india-2016-0 (accessed 20 February 2022).

[80] National Crime Records Bureau, *Crime in India* (New Delhi: National Crime Records Bureau, 2016), https://nalsa.gov.in/services/lok-adalat/national-lok-adalat/national-lok-adalat-2018 (accessed 20 February 2022).

[81] National Crime Records Bureau, *Prison Statistics in India* (New Delhi: National Crime Records Bureau, 2016).

[82] *Lok adalats* are an alternative dispute resolution forum in India where cases pending in courts of law, or at the pre litigation stage are settled. National Crime Records Bureau, 'National Lok Adalat 2018: National Legal Services Authority', 2018, https://nalsa.gov.in/services/lok-adalat/national-lok-adalat/national-lok-adalat-2018 (accessed 12 August 2019).

[83] National Legal Services Authority, 'Disposal of National Lok Adalat Held on 8th December 2018', https://nalsa.gov.in/services/lok-adalat/national-lok-adalat/national-lok-adalat-2018 (accessed 20 February 2022).

commission brought out two reports: one related to delay and arrears in trial courts[84] and another for High Courts and appellate courts[85] with data on both institutions. In the 120th report, the commission produced a report on judicial administration, and provided data on the number of judges serving the population and how efforts could be made to reduce the burden.[86] More recently, the commission in a report on the restructuring of the Supreme Court also provided data on the disposal and pendency of cases from 1950 to 2008 in the court.[87]

A 2014 report of the commission provides an analysis of how backlog in cases were created, and how pendency is being cleared across courts.[88] It also, through an analysis of the data, examines what kinds of cases are causing challenges to the judicial administration, such as with regard to traffic violations, and projects how many additional judges are needed on a priority basis across the different courts.[89] Recently, Niti Aayog proposed introducing judicial performance indicators to address challenges of pendency in cases and delays in trials.[90] The Economic Survey of India also addressed the need for timely justice in order to improve the

[84] Law Commission of India, *Delay and Arrears in Trial Courts*, Report no. 77 (New Delhi, 1978), https://lawcommissionofindia.nic.in/51-100/Report77.pdf (accessed 20 February 2022).

[85] Law Commission of India, *Delay and Arrears in High Courts and Other Appellate Courts*, Report no. 79 (New Delhi, 1979), https://lawcommissionofindia.nic.in/51-100/report79.pdf (accessed 20 February 2022).

[86] Law Commission of India, *Manpower Planning in the Judiciary: A Blueprint*, Report no. 120 (New Delhi, 1987), https://lawcommissionofindia.nic.in/101-169/Report120.pdf (accessed 20 February 2022).

[87] Law Commission of India, *Need for Division of the Supreme Court into a Constitution Bench at Delhi and Cassation Benches in Four Regions at Delhi, Chennai/Hyderabad, Kolkata and Mumbai*, Report no. 229 (New Delhi, 2009, https://lawcommissionofindia.nic.in/reports/report229.pdf (accessed 20 February 2022).

[88] Law Commission of India, *Arrears and Backlog: Creating Additional Judicial (Wo) Manpower*, Report no. 245 (New Delhi, 2014, https://lawcommissionofindia.nic.in/reports/Report245.pdf (accessed 20 February 2022).

[89] Ibid.

[90] Niti Aayog is a policy think tank of the Government of India. NITI Aayog, 'Overview', https://niti.gov.in/content/overview (accessed 9 December 2020); Priya Sundarajan, 'NITI Aayog for Judicial Performance Index to Check Pendency', *Business Line*, 30 April 2017, https://www.thehindubusinessline.com/news/national/niti-aayog-for-judicial-performance-index-to-check-pendency/article9674596.ece (accessed 13 August 2019).

business climate in India and argued for having an efficient and effective legal system for ease of business.[91]

Apart from government organizations, several civil society organizations also collect justice data. A notable example is Daksh, a non-government organization (NGO) in Bengaluru, which conducted a survey in 2015 to study the needs and expectations of litigants who used the judicial system.[92] Through understanding the perceptions of over 9,000 litigants in 305 locations and across 24 states, the survey attempted to study access to justice by asking how easy it was for litigants to access the judicial system, what was the quality of the judicial process, what was their ability to understand the process and finally the socio-economic impacts of the process.[93] The *State of Justice Report* by Daksh largely looked at formal institutions of justice. In their second report, *Approaches to Justice*, Daksh also examined non-judicial bodies with their Paths to Justice survey and had 45,551 responses across 28 states.[94] The survey sought to study what kinds of disputes people had, how they resolved it and at which forums and further the costs of the disputes.[95] A second illustration is a collaborative project the Tata Trusts, a philanthropic foundation, recently published—*India Justice Report*—which measures justice by looking at institutions of the police, prisons and judiciary, while also focusing on legal aid. Each of these factors covered the themes of infrastructure, human resources, diversity, budget,

---

[91] Government of India, 'Chapter 9: Ease of Doing Business' Next Frontier: Timely Justice', in *Economic Survey of India 2017–18,* 131–143 (New Delhi, 2018), https://mofapp. nic.in/economicsurvey/economicsurvey/pdf/131-144_Chapter_09_ENGLISH_ Vol%2001_2017-18.pdf (accessed 20 February 2022).

[92] Harish Narasappa, Kavya Murthy, Surya Prakash B. S. and Yashas C. Gowda, 'Access to Justice Survey: Introduction, Methodology, and Findings', in *State of the Indian Judiciary: A Report by Daksh*, ed. Harish Narasappa and Shruti Vidyasagar (Lucknow: Eastern Book Company, 2016), https://dakshindia.org/state-of-the-indian-judiciary/28_chapter_15.html#_idTextAnchor320 (accessed 20 February 2022).

[93] Ibid.

[94] Padmini Baruah, Shruthi Naik, Surya Prakash B. S. and Kishore Mandyam, 'Paths to Justice: Surveying Judicial and Non-Judicial Dispute Resolution in India', in *Approaches to Justice: A Report by Daksh*, ed. Shruti Vidyasagar, Harish Narasappa and Ramya Sridhar Tirumalai (Lucknow: Eastern Book Company, 2018), https:// dakshindia.org/Daksh_Justice_in_India/12_chapter_02.xhtml#_idTextAnchor011 (accessed 20 February 2022).

[95] Ibid.

workload and trends, and showed how these have evolved over the last five years.[96] A third example from Agami and Civic Data Lab, two organizations working on data and law, is a Justice Hub, an open-source platform for hosting projects and data sets on law and justice in India.[97]

Mapping out these different sources of data on law and justice in India offers a glimpse into the objectives, purposes and focuses of different sources of data. Upon reflecting on these sources, it is possible to hone in on the following themes, which all correspond in some way to measuring justice in an Indian context: the focus of these different data sources on formal judicial institutions; the emphasis on factors that correspond to efficiency and time manifested in ideas like pendency; and the technocratic and administrative aspects of justice data, and the lack of equal importance given to substantive justice.

It is clear that the focus of the data collection is on formal institutions. Take, for example, the NJDG—it presents data in terms of the number of civil and criminal cases pending and disposed of in various courts across the country. What can we deduce from this? The first is that the focus of the data is on courts across the country. Focusing on courts allows the collection of data to be centred on the workings of particular institutions at the level of districts, states or the centre with the Supreme Court. It may seem obvious that courts would be an immediate source of interest for collecting data, but that these institutions are the lenses through which to understand the justice system in India, and not the justice users, is worth noting. The second is that the datasets seek to quantify the functioning of the court by relying on its most obvious function—the disposal of cases. The nature of the data focuses on whether the courts execute their functions in an effective manner or not. The third is in terms of how the court organizes itself, by dealing with matters of civil law and criminal law separately and, in that regard, the data collection responds to the institutional organization of the court. This approach mirrors a supply side approach to justice, where an emphasis is placed on the manner in which legal services are delivered.[98]

---

[96]   Tata Trusts, *India Justice Report: Ranking States on Police, Judiciary, Prisons and Legal Aid* (New Delhi: Tata Trusts, 2019).

[97]   Justice Hub, https://justicehub.in/ (accessed 3 June 2021).

[98]   See generally Catherine R. Albiston and Rebecca L. Sandefur, 'Expanding the Empirical Study of Access to Justice', *Wisconsin Law Review* 2013, no. 1 (2013): 101–120.

There is an emphasis on the administration of justice in terms of infrastructure, personnel, an insight into how courts and judicial institutions are organized and what more needs to be done to improve their functioning. However, when particular aspects of data on justice systems are collected, they are not merely descriptive but also have a structural and normative dimension.[99] For instance, a focus on institutions has manifested in a prioritization of supply side reform, including how to enhance institutional capacity by hiring more judges and reducing vacancies, improving physical court infrastructures and also determining how to make the work of a judge most efficient by reducing other tasks, and in this case it is largely a formal institutional focus.

Along with analysing the institutions that deliver justice, what is interesting to note is the kind of vocabularies that have emerged when quantifying the manner in which institutions function. These include terms like 'backlogs', 'delays', 'disposal', 'arrears' and 'pendency', which have no clear definitions and in many instances are also used interchangeably.[100] This galaxy of terms is important because not only have they become commonplace in the narrative of justice data, but they are also used so often that they have come to be substituted for ideas of reform and change. Evidenced by the number of Law Commission reports that speak of delay, pendency and arrears, there is a narrative that emerges when we speak of reform—we address challenges constructed by these terms. Krishnaswamy et al. show how, due to a lack of empirical rigor, the kind of reforms that

---

[99] Ibid.

[100] The Law Commission of India, on remit from the Supreme Court, which, asked for a rational and scientific definition of 'arrears' and 'delay', tried to evolve some definitions for these terms.

> a. Pendency: All cases instituted but not disposed of, regardless of when the case was instituted.b. Delay: A case that has been in the Court/judicial system for longer than the normal time that it should take for a case of that type to be disposed of.c. Arrears: Some delayed cases might be in the system for longer than the normal time, for valid reasons. Those cases that show unwarranted delay will be referred to as arrears.d. Backlog: When the institution of new cases in any given time period is higher than the disposal of cases in that time period, the difference between institution and disposal is the backlog. This figure represents the accumulation of cases in the system due to the system's inability to dispose of as many cases as are being filed. (Law Commission of India, *Arrears and Backlog*)

are being suggested are often piecemeal rather than systemic when tackling pendency.[101] Successive chief justices of India have also made references to the challenge of pendency of cases and offered solutions.[102] While it is of course a major challenge of the courts, the centrality it receives is undoubtedly also because of the ways in which data signals and frames the nature of the problem.

The process of categorization that is offered by the creation of these key concepts, such as pendency, then presents the possibility for not just the institutions to respond to this but also for policy makers to do the same. Pioneering work by Rajeev Dhavan and others examines the workload of the Indian Supreme Court and the challenges of the pendency of cases.[103] More recently, Nick Robinson has produced an important examination of the workload of the court, which studied the collection and categorization of workload data by the court, how accurate it is, and what accounting practices are used.[104] He argues that such data provides insights into the types of

---

[101] Sudhir Krishnaswamy, Sindhu K. Sivakumar and Shishir Bail, 'Legal and Judicial Reform in India: A Call for Systemic and Empirical Approaches', *Journal of National Law University Delhi* 2, no. 1 (2014): 1–25.

[102] PTI, 'CJI T. S. Thakur Laments Lack of Judges, Pendency in His Farewell Speech', *Mint*, 3 January 2017, https://www.livemint.com/Politics/v4Z20q2nZf2AllrSzyat0O/CJI-TS-Thakur-laments-lack-of-judges-pendency-in-his-fare.html (accessed 20 August 2019); PTI, 'Pendency of Cases Bound to Increase: CJI Altamas Kabir', *Business Standard*, 2 March 2013, https://www.business-standard.com/article/pti-stories/pendency-of-cases-bound-to-increase-cji-altamas-kabir-113030200332_1.html (accessed 20 February 2022); 'Chief Justice Designate Ranjan Gogoi Says Case Pendencies Bring Disrepute', *Scroll.in*, 30 September 2018, https://scroll.in/latest/896415/i-have-a-plan-says-chief-justice-designate-ranjan-gogoi-on-tackling-pendency-of-cases-in-courts (accessed 20 August 2019).

[103] Rajeev Dhavan, *The Supreme Court under Strain: The Challenge of Arrears* (Bombay: N. M. Tripathi, 1978); Rajeev Dhavan, *Litigation Explosion in India* (Bombay: N. M. Tripathi, 1986); Robert Moog, 'Indian Litigiousness and the Litigation Explosion: Challenging the Legend', *Asian Survey* 33, no. 12 (1 December 1993): 1136–1150; Arnab Kumar Hazra and Maja B. Micevska, 'The Problem of Court Congestion: Evidence from Indian Lower Courts', in *Judicial Reforms in India: Issues and Aspects*, ed. Arnab Kumar Hazra and Bibek Debroy, 137–156 (New Delhi: Academic Foundation, in association with Rajiv Gandhi Institute for Contemporary Studies, 2007), https://trove.nla.gov.au/version/38793678 (accessed 17 August 2019).

[104] Nick Robinson, 'A Quantitative Analysis of the Indian Supreme Court's Workload', *Journal of Empirical Legal Studies* 10, no. 3 (2013): 570–601.

cases that courts hear, where these cases come from and the duration of their hearings at court, and also raises challenging questions for the court, including in terms of how it admits cases across different jurisdictions.[105] Other studies, such as by Aparna Chandra et al., by examining the functioning of the Supreme Court as an appellate court in terms of how it admits, reverses or upholds cases, ask whether the court favours individual litigants over government in civil and criminal cases.[106] They suggest that the court remains a court of the people based on how it admits cases.[107] Varun Gauri shows that only 1 per cent of the Supreme Court cases are in relation to Public Interest Litigation, and wins in relation to fundamental rights cases at the Supreme Court usually benefit individuals from more advantageous groups.[108] Each of these studies is grounded in discussions on workload, caseload and pendency of cases, and shape the formation of categories of data and a language to evaluate justice delivery.

Following this language, one of the related themes that can be gleaned from the data is the emphasis on performance. Performance is closely linked to efficiency, where, in the context of justice, there is a definite focus on ideas of productivity, efficacy and outputs, a managerial range of terminologies that shape the outlook of the numbers being collected. This is reflected in the Niti Aayog proposal to establish Judicial Performance indicators, which, according to an official, will probably include 'caseload per judge, duration of proceedings, cost per case, clearance rate, and court budgets among others'.[109] This proposal belies an interest in the administrative nature of justice delivery and continues a trend from the Ministry of Justice in India, who have sought recommendations on how judicial performance indicators

---

[105] Ibid.

[106] Aparna Chandra, William H. J. Hubbard and Sital Kalantry, 'The Supreme Court of India: A People's Court?', *Indian Law Review* 1, no. 2 (2017): 145–181.

[107] Ibid.

[108] Varun Gauri, 'Public Interest Litigation in India: Overreaching or Underachieving?', World Bank Policy Research Working Paper No. 5109, The World Bank, 22 June 2013, https://elibrary.worldbank.org/doi/abs/10.1596/1813-9450-5109 (accessed 20 August 2019).

[109] Yogima Sharma, 'Niti Aayog Working on Proposal to Appraise Judges' Performance, Make Rankings Public', *Economic Times*, 7 May 2019, https://economictimes.indiatimes.com/news/politics-and-nation/niti-aayog-working-on-proposal-to-appraise-judges-performance-make-rankings-public/articleshow/69210175.cms?from=mdr (accessed 30 July 2021).

can improve accountability in the higher judiciary.[110] Some of the metrics proposed by a think tank in Delhi called Vidhi Centre for Legal Policy include number of days the judge worked, number of days absent, quantum of cases decided, nature of cases, and so on.[111] Many of these factors attempt to suggest how the court can be made more efficient by placing importance on getting systems to function as units with particular outputs and outcomes. The other aspect is of time, which is becoming synonymous with justice data and justice reform. This includes the aspect of cases pending over a period of time, the backlogs in courts and the need for timely and speedy justice.[112] A recent paper examined how to study the caseload of the court in terms of how long it hears cases.[113] If we refer back to the example of the work of the National Legal Services Authority, which conducts *lok adalats* in one day, such bodies are celebrated in terms of how many thousands, and sometimes million, cases they can resolve in a single day.[114] The discourse around judicial reform, therefore, becomes more about the numbers of cases disposed of within a period of time, and how this feeds into resolving more administrative challenges of the justice, rather than on the substantive merits of the hearings such as in terms of whether the process was fair and transparent and accountable to the parties involved.[115]

---

[110] Medha Srivastava, Shalini Seetharam and Sumathi Chandrashekaran, *Development and Enforcement of Performance Standards to Enhance Accountability of the Higher Judiciary in India* (New Delhi: Vidhi Centre for Legal Policy, 2017), https://doj.gov.in/sites/default/files/document%282%29.pdf (accessed 30 July 2021).

[111] Ibid.

[112] Law Commission of India, *Need for Speedy Justice: Some Suggestions*, Report no. 221 (New Delhi, 2009), https://lawcommissionofindia.nic.in/reports/report221.pdf (accessed 20 February 2022); Government of India, 'Chapter 9: Ease of Doing Business' Next Frontier'.

[113] Rahul Hemrajani and Himanshu Agarwal, 'A Temporal Analysis of the Supreme Court of India's Workload', *Indian Law Review* 3, no. 2 (2019): 125–158.

[114] PTI, 'CJI Dattu Asks Lok Adalats to Settle at Least 10 Lakh Cases This Year', *Mint*, 6 December 2014, https://www.livemint.com/Politics/3oNDFuIL1MXcHqpg45NRTL/CJI-Datta-asks-Lok-Adalats-to-settle-at-least-10-lakh-cases.html (accessed 20 August 2019).

[115] Siddharth Peter de Souza, 'India's Parallel Justice Systems: Engaging with Lok Adalats, Gram Nyayalayas, Nari Adalats and Khap Panchayats through Human Rights', in *Human Rights in India*, edited by Satvinder Juss, 80–101 (London: Routledge, 2019).

These factors of efficiency and time have resulted in a system of managerialism—an ideology that imparts the ideals of business management, strategic planning and decisions based on outputs and outcomes, and performance indicators.[116] It can be argued that the data being collected, and the ways in which studies and categorization take place, feed into a managerial culture of reform. Further evidence of this is apparent with universities now offering Court Management MBAs,[117] and there are proposals to strengthen the office of court managers (who administer the courtroom proceedings) in order to improve the delivery of justice and improve its administration and functioning.[118]

What is also interesting is how closely the narratives from looking at data sources in India correspond to the kind of data that is being collected in global rule of law indicators, wherein both are reflective of a managerial approach to how we evaluate and assess the functioning of legal systems.

Measuring justice in India: Examining what is not measured

While the last section discussed how different sources of data present managerial perspectives to look at judicial institutions such as efficiency, time, pendency, performance, and so on, this section will examine what is

---

[116] Klikauer, 'What Is Managerialism?'; Sue Shepherd, 'Managerialism: An Ideal Type', *Studies in Higher Education* 43, no. 9 (2018): 1668–1678; Kathleen Lynch, 'Managerialism', in *Encyclopedia of Educational Theory and Philosophy*, ed. D. C. Phillips, 507–511 (Thousand Oaks, CA: SAGE Publications Inc, 2014), http://sk.sagepub.com/reference/ encyclopedia-of-education-theory-and-philosophy/n211.i1.xml (accessed 20 August 2019).

[117] Prachi Srivastava, 'Nalsar Starts Court Management MBA; Coffers to Benefit Rs 2 Cr', *Legally India*, 20 May 2013, https://www.legallyindia.com/lawschools/nalsar-offers-mba-court-management-20130520-3685 (accessed 20 August 2019).

[118] Geeta Oberoi, 'The Curious Case of Court Manager in India: From Its Creation to Its Desertion', *International Journal for Court Administration* 9, no. 1 (2017): 1–9; Somasekhar Sundaresan, 'Courts Need Business Process Reform', *Business Standard India*, 10 May 2016, https://www.business-standard.com/article/opinion/somasekhar-sundaresan-courts-need-business-process-reform-116051001476_1.html (accessed 20 August 2019); Apurva Vishwanath, 'Indian Courts Need MBAs and Not Chief Justice to Deal with Pendency', *The Print*, 5 October 2018, https://theprint.in/opinion/off-court/indian-courts-need-mbas-not-chief-justice-to-deal-with-pendency/129914/ (accessed 20 August 2019).

not being measured. It seeks to investigate what the potential absences and silences are that are emerging as a consequence of the current dominant narrative on data in the justice sector and raise questions on what more can be done.

In many of the datasets that were discussed earlier, there is a predominant focus on judicial institutions, whether courts, police stations or other bodies. These sources offered perspectives of the disposal of cases, pendency of cases and the nature in which the institution functioned. Less focus manifested in matters of substantive justice, particularly on the legal needs of ordinary people. For example, do people have any agency in court and understand its procedures? Do legal processes intimidate those who participate in them? Do they have adequate resources to participate?

Aspects of participation, security and capacity are absent when looking at the factors that are being used to determine judicial performance. There is, therefore, a need to problematize the idea of judicial performance. When we speak of performance, we are not just interested in performance from a purely administrative perspective but also how the judicial performance materializes in terms of the needs of people, that is, which institutions work for what problems, how effective the process is and whether it changes for people of different socio-economic backgrounds.[119] Is it possible to build a framework that adopts a demand-driven approach to access to justice, which focuses on the needs and capabilities of people? In this sense, can we think of judicial performance in terms of justice capabilities and needs? To do this will require changing the locus of measurement from how institutions function to how people experience justice problems through an assessment of their needs, barriers and capabilities to resolve disputes.[120]

---

[119] OECD, *Equal Access to Justice for Inclusive Growth: Putting People at the Centre* (Paris: OECD, 2019), https://www.oecd.org/governance/equal-access-to-justice-for-inclusive-growth-597f5b7f-en.htm (accessed 31 July 2019).

[120] Task Force on Justice, *Justice for All Report: Final Report* (New York: Center on International Cooperation, 2019), https://www.justice.sdg16.plus/report (accessed 2 July 2019); Canadian Bar Association, *Reaching Equal Justice: An Invitation to Envision and Act* (Ottawa: Canadian Bar Association, 2013); Pascoe Pleasence and Nigel Balmer, *Legal Needs Surveys and Access to Justice* (Paris: OECD, 2018), https://iris.ucl.ac.uk/iris/publication/1620815/1 (accessed 7 August 2019); Pascoe Pleasence and Nigel Balmer, *How People Resolve 'Legal' Problems* (Cambridge: Legal Services Board, 2014), https://

Presently, there is a narrative of performance and efficiency of institutions. This is clear also from the manner of reportage on *lok adalats*. In studies about their functioning, we are given figures about how many cases have been settled, and the fact that so many cases are removed from the backlog is heralded. Former Chief Justice Thakur said in a speech a few years ago, 'As on September 30, a total of more than 15.14 lakh *lok adalats* have been organised in the country and 8.25 crore cases, including cases pending in the courts as well as those in the pre-litigation stage, have been settled'.[121] However, who are the people in these numbers and what are their legal needs? How do they overcome barriers and challenges to justice? Many of these questions are absent in data on the efficiency of the legal institution. It is only in changing the locus to looking at what this means for people that we can get a different perspective on the functioning of these systems.

For example, as numerous studies of *lok adalats* have shown,[122] the challenge with these institutions has been that those who avail of these speedy settlements are often those who cannot afford to wait for the formal court to decide their case and are compelled to go to these forums, rather than going of their own volition.[123] In the absence of people-centric methods

---

legalservicesboard.org.uk/wp-content/media/How-People-Resolve-Legal-Problems.pdf / (accessed 20 February 2022).

[121] 'Lok Adalats Settled over 8 Crore Cases in Last 20 Years: T S Thakur', *Indian Express*, 10 November 2015, https://indianexpress.com/article/india/india-news-india/lok-adalats-settled-over-8-crore-cases-in-last-20-years-t-s-thakur/ (accessed 26 August 2019). One lakh is 1 hundred thousand, and 1 crore is 10 million. For reference, 15.14 lakh cases is 1.514 million whereas 8.25 crore cases is 82.5 million cases.

[122] *Lok adalats* are governed by the Legal Services Authority Act 1987. See more 'Lok Adalat: National Legal Services Authority', NALSA, http://nalsa.gov.in/lok-adalat (accessed 3 November 2017).

[123] Studies have shown that while the resolution of disputes are conducted in a speedy manner in *lok adalats*, there is a compromise on the substantive and procedural aspects of these forums. See more in Tameem Zainulbhai, 'Justice for All: Improving the Lok Adalat System in India', *Fordham International Law Journal* 35, no. 1 (2011): 248–278; Marc Galanter and Jayanth K. Krishnan, 'Bread for the Poor: Access to Justice and the Rights of the Needy in India', *Hastings Law Journal* 55 (2004): 789–834; Sarah Leah Whitson, 'Neither Fish, nor Flesh, nor Good Red Herring Lok Adalats: An Experiment in Informal Dispute Resolution in India', *Hastings International and Comparative Law Review* 15, no. 3 (1991): 391–445; de Souza, 'India's Parallel Justice Systems'.

of measuring justice, what emerges will be a list of priorities, which are based on the perspectives of those administering justice. Because of this the vocabulary of justice reform currently is of delays, backlogs and pendency, rather than on needs, capabilities and securities of those who face problems in accessing justice.

Focusing on people's needs involves making people the universal denominator when measuring justice.[124] As we have discussed in the previous chapter, it allows for an examination of the realities within which people live and work, and the difficulties they face. Through this approach, it is possible to understand the everyday justice problems of people, which are the routinized challenges that people face, and how they navigate complex and multi-layered relationships in order to resolve a dispute. For instance, Daksh (the NGO mentioned earlier) has attempted to do this but is by far an exception to the general rule. In their study on access to justice, they found that over 30.2 per cent of cases were on matters related to recovery of money, 29.3 per cent of cases were on matters of land and property and 13.5 per cent of cases were on family matters in the last five years.[125] What this tells us is that if we do not change the focus of measurement of official data from merely the functioning of judicial institutions, we could miss the micro-level challenges that currently prevent the resolution of disputes. These include understanding the costs of processing disputes, the lack of infrastructure to access legal services, the problems of staffing of courts, the poor training of officials, the time taken to resolve a dispute, gender and caste-based discrimination and intimidation and corruption that are rampant in these forums.[126]

Legal needs surveys are therefore important devices to provide a bottom-up perspective because they measure how legal problems are experienced from the perspective of the people rather than institutions

---

[124] See also IDLO, *Comparative Justice Policy Workshop* (Rome: IDLO, 2015), https://www.idlo.int/sites/default/files/pdfs/events/Report%20-%20Comparative%20Justice%20Policy%20Workshop.pdf (accessed 26 August 2019).

[125] Baruah et al., 'Paths to Justice'.

[126] Jayanth K. Krishnan, Shirish N. Kavadi, Azima Girach, Dhanaji Khupkar, Kilindi Kokal, Satyajeet Mazumdar, Nupar, Gayatri Panday, Aatreyee Sen, Aqseer Sodhi, and Bharati Takale Shukla, 'Grappling at the Grassroots: Access to Justice in India's Lower Tier', *Harvard Human Rights Journal* 27 (2014): 151–189.

and professions.[127] These surveys provide a perspective into justiciable problems, whether related to family matters, property matters or consumer disputes, and offer insight into their frequency, urgency and the inequality within which they manifest.[128] They also offer a perspective into how such justiciable problems impact lives through health, livelihood and housing situations. Everyday justice problems can also have related impacts in people lives.

What is demonstrated in the India case is a preoccupation with legal institutions that are state driven. As a result, there is conflation of the access to courts with access to justice.[129] While judicial institutions like courts get primary focus in measuring instruments, other forums—whether based on community, religious or social practices—are not given as much prominence.[130] Yet, as the Daksh survey shows, it was found that 40 per cent of people would not go to the police and over 32 per cent would not go to a lawyer if they had a dispute.[131] In fact over 74 per cent of people would rather go to friends and family to understand the nature of the dispute; others also preferred to go to village elders or local governance authorities over legal services authorities.[132] The relevance of legal pluralism in the resolution of disputes is apparent in how people move between family, religious forums and the state. This raises questions for why we need to incorporate multiplicity in our imagination of legal orders.[133] If we

[127] Pleasence and Balmer, *Legal Needs Surveys and Access to Justice*.

[128] Ibid.; Maurits Barendrecht, Peter Kamminga and Jin Ho Verdonschot, 'Priorities for the Justice System: Responding to the Most Urgent Legal Problems of Individuals', TISCO Working Paper, 2008, https://papers.ssrn.com/abstract=1090885 (accessed 7 August 2019).

[129] Aparna Chandra, 'Indian Judiciary and Access to Justice: An Appraisal of Approaches', in *State of the Indian Judiciary*, ed. Harish Narasappa and Shruti Vidyasagar (Lucknow: Eastern Book Company 2016), https://dakshindia.org/state-of-the-indian-judiciary/33_chapter_18.html#_idTextAnchor412 (accessed 20 February 2022).

[130] Marc Galanter, 'The Displacement of Traditional Law in Modern India', *Journal of Social Issues* 24, no. 4 (1968): 65–90; de Souza, 'India's Parallel Justice Systems'.

[131] Baruah et al., 'Paths to Justice'.

[132] Ibid.

[133] Siddharth Peter de Souza, 'Evaluating "Access to Justice" in Informal Justice Systems: A Suggestive Framework', *Max Planck Yearbook of United Nations Law Online* 19, no. 1 (2016): 469–504; Kalindi Kokal, 'Many Laws, Many Orders: Disputes and Their

incorporate the multiplicity of legal forums that generate justice data, we will be able to incorporate and evaluate the choices that people make and their comparative experiences in different forums.

These aspects of people's needs and everyday problems that otherwise get overlooked raises questions about whose justice we measure and from what perspective. Are we interested in measuring access to justice or judicial efficiency? Are we interested in enhancing judicial performance or in empowering people with more capabilities to use the legal system? Further, if we are only measuring judicial institutions, and not people's legal needs, and also ignore plural legal contexts, is this truly justice data? Or is this in fact much more limited, and instead just judicial data, or court data?

These are questions that animate the final section of this chapter, wherein I seek to unpack what it means to build indicators that incorporate plurality, having reflected upon the managerial and technocratic ways in which data sources work. Having previously laid out in some detail the challenges of persistence, the arguments for engaging the Global South and how to counter managerialism, the next section attempts to bring it all together by looking at how to build plural legal indicators.

Plural legal indicators: how do we build them?

This section builds on the arguments put forward on making persistence political and on the managerial implications that currently influence the ways in which justice systems are assessed. It offers a method for building a framework that integrates the messiness of law in action, and thereafter argues for how plural legal indicators that give cognizance to the South can be built. These include by pluralizing the design of legal institutions, diversifying knowledge centres and focusing on law from below.[134]

Processing in the Non-State Arena', in *State Law, Dispute Processing, and Legal Pluralism: Unspoken Dialogues from Rural India*, 58–72 (Oxon: Routledge, 2019).

[134] I have also developed the idea of a user-centred focus in law in Siddharth Peter de Souza, 'Towards a User-Centered Engagement with Law', *Südasien-Chronik/South Asia Chronicle* 2018, no. 8 (2019): 238–291, https://edoc.hu-berlin.de/handle/18452/20489 (accessed 31 July 2019).

Integrating the 'messiness' of law in action

The managerial nature of how law is evaluated operates in a technical and normative manner that presumes a degree of certainty and uniformity in terms of how the law is operationalized.[135] In practice, however, this is rarely the case.[136] A recent Supreme Court of India judgment (Sabarimala Judgment) addressed a long-standing issue where women who were at a menstruating age were unable to enter a temple in south India because they were seen as impure, and held that this was unconstitutional and in violation of the right to life enshrined in the Indian Constitution.[137] While the court spoke clearly and decisively on matters of gender equality and fundamental rights of women to practice their religion, the judgment of the court has been very difficult to implement by the local government because of political and social pressures of the community.[138] As a result, hardly any women have entered the temple since the judgment. Without considering the merits of the judgment itself, what this incident demonstrates is that the operation of law cannot be divorced from the complexities within which it has to be enforced.[139] How does this connect to a legal indicator?

In a legal indicator that measures the rule of law and the application of fundamental rights and gender equality by courts, this case would demonstrate that India is doing well with a progressive court that protects the rights of women and individual freedom. This, however, is only a part of the story. The problem is not just that the judgment has not been implemented, but also that there is a clear hierarchy within which the law plays out in everyday practice, from social and community pressures to cultural norms. This contestation that emerges in the execution of a legal decision, which impacts the realization of justice, is as important an aspect as the decision itself. This messiness of law in action, which represents the

---

[135] de Souza, 'Evaluating "Access to Justice" in Informal Justice Systems'.

[136] de Souza, 'Towards a User-Centered Engagement with Law'.

[137] *Indian Young Lawyers Association v. State of Kerala*, WP 373 of 2006 (Supreme Court of India).

[138] 'Sabarimala: Women Who First Entered Shrine Were Escorted by Police in Civilian Clothes, Court Told', *Scroll.in*, 25 January 2019, https://scroll.in/latest/910838/sabarimala-women-who-first-entered-shrine-were-escorted-by-police-in-civilian-clothes-court-told (accessed 16 September 2019).

[139] See generally Reza Banakar, *Normativity in Legal Sociology: Methodological Reflections on Law and Regulation in Late Modernity* (Cham: Springer, 2014).

complexity with how law exists in its social context, must be integrated in any evaluation of legal systems to understand how to objectively capture highly subjective contexts at a global level. To counter the language of efficiency, one needs to integrate the social aspects of the law and to consider different factors that acknowledge the consequences of law in its lived reality. But what does it mean to integrate the messiness? How does this change the nature in which legal indicators are imagined, and why is there a benefit in adopting such an approach?

Integrating the messiness of law in action into the development of a legal indicator includes several factors, such as engaging with the phenomenological aspects of law, which are the role of context, the role of space and the role of people.[140] In this sense, it is an exercise to rethink a legal geography, which is otherwise typified by doctrine or institutions.[141] As a starting point, engaging with the social aspects of law is to capture the ways in which the law is realized.[142] There is a well-established dichotomy between law in books and law in action.[143] This means a departure from the texts and doctrine of the law to instead understand the experiences through which it is played out in everyday practice.[144] In this regard, context matters, and acknowledging the ways in which laws operates holds an important sway in terms of how it manifests in the everyday lives of people.[145] The correlation of law as a

---

[140] In research on legal geography, the impact of the intersection of people, place and space assume an important role. See also Luke Bennett and Antonia Layard, 'Legal Geography: Becoming Spatial Detectives', *Geography Compass* 9, no. 7 (2015): 406–422.

[141] David Delaney, 'Beyond the Word: Law as a Thing of This World', in *Law and Geography*, ed. Jane Holder and Carolyn Harrison, 67–83 (Oxford: Oxford University Press, 2003).

[142] See the discussions on a realization approach to justice in Amartya Sen, *The Idea of Justice* (Cambridge, MA: Harvard University Press, 2011).

[143] Roscoe Pound, 'Law in Books and Law in Action', *American Law Review* 44 (1910): 12–36; Eve Darian-Smith, 'Introduction: Sociolegal Scholarship in the Twenty-First Century', in *Laws and Societies in Global Contexts: Contemporary Approaches*, 1–38 (Cambridge: Cambridge University Press, 2013).

[144] Roger Cotterrell, 'Why Must Legal Ideas Be Interpreted Sociologically?', *Journal of Law and Society* 25, no. 2 (June 1998): 171–192, https://onlinelibrary.wiley.com/doi/abs/10.1111/1467-6478.00086 (accessed 8 February 2022).

[145] William Twining, *Law in Context: Enlarging a Discipline* (Oxford: Clarendon Press, 1997); William Twining, *Human Rights, Southern Voices: Francis Deng, Abdullahi*

phenomenon that changes and moves according to the different agents that play a role in its development gives rise to uncovering how context matters.[146]

In addition to the question of context, another related aspect is the importance of space. Blomley argues how 'space offers a powerful ordering framework. The boundary, which delineates and defines "inside" with reference to the "outside", whether at the scale of the State or the home, is a vital modality of ordering'.[147] The implications of space assume importance because, as was seen in the Sabarimala decision, the disconnect between the court and the people was apparent, in that the court was unable to make its judgment enforceable in a space where local customs, traditions and values hold greater authority. In the case of indicators, the recognition of space, whether in the form of formal or informal institutions, families, communities and its antecedent particularities, would result in an indicator that would take into account how the decision of the adjudicatory body moves from the corridors where it is decided to the people it is deciding for. Thus, space plays a role because the location where decisions are made and where they are executed or enforced exist in very different settings, and acknowledging the intricacies of these spaces will allow for a more grounded understanding of how justice is realized. It is important to find a way to build a dialogical framework for the indicator that accounts for the perspective of the institution, people and context, and moves back and forth between formal structures, and the more messiness of law's reality in practice.

An-Na'im, Yash Ghai and Upendra Baxi (Cambridge: Cambridge University Press, 2009); de Souza, 'Towards a User-Centered Engagement with Law'.

[146] Julia Eckert, Zerrin Özlem Biner, Brian Donahoe and Christian Strümpell, 'Law's Travels and Transformations', in *Law against the State: Ethnographic Forays into Law's Transformations*, ed. Julia Eckert, Brian Donahoe, Christian Strümpell and Zerrin Özlem Biner, 1–22 (Cambridge: Cambridge University Press, 2012).

[147] 'Space comes with particular and deeply encoded classifications of appropriate behaviour. Behaviours and people that challenge such classifications, such as the homeless person who urinates in public, are deemed "out of place". Space and identity are also wedded: national and ethnic identities are often assumed to overlap.' See Nicholas Blomley, 'From "What?" to "So What?": Law and Geography in Retrospect', in *Law and Geography*, ed. Jane Holder and Carolyn Harrison, 8–14 (Oxford: Oxford University Press 2003), 8.

The next aspect is that of people; in this regard, what is important to demonstrate is that the experiences of people play an important role in understanding the messiness of law in action. By exploring the legal needs of people and the ways in which they experience and interact with the law, the barriers they face, the choices they make and the decisions they have to work with, it is possible to have a better sense of how the law works in practice, from the perspective of people rather than from a technical standpoint.[148]

Integrating messiness is a counter to managerialism because messiness looks at law as it functions in operation. It engages with people, with context and with spaces. There is a fundamental difference from using a deductive approach, where there is already a pre-established notion of what the law can do and be, to a more inductive approach, which is premised on capturing the different attributes that influence the functioning of law.[149] Triangulating law as a phenomenon with context, space and people introduces a different kind of measurement device. It is one that is more reflexive in terms of its ability to capture difference. It is more reflective of contexts and thereby adopts a more grounded approach, and it is more aware of diversity and difference. By embracing messiness as a methodological device, we make the conscious decision to engineer indicators towards being responsive to the constituencies they study, rather than being prescriptive. Such an approach is in contrast to processes of standardization and involves an iterative design. Engaging in iteration does not imply a lack of rigor or uncertainty. It is a reflection of the fact that only by adopting values of change and reflexivity can the messiness of law in action be concretely used and adopted.[150]

---

[148] Pleasence and Balmer, *Legal Needs Surveys and Access to Justice*; Barendrecht, Kamminga and Verdonschot, 'Priorities for the Justice System'; TISCO et al., *Measuring the Costs and Quality of Access to Justice*; Baxi, 'Voices of Suffering and the Future of Human Rights'.

[149] Banakar, *Normativity in Legal Sociology*; David R. Unruh, 'The Nature of Social Worlds', *Pacific Sociological Review* 23, no. 3 (1980): 271–296; David N. Schiff, 'Socio-Legal Theory: Social Structure and Law', *The Modern Law Review* 39, no. 3 (1976): 287–310.

[150] Siddharth Peter de Souza, 'Beyond Best Practices: How to Use Design Thinking in Rule of Law Promotion', Peace Lab Blog, 2019, https://peacelab.blog/2019/03/beyond-best-practices-how-to-use-design-thinking (accessed 29 August 2019); Deval Desai and Michael Woolcock, 'Experimental Justice Reform: Lessons from the World Bank and Beyond', *Annual Review of Law and Social Science* 11, no. 1 (2015): 155–174.

The challenge of many legal indicators is that they wish to measure phenomenon over a particular period of time and space. However, in many instances, these frameworks might need to be updated given changes in the socio-political context. Failing to acknowledge a changing context into the design of the indicator will lead to the effect that it is the indicator that is driving decision-making, reform initiatives and interventions because of the power of the narrative. This is not the purpose of an indicator, which should be a tool that is responsive to and acknowledges the situation that it is framed to study. While this is a tricky line to draw, given that a comparative study needs to be made over time, the expectation must be that indicators are not built for perpetuity and neither should the construction of legal needs or barriers to justice. These will change and evolve as the demography and political and social contexts change. It is therefore important to make explicit the periods for which indicators are designed rather than keep this open ended.

In the next section, building on the need to embed legal indicators in their social realities, I argue for incorporating pluralism into how we think of legal institutions that are part of the delivery of justice.

Incorporating the reality of pluralism in the design of legal institutions

A central challenge in acknowledging plural legal orders is to evaluate the role of the state and its outsized influence in determining matters concerning the resolution of legal disputes. It involves looking beyond a rule of law orthodoxy that is driven by a particular set of institutions and values and with the technocratic purpose of re-engineering institutions based on transplanting values and ideas disregarding context.[151] In order to do this, a first step is to de-centre the state, which implies allowing for alternative avenues where the law manifests and looking for the

---

[151] Stephen Golub, 'Beyond Rule of Law Orthodoxy: The Legal Empowerment Alternative', Carnegie Endowment for International Peace, 14 October 2003, http://carnegieendowment.org/2003/10/14/beyond-rule-of-law-orthodoxy-legal-empowerment-alternative-pub-1367 (accessed 7 December 2017); Carothers, 'The Rule of Law Revival'; Keebet von Benda-Beckmann and Bertram Turner, 'Legal Pluralism, Social Theory, and the State', *The Journal of Legal Pluralism and Unofficial Law* 50, no. 3 (2018): 255–274.

interconnections between people, places, ideologies and values that influence the ways in which law is produced and delivered.[152] If we are to embark upon this process of de-centring the state, it is important to ask questions that are otherwise presumed, such as what law is, how it works, where we can find it, and engage with law in its descriptive reality rather than its idealized form.[153]

Examining alternatives beyond the state also requires engaging beyond national institutions and markets to also examine history, culture and political economy, which will allow for a more cosmopolitan outlook on the law.[154] This outlook also accounts for whether the law travels and is exported or imported, imposed or adopted, and is a function of experts or of local imaginations.[155] In this movement of law from one jurisdiction to another, it adopts different forms, categories and functions.[156] These functions each hold their own legitimacy and authority, and capturing legal pluralism would mean to capture this dynamism and messiness, as it reveals itself in practice. In moving beyond the state, it is equally important to document resistances and sufferings of people through examining social movements and the grassroots experiences of those who are otherwise marginalized

---

[152] Eve Darian-Smith, 'Reimagining Legal Geographies', in *Laws and Societies in Global Contexts: Contemporary Approaches*, 167–242 (Cambridge: Cambridge University Press, 2013); Eve Darian-Smith, 'Producing Legal Knowledge', in *Laws and Societies in Global Contexts: Contemporary Approaches*, 97–166 (Cambridge: Cambridge University Press, 2013).

[153] de Souza, 'Towards a User-Centered Engagement with Law'; Peter Albrecht and Helena Maria Kyed, 'Introduction: Non-State and Customary Actor in Developing Programs', in *Perspectives on Involving Non-State and Customary Actors in Justice and Security Reform*, ed. Peter Albrecht, Helene Maria Kyed, Deborah Isser and Erica Harper, 3–22 (Rome: IDLO and DIIS, 2011).

[154] See generally Mark Goodale, *Anthropology and Law: A Critical Introduction* (New York: NYU Press, 2017) ; Goodale, 'Introduction'.

[155] Eckert et al., 'Law's Travels and Transformations'; Franz von Benda-Beckmann and Keebet von Benda-Beckmannn, 'The Dynamics of Change and Continuity in Plural Legal Orders', *The Journal of Legal Pluralism and Unofficial Law* 38, nos. 53–54 (2006): 1–44.

[156] Twining, *Law in Context*. See Vidya Kumar, 'Towards a Constitutionalism of the Wretched', *Völkerrechtsblog*, 27 July 2017, https://voelkerrechtsblog.org/towards-a-constitutionalism-of-the-wretched/ (accessed 16 April 2020).

by top-down institutional processes.[157] Such an approach would enable us to also understand the 'subaltern cosmopolitan legality', that is intrinsic to functioning of legal processes.[158] In this approach of de-centring the state, I do not discount the state, but rather argue for one that moves from a homogenous model to a more heterogeneous, polycentric and plural one.[159] This is critical to thinking of a global indicator, because in doing so, there is recognition of the multiplicity of ways in which law is conceptualized, authorized and realized. Thinking of plurality is also not just abstract but also present in real-world approaches such as the case of the Bolivian Constitution. The Preamble offers us a conception of thinking of the state that embraces plural legal ideas drawn from histories and struggles of the country, and acknowledges that different identities exist and there needs to be different models of governance to suit and accommodate the local cultural and ethnic diversities.

> In ancient times mountains arose, rivers moved, and lakes were formed. Our Amazonia, our swamps, our highlands, and our plains

---

[157] These movements play an important role in elevating needs of communities they work with and in holding institutions accountable, while at the same time translating law and human rights into local practices. See generally Kiyoteru Tsutsui, Claire Whitlinger and Alwyn Lim, 'International Human Rights Law and Social Movements: States' Resistance and Civil Society's Insistence', *Annual Review of Law and Social Science* 8, no. 1 (2012): 367–396; Michael McCann, 'Law and Social Movements: Contemporary Perspectives', *Annual Review of Law and Social Science* 2, no. 1 (2006): 17–38.

[158] 'Subaltern cosmopolitan legality seeks to expand the legal canon beyond individual rights and focuses on the importance of political mobilization for the success of rights-centred strategies', in Boaventura de Sousa Santos and Cesar A. Rodríguez-Garavito, 'Law, Politics, and the Subaltern in Counter-Hegemonic Globalization', in *Law and Globalization from Below: Towards a Cosmopolitan Legality*, ed. Boaventura de Sousa Santos and Cesar A. Rodríguez-Garavito, 1–26 (Cambridge: Cambridge University Press, 2005), 15.

[159] Conceptions of the state are in a continuous process of renegotiation and discussion, whether in terms of what institutions are legitimate or how these institutions together portray a notion of governance. See generally Boaventura de Sousa Santos, 'The Heterogeneous State and Legal Pluralism in Mozambique', *Law and Society Review* 40, no. 1 (March 2006): 39–75; Mattias Kumm, 'The Cosmopolitan Turn in Constitutionalism: An Integrated Conception of Public Law', *Indiana Journal of Global Legal Studies* 20, no. 2 (2013): 605–628; Alfred Stepan, Juan J. Linz and Yogendra Yadav, 'The Rise of "State-Nations"', *Journal of Democracy* 21 (2010): 50–68.

and valleys were covered with greenery and flowers. We populated this sacred Mother Earth with different faces, and since that time we have understood the plurality that exists in all things and in our diversity as human beings and cultures. Thus, our peoples were formed, and we never knew racism until we were subjected to it during the terrible times of colonialism.

We, the Bolivian people, of plural composition, from the depths of history, inspired by the struggles of the past, by the anti-colonial indigenous uprising, and in independence, by the popular struggles of liberation, by the indigenous, social and labor marches, by the water and October wars, by the struggles for land and territory, construct a new State in memory of our martyrs.

A State based on respect and equality for all, on principles of sovereignty, dignity, interdependence, solidarity, harmony, and equity in the distribution and redistribution of the social wealth, where the search for a good life predominates; based on respect for the economic, social, juridical, political and cultural pluralism of the inhabitants of this land; and on collective coexistence with access to water, work, education, health and housing for all.[160]

From this text, we are offered an insight into a very different idea of a state; there is a sophisticated framing that captures the diversities of experiences, contexts and histories seen in the everyday negotiation in the lives of people. It acknowledges the trials of colonialism and the effects it has had. It acknowledges the inherent plurality that exists among people, places and things, and how these reinforce, shape and inhabit the ways in which societal experiences are founded.[161] These are ideas that also

---

[160] 'Bolivia (Plurinational State of)'s Constitution of 2009', Constitute, https://www. constituteproject.org/constitution/Bolivia_2009?lang=en (accessed 10 December 2020).

[161] Plurinationalism is not without its challenges in trying to balance the rights of indigenous people through expansion of social rights and market regulation while at the same time maintaining state power over indigenous territory. See generally Roger Merino, 'Reimagining the Nation-State: Indigenous Peoples and the Making of Plurinationalism in Latin America', *Leiden Journal of International Law* 31, no. 4 (2018): 773–792; Lorenza Fontana, 'Plurinational Citizenship in the Making', OxPol, 19 February 2015, https://blog.politics.ox.ac.uk/plurinational-citizenship-making/ (accessed 10 December 2020).

find resonance in other constitutions: in Ecuador, for example, through recognizing the rights of indigenous people, and introducing concepts of interculturality and plurinationalism in their constitutions.[162] In Canada, this is seen in the introduction of First Nations Court, where those accused of crimes can choose to be heard and sentenced according to principles of restorative justice. These principles aim at repairing the harm done by the person accused of a crime. The person is given a healing plan—one that helps them identify why they got into trouble with the law, and what steps they can take in order to take responsibility for the crime and repair the situation with the community and the victim.[163] This provides another example of a more cosmopolitan and plural law where there is an acknowledgment of different ecologies of knowledge and value systems that make up the ways in which people address the legal system. In South Africa, over the past several years, there has been a long debate on the how to integrate traditional courts within the architecture of the other state-administered courts. These concern the scope of the cases that can be dealt with by the traditional courts, the advantages and disadvantages of 'opting in' and 'opting out' procedures, and the concentration of powers into the hands of certain leaders.[164]

What these examples show is that the idea of a pluri-legal state is not just an aspiration but also one that is founded in empirical evidence. It is important to acknowledge that even while ideas of nation states have assumed prominence, there are layers of legality and different forms of governance that show how contested, cosmopolitan and heterogonous the

---

[162] Philipp Altmann, 'Plurinationality and Interculturality in Ecuador: Indigenous Movement and the Development of Political Concepts', *Iberoamericana – Nordic Journal of Latin American and Caribbean Studies* 43, nos. 1–2 (2014): 47–66.

[163] Legal Aid BC, 'First Nations Court: Aboriginal Legal Aid in BC', https://aboriginal. legalaid.bc.ca/courts-criminal-cases/first-nations-court (accessed 11 September 2019).

[164] Sindiso Mnisi Weeks, 'South Africa Still Has a Long Way to Go to Settle Traditional Leadership Challenges', *The Conversation*, 23 June 2019, http://theconversation. com/south-africa-still-has-a-long-way-to-go-to-settle-traditional-leadership-challenges-119009 (accessed 16 April 2020); Sindiso Mnisi Weeks, 'South Africa's Traditional Courts Bill 2.0: Improved but Still Flawed', *The Conversation*, 2 April 2017, http://theconversation.com/south-africas-traditional-courts-bill-2-0-improved-but-still-flawed-74997 (accessed 16 April 2020).

nature of governance is.[165] Exploring these ideas assume relevance for legal indicators because they demonstrate the need to build indicator frameworks that are able to capture this diverse and plural reality. Through relying on the concept of access to justice that can encompass the rule of law, but also include conceptions of legal needs, we have an opportunity to be able to capture law's cosmopolitan reality, and the ways in which contestations are not merely referenced but are instrumental to evaluating the functioning of legal systems. In the next section, I look at how to diversify the locations from where knowledge is curated, and to thereby build an epistemic plurality around the evaluation of justice systems.

Diversifying knowledge and thinking about law from below

A part of building plural legal indicators is also looking at diversifying sources that currently make up the legal imagination such as the types of processes, practices, values and institutions.[166] Bonilla Maldonado, in his study of the political economy of legal knowledge production, discusses how rules and principles govern the development, consumption and sharing of theories and practices of law, in particular due to the effects of colonialism, which has created systems for the flow of legal knowledge.[167] The primacy of certain legal knowledge over others is a function of the institutions that produce it, and cultures enable and sustain it.[168] The flow of legal knowledge is also determined by the types of concepts that are used, the epistemic categories generated, such as whether they are

---

[165] H. Patrick Glenn, 'Preface', in *The Cosmopolitan State*, vii–viii (Oxford: Oxford University Press, 2013).

[166] Darian-Smith, 'Producing Legal Knowledge'; Darian-Smith, 'Introduction'; Peter Ronald de Souza, 'The Recolonization of the Indian Mind', *Revista Crítica de Ciências Sociais* 114 (2017): 137–160.

[167] Daniel Bonilla Maldonado, 'The Political Economy of Legal Knowledge', in *Constitutionalism in the Americas*, ed. Daniel Bonilla and Colin Crawford, 29–78 (Cheltenham: Edward Elgar, 2018).

[168] Anthea Roberts, 'The Divisible College of International Lawyers', in *Is International Law International?*, 1–17 (Oxford: Oxford University Press, 2017); Luis Eslava, 'The Teaching of (Another) International Law: Critical Realism and the Question of Agency and Structure', *The Law Teacher* 54, no. 3 (2020): 368–384.

local or universal and whether they are self-generated or replicated.[169] It is important to recognize the hegemonic structures that dominate legal knowledge production by asking whose knowledge is silenced or erased by dominant narratives, whose knowledge is in use, and how such narratives lead to particular views that then become universalized.[170]

If we are interested in building global legal indicators that are able to capture the diversity and plurality of law in action, then it is pertinent to be able to embed resistances and struggles in international law, because it is not just in its institutions that we will have to evaluate justice systems but also in terms of the realities of those who have worked outside these institutions. In order to do this, the indicators as global devices will need to be able to capture not just institutional functioning but also instances where there is resistance, capturing what the resistance is against, what ends it serves, what strategies are used and what role plural, fragmented and postcolonial imaginations have to play in such thinking.[171] An example from the field of development studies comes from Rajagopal, who, through using narratives from social movements, offers a technique for how to think of questions of development and modernity from the ground. He argues that oftentimes poverty and the destruction of livelihood are seen as a

---

[169] Bonilla Maldonado, 'The Political Economy of Legal Knowledge'. See also Santos, *Toward a New Legal Common Sense*; Dann, Riegner and Bönnemann, 'The Southern Turn in Comparative Constitutional Law'; Achille Joseph Mbembe, 'Decolonizing the University: New Directions', *Arts and Humanities in Higher Education* 15, no. 1 (2016): 29–45.

[170] Darian-Smith, 'Reimagining Legal Geographies'; Boaventura de Sousa Santos, 'From University to Pluriversity and Subversity', in *The End of the Cognitive Empire: The Coming of Age of Epistemologies of the South*, 269–292 (Durham: Duke University Press 2018); Boaventura de Sousa Santos, João Arriscado Nunes and Maria Paula Meneses, 'Introduction: Opening Up the Canon of Knowledge and Recognition of Difference', in *Another Knowledge Is Possible: Beyond Northern Epistemologies*, ed. Boaventura de Sousa Santos, xix–lxii (New York: Verso, 2008).

[171] Balakrishnan Rajagopal, 'Writing Third World Resistance into International Law', in *International Law from Below: Development, Social Movements and Third World Resistance*, 9–23 (Cambridge: Cambridge University Press, 2003). See also the case of thinking about personal laws and the uniform civil code in India through women's movements in Tanja Herklotz, 'Dead Letters? The Uniform Civil Code through the Eyes of the Indian Women's Movement and the Indian Supreme Court', *Verfassung in Recht und Übersee* 49, no. 2 (2016): 148–174.

consequence of the lack of development. But from the perspective of social movements, they are seen as an outcome of the process of development itself.[172] This is an important argument to avoid an excessive reliance on experts who often prescribe solutions and advise on technical matters while being divorced from the realities of the struggles that people face.[173] In building indicators, while experts play an important role in providing concepts and methods for evaluation, capturing more grounded realities should not be discounted if the indicator envisages providing space for voices from below.

One way of capturing such instances of lived realities of people is to rely more on the use of ethnographies in international law.[174] This will help in understanding the frameworks of law beyond it being an ideological project, to also being a material project. It will also help identify new locations for international law, beyond its traditional sites for enactment and performance, such as in administrative procedures, into other sources like artefacts or objects.[175] Each of these disaggregated sources play a role in effecting the way law is manifested and if these different objects and sites to find concepts of law are considered, we could arrive at a more accurate and holistic way of building a legal indicator. We, thus, have an opportunity to look at the practices and effects of international law that exist far away from the mere formal institutions that govern it, and pay attention to the kinds of narratives that are emerging from plural legal institutions.[176] This will allow for other diversities to be given space and weightage, particularly those that

---

[172] Balakrishnan Rajagopal, 'Introduction', in *International Law from Below: Development, Social Movements and Third World Resistance*, 1–6 (Cambridge: Cambridge University Press, 2003).

[173] David Kennedy, 'Introduction: Could This Be 1648?', in *A World of Struggle: How Power, Law, and Expertise Shape Global Political Economy*, 1–20 (Princeton: Princeton University Press, 2016).

[174] Luis Eslava and Sundhya Pahuja, 'Beyond the (Post)Colonial: TWAIL and the Everyday Life of International Law', *Verfassung und Recht in Übersee/Law and Politics in Africa, Asia and Latin America* 45, no. 2 (2012): 195–221.

[175] Ibid. See also Nick Cheesman, 'Rule-of-Law Ethnography', *Annual Review of Law and Social Science* 14, no. 1 (2018): 167–184.

[176] Sujith Xavier, 'Learning from Below: Theorising Global Governance through Ethnographies and Critical Reflections from the Global South', *Windsor Yearbook of Access to Justice* 33, no. 3 (2016): 229–255, https://papers.ssrn.com/sol3/papers.cfm?abstract_id=2979384&download=yes## (accessed 31 August 2019).

are currently seen as marginal and peripheral to the development of legal indicators.[177]

Another pivotal axis to pluralizing the knowledge centres of international law is to focus on the experiences of the justice user, that is, to understand the experiences, resistances, challenges and difficulties that a person has when they negotiate the dispute resolution system. The benefit of focussing on a demand-centred perspective is that it will be able to capture different experiences and also be flexible enough to not be constrained by the specificity of institutions. A demand-oriented view will look expansively at barriers for users manifested in spatial, symbolic, linguistic, financial and other aspects.[178] This involves thinking not of transplantation and best practice, but actively immersing oneself in the context, framing an understanding from a user-centred view, discussing what works and not what ought to work, and finally iterating with perspectives from the contexts of the users.[179]

Conclusion

This chapter began by describing how quantification is becoming more and more pervasive. In light of the pervasive presence of numbers, it is important to build an epistemic plurality, such that the ways in which legal indicators are conceptualized become more representative of contexts outside dominant knowledge centres. It argues that it is impossible to go

---

[177] For an engagement with discussions on how law making and institutions function with intersecting influences from tradition to religion and custom, see generally Matthias Kötter, Tilmann J. Röder, Gunnar Folke Schuppert and Rüdiger Wolfrum (eds.), *Non-State Justice Institutions and the Law: Decision-Making at the Interface of Tradition, Religion and the State* (London: Springer, 2015).

[178] Martin Gramatikov and Robert B. Porter, 'Yes, I Can: Subjective Legal Empowerment—Tisco Working Paper Series on Civil Law and Conflict Resolution Systems', *Georgetown Journal on Poverty Law and Policy* 18, no. 2 (Spring 2010): 169–200; Mike de Langen and Maurits Barendrecht, 'Legal Empowerment of the Poor: Innovating Access to Justice', in *The State of Access: Success and Failure of Democracies to Create Equal Opportunities*, ed. Jorrit de Jong and Gowher Rizvi, 250–271 (Washington, DC: Brookings Institution Press, 2009); de Souza, 'Towards a User-Centered Engagement with Law'; de Souza, 'Evaluating "Access to Justice" in Informal Justice Systems'.

[179] de Souza, 'Beyond Best Practices'.

back to a world before indicators, and therefore persisting with indicators and finding new ways and concepts for evaluation through persistence can be, and is, a political action. Through examining different methods of persistence, this chapter argues that it is possible to pluralize the vocabulary of legal indicators by introducing and representing different concepts and values.

One of the major challenges of indicators is the language of experts and the managerial focus of quantification tools that emphasize technocracy. Through looking at instances of such technocracy from cases of empirical legal data from India, the chapter suggests instead that the messiness of law in action must be integrated into the frameworks of indicators. This is because such frameworks cannot be static and non-responsive devices but instead must continuously and iteratively respond to changing dynamics of how law is realized. Additionally, the chapter advances that to build plural legal indicators, it is important to de-centre and pluralize the state, which otherwise plays an outsized role in conceptualizing legal indicators, and further that it is essential to diversify knowledge centres and acknowledge different normative universes that exist. This expansion in the discourse happens because of the introduction of the idea of law from below.

5

A Capability Approach to Access to Justice in Plural Legal Systems

This chapter seeks to build upon the argument for epistemological diversity proposed in the last chapter by embracing legal plurality and including bottom-up perspectives in understanding and evaluating access to justice, and how people use the law to resolve their grievances. It also calls for engaging with concepts and narratives from the Global South, with the understanding that there are many worlds with different knowledge systems and there is a need to engage with these epistemologies and values to present a truly global legal indicator.[1] To do this, this chapter draws on recent work that recognizes the need for people-centred approaches to address justice problems,[2] and extends these approaches by offering a framework and methodology to measure access to justice in plural legal systems where there are competing forums for dispute resolution, and varied principles, ideas and norms.

Having introduced concepts of 'access to justice' and 'legal pluralism' in the previous chapters, this chapter analyses how these two concepts can be developed using the capability approach first proposed by Amartya

---

[1] Boaventura de Sousa Santos, *Toward a New Legal Common Sense: Law, Globalization, and Emancipation* (Cambridge: Cambridge University Press, 2002); Marisol de la Cadena and Mario Blaser, 'Pluriverse: Proposals for a World of Many Worlds', in *A World of Many Worlds*, 1–22 (Durham: Duke University Press, 2018).

[2] See the report by OECD, which focuses on the importance on developing approaches to access to justice that centre people, in *Equal Access to Justice for Inclusive Growth: Putting People at the Centre* (Paris: OECD, 2019), https://www.oecd.org/governance/equal-access-to-justice-for-inclusive-growth-597f5b7f-en.htm (accessed 31 July 2019).

Sen.[3] The purpose of focussing on human capability is to understand and map effective opportunities that people have in order to lead lives that they consider valuable, and in this regard understand how they can also have meaningful access to justice.[4] I argue that if we wish to evaluate how justice systems function, we need to do so by understanding them from a user perspective and by looking at how people experience them and find ways to resolve their grievances.

There are several existing legal indicators. However, a majority of them are designed primarily to measure the rule of law from an institutional approach, with a state-centric notion of justice delivery.[5] In these evaluative tools, the rule of law is measured in terms of institutions responsible for the administration of justice, such as the police, prisons, and courts.[6] The conceptual aspects of these tools are designed primarily for formal justice systems, which are then seen as aspirational models of justice delivery and

---

[3] Amartya Sen, 'Equality of What?', in *Tanner Lectures on Human Values,* ed. S. McMurrin, vol. 1, 197–220 (Cambridge: Cambridge University Press, 1980); Amartya Sen, 'Introduction: Development as Freedom', in *Development as Freedom,* 3–12 (Oxford: Oxford University Press, 2001).

[4] Ingrid Robeyns, 'The Capability Approach: A Theoretical Survey', *Journal of Human Development* 6, no. 1 (2005): 93–117; Sabina Alkire, Mozaffar Qizilbash and Flavio Comim, 'Introduction', in *The Capability Approach: Concepts, Measures and Applications,* ed. Flavio Comim, Mozaffar Qizilbash and Sabina Alkire, 1–25 (Cambridge: Cambridge University Press, 2008).

[5] Please refer to Chapter 3 for an engagement with rule of law indicators. In addition to the state-centric measurement frameworks, I also look at a user-centred approach to measuring justice in The Hague Model of Access to Justice. This approach emphasizes the importance of capturing the voices of the persons who embark on a path to justice. The framework that I develop complements the work from the Measuring Access to Justice project. It focuses not just on needs but also on how these needs are realised through an emphasis on capabilities. In addition to this, the framework is designed with an understanding of legal plurality at its core. This is to account for not just the fact that there are competing legal systems but also that concepts of dispute resolution emerge not just from different sources.

[6] See the comparison of rule of law tools carried out by Wolfgang Merkel. Wolfgang Merkel, 'Measuring the Quality of Rule of Law', in *Rule of Law Dynamics: In an Era of International and Transnational Governance,* ed. Michael Zürn, André Nollkaemper and Randy Peerenboom, 21–47 (Cambridge: Cambridge University Press, 2012).

models to be replicated in other geographies.[7] These indicators, as we have shown in the previous chapter, do not accurately represent the Global South due to the pluralities of dispute resolution institutions that operate with different concepts, procedures and substantive values. Concentrating only on state-centric forums, which are dominant in the Global North, implies advocating for a transplantation of norms, regulations and institutional forms without reference to contextual realities.[8] As a result of this formalistic approach, the specificities of the challenges of plural legal systems based on community, religion or custom are not mapped out in these indicators.[9] These assumptions of legal systems as transplantable commodities need to be rethought in acknowledgement of the intricacies of different cultures.[10] This argument is reiterated because it needs to be addressed in order to build a more accurate and inclusive understanding of the evaluation of justice systems that is rooted in plurality.

The Justice Capabilities Framework (JCF) that I offer in this chapter is designed to be a step in this direction. It focuses on access to justice, defined in terms of its attributes of networks, processes and user focus as discussed in Chapter 3, and draws from the capability approach to present capabilities and indicators to evaluate the functioning of plural legal systems. This

---

[7] Siddharth Peter de Souza, 'Evaluating "Access to Justice" in Informal Justice Systems: A Suggestive Framework', *Max Planck Yearbook of United Nations Law Online* 19, no. 1 (2016): 469–504; Deval Desai, 'In Search of "Hire" Knowledge', in *The International Rule of Law Movement: A Crisis of Legitimacy and the Way Forward*, ed. David Marshall, 42–83 (Cambridge, MA: Harvard University Press, 2014).

[8] Stephen Golub, 'Beyond Rule of Law Orthodoxy: The Legal Empowerment Alternative', Carnegie Endowment for International Peace, 14 October 2003, http://carnegieendowment.org/2003/10/14/beyond-rule-of-law-orthodoxy-legal-empowerment-alternative-pub-1367 (accessed 7 December 2017)'; Brian Z. Tamanaha, 'The Rule of Law and Legal Pluralism in Development', *Hague Journal on the Rule of Law* 3, no. 1 (2011): 1–17; Stephen Golub, 'Make Justice the Organizing Principle of the Rule of Law Field', *Hague Journal on the Rule of Law* 1, no. 1 (2009): 61–66.

[9] A further discussion on the absence of an engagement with legal pluralism in rule of law indicators is discussed in Chapter 3.

[10] The work of Desai and Isser explores the transplantation of legal systems. Desai, 'In Search of "Hire" Knowledge'; Deborah H. Isser, 'The Problem with Problematizing Legal Pluralism', in *Legal Pluralism and Development: Scholars and Practitioners in Dialogue*, ed. Brian Z. Tamanaha, Caroline Sage and Michael Woolcock, 237–248 (Cambridge: Cambridge University Press, 2012).

framework focuses on the perspectives, experiences and accompanying capabilities of the justice user. It recognizes that an access to justice indicator requires a bottom-up approach that engages with the power, opportunity and capacity that impacts how an individual participates in a dispute resolution process. In doing so, the framework aims to offer a global tool for measurement of access to justice that is designed to be reflexive in understanding how people bargain and mediate between different legal systems, what factors animate their decisions to choose a particular forum, and how these factors influence their quest for meaningful access to justice outcomes. In taking a global approach, it builds on the idea that de Sousa Santos advances, that for global social justice, you need global cognitive justice.[11] It also addresses some of the challenges of measuring plural legal systems where there are gaps in knowledge as to what actually improves the delivery of justice within the legal system.[12]

This chapter contributes to the literature on the capability approach through its application to the framing of access to justice in plural legal contexts, by arguing for how the capability approach can be a useful framework to evaluate justice delivery in diverse contexts.[13] The chapter

---

[11] Cognitive justice is the idea that there is a plurality of knowledge, and these must be recognized and allowed to co-exist. See generally Boaventura de Sousa Santos, *Epistemologies of the South: Justice Against Epistemicide* (London: Routledge, 2015); Shiv Visvanathan, 'The Search for Cognitive Justice', *Seminar Magazine* 597 (May 2009), https://www.india-seminar.com/2009/597/597_shiv_visvanathan.htm (accessed 30 September 2020).

[12] Isser, 'The Problem with Problematizing Legal Pluralism'; Daniel Adler and Sokbunthoeun So, 'Towards Equity in Development When the Law Is Not the Law: Reflections on Legal Pluralism in Practice', in *Legal Pluralism and Development: Scholars and Practitioners in Dialogue*, ed. Brian Z. Tamanaha, Caroline Sage and Michael Woolcock, 83–92 (Cambridge: Cambridge University Press, 2012)'.

[13] Work on access to justice and the capability approach has been explored through case studies of legal aid services in India and comparative work on legal services in the European Union and the United States. See Promit Chatterjee and Sreerupa Chowdhury, 'A Capabilities Approach to Access to Justice', *Journal of Indian Law and Society* 20, no. 4 (Winter 2012): 107–129; Marco Segatti, 'A Capabilities Approach to Access to Justice: Unfulfilled Promises, and Promising Strategies in the US and in Europe', *Teoria Politica (Nuova serie Annali)* 6 (2016): 335–359. In this book, the capability approach is examined in the context of the intersection of legal pluralism and access to justice.

also engages with discussions on the technicalities of operationalizing the capability approach by arriving at a list of capabilities that can be considered basic and essential for meaningful access to justice, and through building upon methods that have been used to ensure that the process of arriving at such dimensions is participative and deliberative.[14]

The chapter is organized as follows. The second section introduces key technical vocabulary of the capability approach and argues for its use, while at the same time addressing its key challenges in the third section. It goes on to examine how access to justice in plural legal systems can be understood in terms of human capabilities theoretically, before it is operationalized. This section explores the methods to arrive at a list of basic capabilities and dimensions more generally before introducing the framework and elements of the JCF, which is explored in further detail in the fourth section. The final section of the chapter provides details on the kind of data required for the framework and the means of collecting such data, in order to be able to measure access to justice in terms of capabilities.

The capability approach to framing access to justice

Access to justice in plural legal systems is envisaged as a concept that includes looking at different aspects of 'access' to reflect the various unmet legal needs of people; it explores the issue of how people resolve disputes irrespective of the institutional specificities in different jurisdictions and locates the processes involved, which consist of a series of relations and networks that play an important role in order for the dispute resolution processes to reach a conclusion.[15]

In this section, I argue that there is value in thinking of access to justice in terms of the capability approach because it focuses on the individual,

---

[14] I will draw on studies that have examined how the capability approach has been operationalized for human rights instruments, such as in the work by Tania Burchardt and Polly Vizard, '"Operationalizing" the Capability Approach as a Basis for Equality and Human Rights Monitoring in Twenty-First-Century Britain', *Journal of Human Development and Capabilities* 12, no. 1 (2011): 91–119; Polly Vizard, 'Specifying and Justifying a Basic Capability Set: Should the International Human Rights Framework Be Given a More Direct Role?', *Oxford Development Studies* 35, no. 3 (2007): 225–250.

[15] Please refer to Chapter 3 for a detailed overview of access to justice as a concept.

instead of the institutions, and is more flexible as a framework where there are competing authorities and jurisdictions, such as in a plural legal system. It places an emphasis on choice and autonomy for an individual to choose between different dispute resolution forums and examines the real freedoms people have to make decisions to resolve their disputes given the social relations at play. It allows for an analysis of individual capabilities, as well as how social arrangements and relations in the community impact the ways in which a person is able to make choices to achieve certain outcomes to address barriers to justice. In this sense, I argue for why it is a valuable framework from where we can articulate and evaluate the experiences of the justice user.

What is the capability approach and why should we use it?

The capability approach is a conceptual framework that focuses on what people are really able to 'be' and 'do' and what they can achieve in order to live a meaningful life.[16] It emphasizes the real freedoms that people have in order to achieve a level of well-being that is valuable to them.[17] People's ability to achieve a degree of well-being is also based on the opportunities that they have to be and do things that they value, and it also involves an assessment of social arrangements that impact these opportunities.[18]

---

[16] Sen, 'Equality of What?'; Sen, 'Introduction: Development as Freedom'; Martha Nussbaum and Amartya Sen, *The Quality of Life* (Oxford: Oxford University Press, 1993); Ingrid Robeyns, 'The Capability Approach', in *The Stanford Encyclopedia of Philosophy*, ed. Edward N Zalta (Winter 2016 edition, Metaphysics Research Lab, Stanford University, 2016), https://plato.stanford.edu/archives/win2016/entries/capability-approach/ (accessed 11 October 2019).

[17] Please note, I will be using terms such as 'functionings', 'capabilities' and 'beings and doing' or 'to be and do', which are terms from the capability approach and its particular vocabulary. Amartya Sen, 'Well-Being, Agency and Freedom: The Dewey Lectures 1984', *The Journal of Philosophy* 82, no. 4 (April 1985):169–221; Robeyns, 'The Capability Approach'; Séverine Deneulin and Lila Shahani (eds.), *An Introduction to the Human Development and Capability Approach: Freedom and Agency* (London: Earthscan and IDRC, 2009), 3–21.

[18] Ingrid Robeyns, *Wellbeing, Freedom and Social Justice: The Capability Approach Re-Examined* (Cambridge: Open Book Publishers, 2017); Alkire, Qizilbash and Comim, 'Introduction'.

Over the years, the capability approach has been used to study and assess poverty, inequality and human development by providing an evaluative framework to understand these phenomena.[19] It offers a contrast to other approaches examining phenomena such as poverty and inequality on the basis of people's income and expenditure or utility.[20] In this regard, it focuses on a departure from the means that a person has to the actual opportunities available to them in order to achieve desirable outcomes.[21] For example, having the income to hire a lawyer is not sufficient if there are barriers and pressures that prevent an individual from independently seeking out a lawyer to address a grievance due to, for instance, familial, gender, caste or community standing. The capability approach can be seen as a framework to measure the quality of life of people by taking each person as an end and examining their ability to achieve real freedoms for a flourishing life, while recognising that there are differences in how each person makes choices to exercise their freedoms.[22]

The capability approach introduces a new technical vocabulary that involves a number of key concepts. The first concept is the idea of a 'functioning', which is the different activities that a person may value 'being or doing'.[23] These include activities that play a role in making up a person's well-being such as having an education and being healthy. Examples of 'beings' can include being educated or being well fed whereas examples

---

[19] The capability approach has been used to develop measurement frameworks such as the Human Development Index and the Multi-Dimensional Poverty Index. See UNDP, 'Human Development Index (HDI)', *Human Development Reports*, http://hdr.undp.org/en/content/human-development-index-hdi (accessed 19 April 2020); OPHI, 'Global Multidimensional Poverty Index', , https://ophi.org.uk/multidimensional-poverty-index/ (accessed 14 December 2020).

[20] Sen, 'Introduction: Development as Freedom'.

[21] Amartya Sen, 'Lives: Freedoms and Capabilities', in *The Idea of Justice*, 225–252 (Cambridge, MA: Harvard University Press, 2009).

[22] For instance, a person may address a grievance by going to a lawyer, but someone else may seek a settlement. Both are interested in resolving their disputes, and through the capability approach, there is a possibility to evaluate how they are able to assess the different options. See generally Martha C. Nussbaum, 'The Central Capabilities', in *Creating Capabilities: The Human Development Approach*, 17–45 (Cambridge, MA: Harvard University Press, 2011).

[23] Amartya Sen, 'Functionings and Capabilities', in *Inequality Reexamined*, 39–55 (Cambridge, MA: Harvard University Press, 1995).

of 'doings' can include going out to shop or taking part in a concert. Functionings are basic elements and actions that constitute a human life and are central to a self-understanding of what a human life is.[24]

The second concept is that of 'capability', which Sen defines as various combinations of functionings, or *beings* and *doings*, that make it possible for a person to lead a valuable life.[25] Capabilities are concerned with the real freedoms that people have to make choices about their lives, and through these choices achieve outcomes that enhance their well-being.[26] For instance, while studying is a 'functioning', the opportunity to study is a 'capability'. The distinction between capabilities and functionings are that while the former includes the opportunities to achieve particular aspects of value, the latter is concerned with what is then realized.[27] The value of focusing on capabilities is that it allows for an examination of a combination of functionings that can help a person achieve what they value. A key aspect that distinguishes the capability approach from, for instance, Rawl's primary goods approach[28] is in the analytical distinction between means and ends. The capability approach argues for not only primary goods, but also the person's ability to convert these primary goods to meet her ends.[29] In this sense, through the capability approach, policies or phenomena are

---

[24] Ingrid Robeyns, 'Core Ideas and the Framework', in *Wellbeing, Freedom and Social Justice: The Capability Approach Re-Examined*, 21–88 (Cambridge: Open Book Publishers, 2017); Sabina Alkire and Séverine Deneulin, 'The Human Development and Capability Approach', in *An Introduction to the Human Development and Capability Approach: Freedom and Agency*, ed. Séverine Deneulin and Lila Shahani, 22–48 (London: Earthscan and IDRC, 2009).

[25] Sen, 'Functionings and Capabilities'; Sterling M. McMurrin (ed.), *Tanner Lectures on Human Values*, vol. 1 (Cambridge: Cambridge University Press 1980).

[26] Sen, 'Functionings and Capabilities'; Nussbaum, 'The Central Capabilities'.

[27] Robeyns, 'The Capability Approach'; Sabina Alkire, 'Why the Capability Approach?', *Journal of Human Development* 6, no. 1 (2005): 115–135.

[28] Primary goods are those goods which a person would like more of than others. They include aspects like rights, liberties, opportunities and wealth. See also John Rawls, 'Principles of Justice', in *A Theory of Justice*, 47–101 (Cambridge, MA: Harvard University Press, 1971).

[29] Sen, 'Equality of What?'; Ingrid Robeyns and Harry Brighouse, 'Introduction: Social Primary Goods and Capabilities as Metrics of Justice' in *Measuring Justice: Primary Goods and Capabilities*, ed. Harry Brighouse and Ingrid Robeyns, 1–14 (Cambridge: Cambridge University Press, 2010).

evaluated based on how they affect people's freedoms to make choices and achieve outcomes in terms of what they are actually able to realize.[30] If people are to have meaningful access to justice, it is not just about the means necessary to achieve this such as access to knowledge, finance and security but whether they can convert these means to actually be able to achieve outcomes that enhance their access to justice such as a fair hearing or a just settlement.

First, the capability approach assumes importance as a framework to study access to justice because it allows for a focus on real or effective opportunities that people have rather than merely an evaluation of the resources that they have.[31] For instance, we will be able to study whether people can actually choose which dispute resolution forum they would like to attend rather than just whether there are options of multiple forums to resolve a dispute.

Second, the capability approach allows for different interactions of individuals to be mapped out because it captures the complexity of people and the varied ways in which people use different capabilities to achieve particular valuable outcomes.[32] In this instance, we will be able to evaluate, for instance, why particular demographics use particular dispute resolution forums in one way or another depending on gender or community lines, or how factors such as disability play a role in people meeting their justice needs. This approach examines the manner in which individuals convert the resources they have into capabilities depending upon personal, social and environmental factors.[33]

---

[30] Amartya Sen, 'Introduction: Questions and Themes', in *Inequality Reexamined*, 1–11 (Cambridge, MA: Harvard University Press, 1995).

[31] Ibid.; Robeyns, 'The Capability Approach'; Martha Nussbaum, 'Capabilities as Fundamental Entitlements: Sen and Social Justice', *Feminist Economics* 9, nos. 2–3 (2003): 33–59.

[32] Elizabeth Anderson, 'Justifying the Capabilities Approach to Justice', in *Measuring Justice: Primary Goods and Capabilities*, ed. Harry Brighouse and Ingrid Robeyns, 81–100 (Cambridge: Cambridge University Press, 2010); Amartya Sen, 'Human Rights and Capabilities', *Journal of Human Development* 6, no. 2 (2005): 151–166; Robeyns, 'Core Ideas and the Framework'.

[33] Amartya Sen, 'Capabilities, Lists, and Public Reason: Continuing the Conversation', *Feminist Economics* 10, no. 3 (2004): 77–80; Anderson, 'Justifying the Capabilities Approach to Justice'.

Thirdly, the capability approach uses a language of what a person is able to be and do; it does not privilege one tradition over another. It speaks squarely in terms of people's experiences and how they manage to do certain things.[34] It primarily evaluates the extent of freedom people have to promote or achieve the things that they value.[35] I have adopted the capabilities approach in constructing this indicator framework because it is sensitive to structural, psychological and social injustices, as evidenced by its use in the development of indices such as the Human Development Index or measuring multi-dimensional poverty. In measuring access to justice, using such an approach is meant to determine the ability of people to make choices within a justice system, such that through those choices they find outcomes that they consider meaningful and valuable.[36]

Framing a capability approach to access to justice in plural legal systems

The previous section provided an outline of the capability approach and the potential it has in its application to access to justice by arguing for the flexibility of the framework. This section addresses how to think about capabilities while integrating legal plurality that comes when aspects of access to justice need to be understood in a situation where there are distinct forums, contexts and histories that compete for legitimacy and have varying degrees of authority.

Examining how legal pluralism impacts the manner in which people resolve their disputes is critical to conceptualizing what kind of capabilities

---

[34] Martha C. Nussbaum, 'Capabilities, Entitlements, Rights: Supplementation and Critique', *Journal of Human Development and Capabilities* 12, no. 1 (2011): 23–37. See generally Martha C. Nussbaum, 'Capabilities across National Borders', in *Frontiers of Justice: Disability, Nationality, Species Membership*, 273–324 (Cambridge, MA: Harvard University Press, 2009).

[35] See generally Marcos Segatti, 'The Point of Equal Access to Justice: On the Duty to, at All Times and Provisionally, Pause, Cool Down and Listen', JSD diss., University of Chicago, 2019, https://chicagounbound.uchicago.edu/jsd_dissertations/69 (accessed 30 July 2021).

[36] Sen, 'Human Rights and Capabilities'; Sakiko Fukuda-Parr, 'The Human Development Paradigm: Operationalizing Sen's Ideas on Capabilities', *Feminist Economics* 9, nos. 2–3 (2003): 301–317; Chatterjee and Chowdhury, 'A Capabilities Approach to Access to Justice'.

are required to navigate a dispute resolution process.[37] As has been previously examined, the idea of legal pluralism envisions more than one legal system, coexisting beyond the state, with multiple influences, values and spaces of legitimacy within the same geographical space.[38] This means that there are different forums, and each has a stake and a claim to authority. There are also norms that conflict with each other, and there are multiple procedures with respect to how a dispute can be resolved.[39]

As discussed in the introduction, some of the recurrent themes in discussions on legal pluralism are the role that 'law', the 'state', the 'community' and finally 'space' play in a resolution of disputes.[40] It is important to note that each of the above factors play a role in influencing and shaping the nature of dispute resolution. These themes are also flagged because in thinking about access to justice and capabilities, these will influence how we arrive at a basic set of capabilities.

The first aspect of law brings forth the question of what constitutes the law and the distinction between law and other forms of normative orderings.[41] Can law be anything that justice users perceive it to be? [42] In order to answer this, we need to think beyond legal centralism and engage in a more descriptive analysis of how legal systems function by dealing with the empirical realities of law.[43] We have also discussed in Chapter 3 the value of 'inter-legality', and the fact that even when people find ways

---

[37] I have focused on the dispute resolution process because, as outlined in Chapter 3, I am interested in examining the paths that people take to find meaningful resolutions to their disputes.

[38] Sally Engle Merry, 'Legal Pluralism', *Law and Society Review* 22, no. 5 (1988): 869–896.

[39] Brian Z. Tamanaha, 'Understanding Legal Pluralism: Past to Present, Local to Global', *Sydney Law Review* 30, no. 3 (2008): 375–411.

[40] Michaels does a survey of common themes of legal pluralism as prerequisites in understanding the implications of globalization. It assumes a useful framework to also signal issues that would impact a global legal indicator. Ralf Michaels, 'Global Legal Pluralism', *Annual Review of Law and Social Science* 5, no. 1 (2009): 243–262.

[41] Merry, 'Legal Pluralism'; John Griffiths, 'What Is Legal Pluralism?', *The Journal of Legal Pluralism and Unofficial Law* 18, no. 24 (1986): 1–55.

[42] Brian Z. Tamanaha, 'A Non-Essentialist Version of Legal Pluralism', *Journal of Law and Society* 27, no. 2 (2000): 296–391.

[43] Griffiths, 'What Is Legal Pluralism?'

to access justice, they have to confront competing orders that sometimes intertwine and intersect with each other.[44]

The second aspect is the influence of the state and whether state institutions monopolize the ways in which justice is delivered to people.[45] In a polycentric world, it becomes apparent that the state is just one of many justice delivery options, and that there are a great wide variety of legal orders from exchanges that take place at home, at work, through communities and in businesses.[46] This is relevant because, as we have discussed, law cannot just be limited to its formal and official frameworks, but must also emerge from the social practices around it.[47] In countries that have been affected by colonialism, this coexistence of competing legal systems is very widespread. This is because there were several pre-existing forums for dispute resolution, and where state law, emerging from colonial rule, competes with and dominates local legal traditions.[48] In the previous chapter, I mentioned the preamble to the Bolivian Constitution which spoke to the challenge of moving from colonialism to appreciating the diversity that comes with representing and including different histories and forms of dispute resolution.[49] The capabilities for access to justice thus require an imagination and an inclusion of institutions, concepts and categories that move beyond those inspired and mandated by the state.

The third aspect to consider when thinking of access to justice in plural legal systems is the role that different communities play in influencing norms that are accepted and incorporated in the administration of justice. Hoekema extends the idea of inter-legality to argue that we need to think not just of how the state or a dominant legal system influences the local, but also focus on

---

[44] Boaventura de Sousa Santos, 'Law: A Map of Misreading—Toward a Postmodern Conception of Law', *Journal of Law and Society* 14, no. 3 (Autumn 1987): 279–302.

[45] Keebet von Benda-Beckmann and Bertram Turner, 'Legal Pluralism, Social Theory, and the State', *Journal of Legal Pluralism and Unofficial Law* 50, no. 3 (2018): 255–274.

[46] Baudouin Dupret, 'What Is Plural in the Law? A Praxiological Answer', *Égypte/Monde Arabe* 1 (2005): 159–172.

[47] David Nelken, 'Eugen Ehrlich, Living Law, and Plural Legalities', *Theoretical Inquiries in Law* 9, no. 2 (2008): 448–471.

[48] Tamanaha, 'Understanding Legal Pluralism'; Merry, 'Legal Pluralism'.

[49] Donna Lee Van Cott, 'A Political Analysis of Legal Pluralism in Bolivia and Colombia', *Journal of Latin American Studies* 32, no. 1 (February 2000): 207–234.

an actor-oriented perspective which engages with multiple legal systems.[50] Take, for example, the concept of *ubuntu*, which is increasingly incorporated by the South African Constitutional Court in their jurisprudence and includes ideas of humanity, reciprocity and compassion.[51] In a case related to the death penalty, the court said:

> The adoption of this Constitution lays the secure foundation for the people of South Africa to transcend the divisions and strife of the past, which generated gross violations of human rights, the transgression of humanitarian principles in violent conflicts and a legacy of hatred, fear, guilt and revenge. These can now be addressed on the basis that there is a need for understanding but not for vengeance, a need for reparation but not for retaliation, a need for *Ubuntu* but not for victimisation.[52]

The concept of *ubuntu* in this regard is influencing and penetrating the western concepts of justice currently applied in the courts, and it offers an example for how community practice can influence the nature of dispute resolution and the kind of expectation that people have when they go to a court to resolve their disputes and grievances. Acknowledging the existence of different categories and norms is fundamental to building a more plural legal indicator. It is an opportunity to think about the alternative ways of conceptualizing and seeing justice by referring to different cosmologies, such as in terms of engaging with *ubuntu*. In doing so, at the time of operationalizing the capability approach, close attention is paid to the need to replace a 'monoculture of scientific knowledge' by 'ecologies of

[50] André J. Hoekema, 'European Legal Encounters between Minority and Majority Cultures: Cases of Interlegality', *The Journal of Legal Pluralism and Unofficial Law* 37, no. 51 (2005): 1–28.

[51] *Ubuntu* means humanity towards others and a universal bond of sharing. See also Sibusiso Blessing Radebe and Moses Retselisitsoe Phooko, 'Ubuntu and the Law in South Africa: Exploring and Understanding the Substantive Content of Ubuntu', *South African Journal of Philosophy* 36, no. 2 (2017): 239–251.

[52] *State v. Makwanyane and Another*, (CCT3/94) [1995] ZACC 3; 1995 (6) BCLR 665; 1995 (3) SA 391; [1996] 2 CHRLD 164; 1995 (2) SACR 1 (6 June 1995), http://www.saflii.org/za/cases/ZACC/1995/3.html (accessed 8 October 2019).

knowledge'.[53] This will allow for the epistemic diversity needed to construct a global indicator that is inclusive and plural.

The fourth aspect is that of space, in terms of the location of the forum and the kinds of values and language it evokes based on its setting. For example, how would a concept of dignity and *ubuntu* play out in a customary court and a constitutional court? Is it a concept that could work in both places? Does the space matter in terms of how it manifests in the decision making of the people? Twining, in his paper about how legal concepts travel, argues for two tests: first, whether the concept travels well; and second, whether it travels far—and if so, does it fit or does it work?[54] He asks,

> Assumptions that 'one size fits all' are a common target of the critics. I suggest that there is a conceptual aspect to these concerns. Where concepts such as court or constitution or corruption or lawyer have deep roots in local history or have acquired strong cultural or ideological baggage, the dangers `of ethnocentric projection are obvious. So it is worth asking, how much of our stock of concepts is local and context specific?[55]

In thinking about pluralities of context, and attempting to build a set of central capabilities, these are questions that require consideration.

How do we capture and conceptualize access to justice when there are multiple understandings of laws, institutions, procedures, languages and communities, which each play a role in determining the networks, processes and abilities that a person has to obtain an outcome that is valuable for them? We need to think deeply and acknowledge that law is a plural and cosmopolitan enterprise, and for that there must be fluidity in how we can

---

[53] Boaventura de Sousa Santos, João Arriscado Nunes and Maria Paula Meneses, 'Introduction: Opening Up the Canon of Knowledge and Recognition of Difference', in *Another Knowledge Is Possible: Beyond Northern Epistemologies*, ed. Boaventura de Sousa Santos, xix–lxii (New York: Verso, 2008), xx. See also Boaventura de Sousa Santos, 'Introduction: Why the Epistemologies of the South? Artisanal Paths for Artisanal Futures', in *The End of the Cognitive Empire: The Coming of Age of Epistemologies of the South*, 1–35 (Durham: Duke University Press, 2018).

[54] William Twining, 'Have Concepts, Will Travel: Analytical Jurisprudence in a Global Context'. *International Journal of Law in Context* 1, no. 1 (2005): 5–40.

[55] Ibid., 34.

measure and interpret the ways in which people negotiate different spaces that they live in.

Keeping this in mind, it becomes imperative not to focus on thinking of access to justice only in terms of who the supplier of justice is, because the institutions vary, change, compete, and often do not travel well or far. Instead, we should focus, as mentioned earlier in Chapter 3, on how people resolve their disputes, what their experiences are and especially how they manage the plurality of the different forums before them. In summary, this entails that access to justice must focus on what works, rather than what ought to work according to western normative frameworks, it must incorporate a plurality of experiences, because disputes do not take a linear path to their resolution, and finally it must address a mismatch between rule of law principles and the realities of everyday justice.

Access to justice in plural legal systems can be defined as the capability or freedoms that a person has to negotiate and derive a valuable outcome that addresses their justice problems. This may mean that through having the freedom to decide how to address multiple networks, differentiated processes and competing forums, where each influence the path to the resolution of the dispute. This definition acknowledges that there are several factors at play (knowledge, finance, geography, physical and social ability) and each is able to influence how a dispute is being resolved. It also acknowledges that there are several competing forums, and in order to avail of a resolution there are decisions that require different capabilities to be able to be successful. In this context, access to justice in terms of capabilities is understood as evaluating how a user is able to access a plural justice system and achieve an outcome that they consider just and fair.

Constructing the Justice Capabilities Framework (JCF)

This section begins by highlighting and addressing some of the criticisms of the capability approach and ways to address them. This includes whether the capability approach focuses on individuals or on communities, and also on the question of how to arrive at a list of canonical capabilities. I then go on to explain what kinds of methods can be used in order to arrive at a set of basic justice capabilities.

I examine the ways a list of basic capabilities can be arrived at for a global understanding of access to justice, keeping in mind the concerns of capability theorists as well the importance of focusing on people and experiences from the Global South. I will draw from the idea of a global cognitive justice that considers diversity not just in abstract but also materially in terms of how it is integrated into the development of frameworks and evaluation exercises.[56]

I will then highlight the key elements and the conceptual framework for a JCF that takes into account aspects of plurality, contestation and the different ways in which legal systems operate and interact with each other in order to build and operationalize an understanding of access to justice.

Understanding the critiques and challenges of the capability approach

There are two recurrent criticisms of the capability approach that are relevant to this study. The first is that the approach focuses too much on the individual and doesn't focus on groups and communities and their effects on individual well-being.[57] It also does not examine the implications of individual freedoms on the freedoms of others.[58] In the context of plural legal orders that are not always individual centric, this is problematic. However, a counter to this argument is that while the capability approach focuses on the individual, it pays equal attention to the interactions and influences that various factors have on the individual, such as community, social or environmental factors.[59] As a result, while focused on the individual, it shows how the individual is able to interact and undertake certain actions depending upon the factors around them.[60] While individual

---

[56] See generally Visvanathan, 'The Search for Cognitive Justice'; Santos, Nunes and Meneses, 'Introduction'.

[57] Charles Gore, 'Irreducibly Social Goods and the Informational Basis of Amartya Sen's Capability Approach', *Journal of International Development* 9 (1997): 235–250.

[58] Nussbaum, 'Capabilities as Fundamental Entitlements'.

[59] The role of groups and collectives also play a role in influencing people's choices and freedoms, as well as their ability to accomplish outcomes. Frances Stewart, 'Groups and Capabilities', *Journal of Human Development* 6, no. 2 (2005): 185–204; Graciela Tonon, 'Communities and Capabilities', *Journal of Human Development and Capabilities* 19, no. 2 (2018): 121–125; Anderson, 'Justifying the Capabilities Approach to Justice'.

[60] Burchardt and Vizard, '"Operationalizing" the Capability Approach'; Michael Murphy, 'Self-Determination as a Collective Capability: The Case of Indigenous Peoples', *Journal of Human Development and Capabilities* 15, no. 4 (2014): 320–334; Peter

freedoms and agency form a critical part of the capability approach, it is a 'quintessentially social product' because it connects the social and institutional arrangements to individual agency.[61] These social interactions and communities can also play a role in the expansion of capabilities.[62] In this sense, the individual exists in relation to the community and not as an atomistic individual. For example, while a person may have a constitutional right to freedom of religion, if the community where they lived denied them the possibility to go to a place of worship then this freedom would be constrained by the environment in which they lived. So, the capability or real freedom to practice their religion would depend on being able to find ways to materialize that freedom in realized outcomes.

The second critique is whether there can be a canonical list of capabilities that can meet different situations and contexts. Such a list, Sen has argued, would go against any possibility of progress in social understanding, and without social discussion or public reasoning such a list would be misrepresentative of what people really value in order to live a flourishing life.[63] He argues that making such a list should not be embedded in technocracy but be open to challenge and deliberation. Others such as Nussbaum have argued that a list of domains or critical capabilities would be essential to give the theoretical frame of the capability approach a critical focus.[64] In defining her list, Nussbaum develops it at an abstract level that can still be translated at a local level and accommodate difference.[65] Nussbaum argues that having a list adds weight to the theoretical framework of the capability approach by making it more concrete and specific.[66]

This book also argues, in agreement with Nussbaum, for developing a list and advances that the means to developing such a list of basic

Evans, 'Collective Capabilities, Culture, and Amartya Sen's Development as Freedom', *Studies in Comparative International Development* 37 (2002): 54–60.

[61] Sen, 'Introduction: Development as Freedom', 31.

[62] Solava S. Ibrahim, 'From Individual to Collective Capabilities: The Capability Approach as a Conceptual Framework for Self-Help', *Journal of Human Development* 7, no. 3 (2006): 397–419.

[63] Sen, 'Capabilities, Lists, and Public Reason'.

[64] Nussbaum, 'Capabilities as Fundamental Entitlements'.

[65] Robeyns, 'The Capability Approach'.

[66] Flavio Comim, 'Measuring Capabilities', in *The Capability Approach: Concepts, Measures and Applications*, ed. Flavio Comim, Mozaffar Qizilbash and Sabina Alkire, 157–200 (Cambridge: Cambridge University Press, 2008).

capabilities for access to justice must be rigorously explained. This list is not to be developed for perpetuity but is rather something that is iterative and subject to change as the environment and context changes. It is also meant to be responsive because it concerns a plurality of legal systems and how they continuously negotiate and adapt to different situations. In the next section, I examine how capability theorists have gone about operationalizing the capability approach, and the methods they have chosen and employed in order to specify and justify a basic list of capabilities.

Operationalizing the capability approach

Before getting into the conceptual framework of the JCF, the first step is to discuss what methods could be used to build such a framework, and how to justify the selection of a basic set of capabilities. As a general approach to determining basic capabilities, Sen has argued that such a choice must be made with a method that is deliberative and takes into account the purpose, context and trajectory of a particular project.[67] This means that it is important to have a comprehensive understanding of the outcomes (capabilities) by examining the processes that determine the outcomes.[68] This is better than a consequentialist approach, which only looks at outcomes cumulatively and focuses only on the content of the capabilities but not at the process of arriving at it.[69]

Capability theorists have offered different roadmaps for how to arrive at a list of capabilities. Robeyns has argued that when developing a capability list for a particular project, four aspects are crucial.[70] First, it is critical for the list to be explicitly formulated and open to discussion and feedback such that it could be defended. Second, the methodology used to generate such a list must be justified and clarified in order to explain how particular dimensions were arrived at. Third, there should be different degrees of

---

[67] Sen, 'Capabilities, Lists, and Public Reason'; Francesco Burchi, Pasquale De Muro and Eszter Kollar, 'Which Dimensions Should Matter for Capabilities? A Constitutional Approach', *Ethics and Social Welfare* 8, no. 3 (2014): 233–247.

[68] Amartya Sen, 'Capability and Well-Being', in *The Quality of Life*, ed. Martha Nussbaum and Amartya Sen, 30–53 (Oxford: Oxford University Press, 1993).

[69] Ibid.; Burchi, Muro and Kollar, 'Which Dimensions Should Matter for Capabilities'.

[70] Ingrid Robeyns, 'Selecting Capabilities for Quality of Life Measurement', *Social Indicators Research* 74 (2005): 191–215.

generality, which must be at two levels: an ideal list that does not take into account limitations of measurement or data collection and a more pragmatic list that does. And fourth, it should be an exhaustive list, such that nothing important is omitted.[71]

In order to operationalize and build an empirical basis for the capability approach, Alkire offered different selection methods to choose domains and indicators.[72] These included using *existing data* where the availability of data was a primary consideration; making certain *normative assumptions* on what people value; adopting universal standards evolved through *public consensus* like the Universal Declaration of Human Rights which have been consistent over time; developing an *ongoing deliberative process* that would involve conducting activities like focus group interviews to reach a list of what people value; and using *empirical evidence* to arrive at a list of capabilities by taking recourse to evidence, such as existing surveys.[73]

I have referred to the work of Robeyns and Alkire because they provide a basis and a method in order to determine a basic list of capabilities and indicators. In order to proceed, I draw from the work by Alkire on the different ways to build an empirical basis for the capability approach, while also keeping in mind the guidelines offered by Robeyns when developing a list.

I adopt a two-part approach to identifying the indicators for the JCF. The first is to engage with concepts, materials and principles that have travelled and have achieved public consensus through a deliberative process. These include ideas such as *ubuntu, swaraj*, Rule of Law and the Universal Declaration of Human Rights,[74] which have influenced the ways in which institutions respond and develop policies on access to justice.

---

[71] Ibid., the discussion for the quality criteria for developing a list is on pages 205–206; Ligia Noronha and Subrahmanya Nairy, 'Assessing Quality of Life in a Mining Region', *Economic and Political Weekly* 40 (2005): 72–78.

[72] Sabina Alkire, 'Choosing Dimensions: The Capability Approach and Multidimensional Poverty', Chronic Poverty Research Centre Working Paper No. 88, 1 August 2007, https://papers.ssrn.com/sol3/papers.cfm?abstract_id=1646411 (accessed 17 February 2022), see pages 7–13.

[73] Ibid.

[74] I have deliberately used these four concepts next to each other because if we speak of the rule of law as if it is a global concept, we need to also acknowledge the 'global' potential of *ubuntu* and *swaraj*. Providing it with space is the first step to building such a vocabulary that is plural, diverse and multi-locational.

Second, I also refer to existing empirical evidence that has insights into how people are resolving disputes and achieving access to justice. This includes sources such as analysis of legal needs surveys and ethnographic studies that have studied how people resolve their disputes and what their urgent requirements are.[75]

Through looking at both empirical data and concepts that have achieved a public consensus like *ubuntu* or human rights, I am interested in building a set of basic capabilities that are able to articulate what real freedoms people require in order to overcome barriers inhibiting them in their quest for access to justice in plural legal orders. These capabilities must also reflect a new vocabulary that responds to how people experience the resolution of disputes and the challenges they encounter. By examining various sites to study such legal phenomenon, I make two active choices: one, that in this plurality, there is an acknowledgment of difference, and, second, that we need more ground-up experiences of legal problems. The advantage of such an approach is that it can allow for comparisons across time and space because such a measurement framework integrates an expansive vocabulary of experiences and concepts, and in doing so aims to have a co-produced outlook that takes into account the needs and demands of the users in plural legal orders. Such an indicator framework will aim to integrate the messiness of law in action, refer to people-centred needs and, on that basis, use the existing data available to offer an examination of how the most urgent needs of people can then translate into attendant capabilities.

---

[75] I examine a wide variety of legal needs surveys (studies to understand the pressing legal problems that people face) to identify the common findings while studying people's justice experiences. See Pascoe Pleasence, Nigel Balmer and Rebecca Sandefur, *Paths to Justice: A Past, Present and Future Roadmap* (London: Nuffield Foundation, 2013) https://www.nuffieldfoundation.org/sites/default/files/files/PTJ%20Roadmap%20 NUFFIELD%20Published.pdf (accessed 8 October 2020); Pascoe Pleasence and Nigel Balmer, *Legal Needs Surveys and Access to Justice* (Paris: OECD, 2018), https://iris. ucl.ac.uk/iris/publication/1620815/1 (accessed 7 August 2019); Hazel Genn, 'The Landscape of Justiciable Problems', in *Paths to Justice: What People Do and Think about Going to Law*, 21–66 (Oxford: Hart Publishing, 1999); de Souza, 'Evaluating "Access to Justice" in Informal Justice Systems'; Maurits Barendrecht, Peter Kamminga and Jin Ho Verdonschot, 'Priorities for the Justice System: Responding to the Most Urgent Legal Problems of Individuals', TISCO Working Paper, 2008, https://papers.ssrn.com/ abstract=1090885 (accessed 7 August 2019).

Elements of the JCF

The JCF evaluates the basic capabilities that a justice user would require to overcome the barriers and challenges they would face in a plural legal order. It will break down the capabilities on the basis of the different aspects and stages in a dispute resolution process and specific capabilities required at each stage. The JCF aims to measure the quality of access to justice in terms of the capabilities that justice users have to understand, negotiate, participate in and reintegrate into their communities after resolving a dispute in a plural legal order. In doing so, the JCF assesses the ability of plural legal orders to provide opportunities to users to make the best decisions based on the resources and opportunities available to them.

In Chapter 3, during the discussion on conceptualizing access to justice, I discussed the idea of a dispute tree and how it could be a useful metaphor to capture the heterogeneity of options that an individual faces in plural legal settings.[76] I also discussed the different steps and decisions that go into a dispute resolution process, such as meeting, talking, sharing, deciding and stabilizing.[77] Focusing on access to justice as a process and a network is to build on the idea of paths to justice that an individual can take when navigating a dispute resolution process.[78] Related to these discussions, I have argued in earlier work that a dispute resolution process has four key moments or stages for any individual who wants to resolve a grievance.[79] This would include:

---

[76] Catherine R. Albiston, Lauren B. Edelman and Joy Milligan, 'The Dispute Tree and the Legal Forest', *Annual Review of Law and Social Science* 10, no. 1 (2014): 105–131.

[77] Maurits Barendrecht, 'In Search of Microjustice: Five Basic Elements of a Dispute System', Tilburg University Legal Studies Working Paper No. 02/2009, 2009, http://www.ssrn.com/abstract=1334644 (accessed 2 September 2019).

[78] Work on legal needs has focused on the experiences and attitudes of the public and the ways in which they interact and engage with justice systems. Genn, 'The Landscape of Justiciable Problems'; Tilburg Institute for Interdisciplinary Studies of Civil Law and Conflict Resolution Systems (TISCO), Martin Gramatikov, Maurits Barendrecht, Malini Laxminarayan, Jin Ho Verdonschot, Laura Klaming and Corry van Zeeland, *A Handbook for Measuring the Costs and Quality of Access to Justice* (Apeldoorn, Antwerpen and Portland: Maklu Publishers, 2010).

[79] These four stages are based on identifying key moments when a decision is needed to be taken in order to move towards the resolution of a grievance, and it goes

- Understanding the contours of the dispute and the nature of the grievance and determining ways to take action
- Negotiating the details of the dispute and determining the best strategy to achieve a desired outcome
- Deciding on the forum and the types of procedures that will be used to determine the response to the dispute
- Finding a resolution, where there is a possibility to manage ways to enforce or challenge the particular resolution

The JCF is designed to take into account the non-linear ways in which disputes are resolved. It will account for the impacts of different social environments, the fluid interactions between people's needs, and the institutions and procedures that they engage with. Building upon the discussions and conclusions from Chapters 3 and 4 about ways to evaluate access to justice for a plural legal order, the following three steps will guide the development of the JCF as an indicator to measure access to justice globally. The first step involves examining what the justice user or seeker needs and is capable of doing to achieve access to justice in a plural legal order by focusing not on institutions but on people. The second step involves understanding the interactions of the justice user in the justice process. The third step involves identifying the types of basic capabilities required by a justice user in a justice system.

---

beyond merely access to the dispute resolution forum but also relates to having access to information about the dispute, knowledge about options between forums and negotiating between both options, deciding what procedure to take, and finally determining how best to come to a resolution. In previous work, I first explore these stages in de Souza, 'Evaluating "Access to Justice" in Informal Justice Systems'. In their seminal work, Miller and Sarat examine the process that a dispute takes from a perceived injury to actual legal proceedings, demonstrating how many cases actually resulted in a legal proceeding and resolution. Richard E. Miller and Austin Sarat, 'Grievances, Claims, and Disputes: Assessing the Adversary Culture Special Issue on Dispute Processing and Civil Litigation: Part Two – The Civil Litigation Research Project: A Dispute-Focused Approach: Surveying Disputes', *Law and Society Review* 15, no. 3/4 (1980): 525–566. See also Marc Galanter, 'Reading the Landscape of Disputes: What We Know and Don't Know (and Think We Know) about Our Allegedly Contentious and Litigious Society', *UCLA Law Review* 31, no. 1 (October 1983): 4–71.

a. The demand or user perspective

A demand-based approach uses a bottom-up narrative where the voices of the user are recorded, where needs are studied, and where the priorities that most inhibit or challenge the delivery of the justice are mapped and responded to.[80] The advantage of a demand approach is the ability to focus on why users make the choices that they do, how they determine these choices and whether they are satisfied with their choices. It seeks to explain how individuals respond to institutions, whether formal institutions operated by the state, or non-state based on custom, religion and traditions. It further seeks to evaluate how interactions with the community affect the ways in which users make choices; for example, does the fear of social sanction impact the decision to pursue a dispute? In this way, as argued previously, focusing on a demand perspective will evaluate the choices a user makes, what kind of sufferings and challenges impact the decisions of users, and how they resist or accept the nature of the process to gain access to justice. Focusing on a demand-based approach is to ensure that these accounts of users are not silenced but amplified when we are thinking of measuring justice, the experiences of dispute resolution and how this translates into indicators (this will be explained in the subsequent sections).

b. The interactions with the justice system

The second step involves giving shape to the experiences and expectations of the justice user or seeker when they are participating in the justice process. Access to justice, as outlined before, involves different stages, networks and processes. In this sense it becomes a communicative process that requires interactions in the forms of dialogues, negotiations and compromises. This can involve talking between parties to settle a dispute, speaking with a village elder or judge to make a case, or strategizing with a lawyer or other representative on what is the best course of action to resolve the dispute. Kokal also describes a performative aspect to dispute resolution, a *tamasha*

---

[80] Pleasence and Balmer, *Legal Needs Surveys and Access to Justice*; Pascoe Pleasence and Nigel Balmer, *How People Resolve 'Legal' Problems* (Cambridge: Legal Services Board, 2014), https://legalservicesboard.org.uk/wp-content/media/How-People-Resolve-Legal-Problems.pdf/ (accessed 20 February 2022); Barendrecht, Kamminga and Verdonschot, 'Priorities for the Justice System'; Genn, 'The Landscape of Justiciable Problems'.

(theatre), which is used as a tool of communication and self-preservation in deciding which course of action to take to resolve a dispute.[81] In their work on divorce, Mnookin and Kornhauser show that while formal institutions establish the procedures and rules for divorce, much of the negotiation and bargaining takes place outside in matters of custody and property—these are also important aspects of the procedure and more than just the rule of the court based on law.[82] In the case of plural legal systems of the kind we have discussed in this book, there is a continuous dialogue that takes place between users and institutions, and it is this dynamism and fluidity that the indicators identified in the next sections will seek to exemplify.

c. Basic capabilities required

The third step involves deciding the types of basic capabilities required by a justice user in a justice system. It asks two questions:[83]

- What are the basic capabilities required in a plural legal order in order to ensure a user has access to justice?
- What are the ways of defining the dimensions to measure access to justice, if denial of access to justice is a capability deprivation?

The illustration below (Figure 5.1) highlights the key steps that would make up this approach: (*a*) demand based, (*b*) the framing of capabilities as interactions that take place between justice users, justice institutions and the community at large, and (*c*) the basic capabilities required at each stage of the access to justice process.

The indicators in the following section are chosen to reflect capabilities to navigate the four stages of understanding, negotiating, deciding and resolving. At each stage, it is critical to identify the basic capabilities that an individual is required to have to navigate that stage. These capabilities are meant to evaluate what the valuable outcomes are for a person to find access

---

[81] Kalindi Kokal, 'Tamāshā: The Theatrics of Disputing and Non-State Dispute Processing', in *Normative Pluralism and Human Rights*, ed. Kyriaki Topidi, 189–206 (Oxon: Routledge, 2018).

[82] Robert H. Mnookin and Lewis Kornhauser, 'Bargaining in the Shadow of the Law: The Case of Divorce', *The Yale Law Journal* 88, no. 5 (April 1979): 950–997.

[83] de Souza, 'Evaluating "Access to Justice" in Informal Justice Systems'.

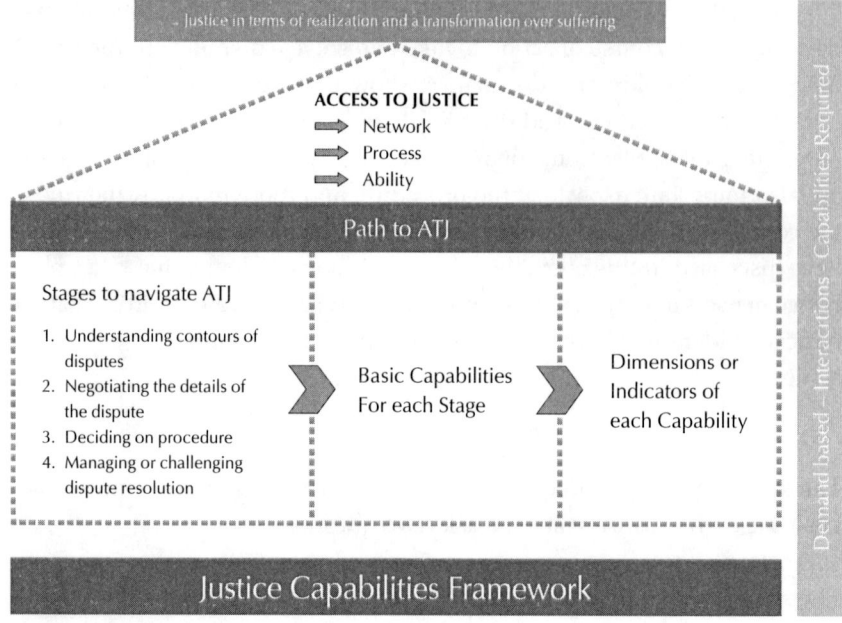

Figure 5.1 The Justice Capabilities Framework (JCF)

Source: Author.

to justice within a plural justice system. At each stage, two basic capabilities are listed to explain the ability of the individual to make choices to achieve a valuable outcome. These basic capabilities are further broken down into three further dimensions which are the indicators of capabilities to access justice in plural legal system.

The key idea behind the JCF is to show how justice users respond to questions that encapsulate the four stages as described earlier:[84]

---

[84] Ibid.; in this paper, I examined this four-step process for informal justice systems and have further examined how the four stages can be built upon to also consider plural systems that also include the state as well as non-state justice systems. I further aim to problematize the idea of consensus concepts by showcasing how concepts from the South, such as *swaraj* and *ubuntu*, must also travel and how they can fit if we expand our conceptual vocabularies beyond those related to ideas such as the rule of law. 'Twelve basic capabilities based on a human rights-based capability selection that a user is required to have in order to have a purposeful and a dignified interaction within an informal justice system. These include the capacity to: *Understand, Access,*

- Whether they have the capacity to name and recognize the nature of the injury and dispute
- Whether they have the capacity to negotiate the possible solution
- Whether they have the capacity to participate and decide on a procedure
- Whether they have the capacity to enforce a resolution and stabilize the conflict

In the next section, these questions are further explained by examining a basic set of capabilities that are required in order to have the opportunity to achieve a valuable outcome at each stage.

Examining basic capabilities for engaging in a dispute resolution process

The stages of dispute, negotiation, deciding and resolution constitute four critical elements of a path to justice. However, each of these different stages have particular factors that influence people's behaviours and how they are able to transcend these different stages of a dispute process.

For the JCF, there are 8 basic capabilities, each of which has 3 dimensions. These 24 dimensions (8 capabilities with 3 dimensions each) are the indicators of capabilities required to access justice in a plural legal system. While I have examined the different ways in which capabilities can be chosen, I also provide an explanation with regard to how these capabilities have been unpacked and determined.

Capability to understand a dispute

The first criterion of understanding a dispute is taken from an analysis of studies that have examined legal needs in different jurisdictions. These studies have shown that at the first stage in a path to justice it is important to understand the nature of the dispute, recognize legal injury and examine how it evolves; in this regard, there is an engagement with a public understanding of justice issues, an analysis of the confidence in

---

Be secure, Be respected, Consent, Predict, Participate, Be treated equally, Contest, Reconcile, Enforce, Reintegrate' (ibid., 501–503).

different institutions and an exploration of the abilities to take action.[85] The two key capabilities that assume importance are (*a*) the capability to name, which entails recognising an injury and identifying the rights and responses available, and (*b*) the capability to choose how to address the problem. This is because prior to joining a process designed to resolve a dispute, it is critical for the individual to understand that an injury has been committed and that there are avenues to resolve such a dispute.

Take the case of domestic violence; women do not report cases because often these instances are not self-perceived and because they do not have the security that they can report without consequences for their homes.[86] For instance, in India, the Tamil Nadu Muslim Women's Jamaat was established to provide a safe space for Muslim women to discuss their domestic problems because the existing state and non-state forums were not sufficient. One of the first approaches adopted by the forum was to

---

[85] See Miller and Sarat, 'Grievances, Claims, and Disputes'; William L. F. Felstiner, Richard L. Abel and Austin Sarat, 'The Emergence and Transformation of Disputes: Naming, Blaming, Claiming ....' *Law and Society Review* 15, no. 3/4 (1980): 631–654. See also detailed research on legal needs surveys by Pleasence and Balmer, *Legal Needs Surveys and Access to Justice*; Pleasence and Balmer, *How People Resolve 'Legal' Problems*. This also includes questions of legal plurality. See also Marc Galanter, 'Justice in Many Rooms: Courts, Private Ordering, and Indigenous Law', *The Journal of Legal Pluralism and Unofficial Law* 13, no. 19 (1981): 1–47; Cott, 'A Political Analysis of Legal Pluralism'; Kalindi Kokal, 'Many Laws, Many Orders: Disputes and Their Processing in the Non State Arena', in *State Law, Dispute Processing, and Legal Pluralism: Unspoken Dialogues from Rural India*, 58–72 (Oxon: Routledge, 2019); Siddharth Peter de Souza, 'Non-State Justice Systems', in *Max Planck Encyclopedia of Comparative Constitutional Law*, 2020, https://oxcon.ouplaw.com/view/10.1093/law-mpeccol/law-mpeccol-e650 (accessed 9 April 2020). While also thinking of the landscape of justiciable problems, see also Barendrecht, Kamminga and Verdonschot, 'Priorities for the Justice System'; Genn, 'The Landscape of Justiciable Problems'; HiiL, 'HiiL Justice Dashboard: Justice Data at Your Fingertips', https://justice-dashboard.hiil.org/ (accessed 6 May 2020). See generally the 'International Covenant on Civil and Political Rights 1966', United Nations Treaty Series no. 14688, 23 March 1976, https://treaties.un.org/doc/publication/unts/volume%20999/volume-999-i-14668-english.pdf (accessed 30 July 2021).

[86] 'Facts and Figures: Ending Violence against Women—What We Do', UN Women, https://www.unwomen.org/en/what-we-do/ending-violence-against-women/facts-and-figures (accessed 14 December 2020).

enable participants to understand the nature of injury (in this case, matters of domestic violence), before determining how to proceed with and evolve a strategy to respond to the offence.[87] Both factors are critical because without self-perception and knowledge, there is no possibility to remedy the dispute or determine an appropriate course of action, and without confidence and choice, there is a hesitancy to take appropriate actions.

These basic capabilities of naming and choosing are a way to understand a dispute, and are further broken down into the following six indicators:

Basic Capability	Dimensions of capability
Name injury	• Capability to recognize the nature of the injury • Capability to know how to proceed with remedying the injury • Capability to anticipate the consequences of decisions taken to remedy the injury
Choose dispute resolution forum	• Capability to determine the best dispute forum to resolve the injury • Capability to act freely to resolve the dispute without bodily or mental injury • Capability to have access to the forum keeping in mind cost and time.

Naming represents the capability to have the self-perception to understand that an injury has occurred, to know how to move forward from recognizing it and to determine a course of action that is also conscious of the consequences. This, coupled with the aspect of choosing, is to highlight the nature of plural legal systems and the fact that users have the capacity to determine which forum is best suited to their needs. Keeping this aspect of choice in mind raises questions of the legitimacy, authority and safety of the forum along with whether it is economical and timely in terms of dispensing justice. These are factors that determine how parties are able to chart a practical course of action after naming injuries.

---

[87] V. Geetha, 'Justice in the Name of God: Organizing Muslim Women in Tamil Nadu', in *Indian Feminisms: Individual and Collective Journeys*, ed. Poonam Kathuria and Abha Bhaiya (New Delhi: Zubaan, 2018).

Capability to negotiate a solution

The stage of negotiation is an important step, wherein an individual must evaluate the potential costs and benefits of resolving a dispute. For this, it is important to determine what the impact of engaging with a particular solution could be, and how this would work for both the individual and community. At the stage of negotiation, an individual bargains between potential options available and this can lead to forum shopping as well. In plural legal systems, there are continuous evaluations between which forums would provide the most suitable resolutions, and oftentimes there is a tendency to use non-state forums over state court systems because these forums carry greater legitimacy in the community.[88] Take, for example, the case of *tara bandu* in Timor-Leste, which I introduced in Chapter 3. In this instance, the community went back to an age-old tradition because they felt that it was a better set of rules and practices to balance the complexities of natural resource governance.[89] In other cases, however, where forums

---

[88] Danish Institute for Human Rights, 'Informal Justice Systems: Charting a Course for Human Rights-Based Engagement', UNDP, UNICEF and UN Women, 2013, http://www.undp.org/content/undp/en/home/librarypage/democratic-governance/access_to_justiceandruleoflaw/informal-justice-systems.html (accessed 7 December 2017); Ewa Wojkowska, *Doing Justice: How Informal Justice Systems Can Contribute* (UNDP, 2006), https://www.un.org/ruleoflaw/blog/document/doing-justice-how-informal-justice-systems-can-contribute/ (accessed 3 February 2018); International Council on Human Rights Policy, *When Legal Worlds Overlap: Human Rights, State and Non-State Law* (Geneva: International Council on Human Rights Policy, 2009); Fernanda Pirie, *The Anthropology of Law* (Oxford: Oxford University Press, 2013); Mark Goodale, *Anthropology and Law: A Critical Introduction* (New York: NYU Press, 2017); Matthias Kötter, Tilmann J. Röder, Gunnar Folke Schuppert and Rüdiger Wolfrum (eds.), *Non-State Justice Institutions and the Law: Decision-Making at the Interface of Tradition, Religion and the State* (London: Springer, 2015); Peter Albrecht, Helene Maria Kyed, Deborah Isser and Erica Harper (eds.), *Perspectives on Involving Non-State and Customary Actors in Justice and Security Reform* (Rome: IDLO and DIIS, 2011).

[89] Bikash Kumar Bhattacharya, 'Timor-Leste: Maubere Tribes Revive Customary Law to Protect the Ocean', *Mongabay Environmental News*, 26 October 2018, https://news.mongabay.com/2018/10/timor-leste-maubere-tribes-revive-customary-law-to-protect-the-ocean/ (accessed 9 April 2020); Bikash Kumar Bhattacharya, 'Timor-Leste: With Sacrifice and Ceremony, Tribe Sets Eco Rules', *Mongabay Environmental News*, 8 November 2018, https://news.mongabay.com/2018/11/timor-leste-with-sacrifice-and-ceremony-tribe-sets-eco-rules/ (accessed 22 April 2020); Bikash Kumar

prioritize conciliation at a community level over individual autonomy, there can be serious impacts. As with the case of Khap Panchayats from India, in matters related to marital disputes among inter-caste couples, the needs of a couple are second to that of family honour. This results in threats to the lives of the couples who then have to look for other forums outside the village to ensure their safety.[90] These examples demonstrate the importance of negotiation in determining how to proceed with redressing a dispute. It requires the individual to think both at a strategic level in terms of the options available and the impact of the choices made on their own life and well-being, but also at a personal level that considers which forum is familiar, comfortable and participative in terms of their rules and procedures.

While evaluating capabilities at the negotiation stage, two aspects hold importance: the capability to strategize and the capability to be valued. In order to determine these indicators, I looked at the legal needs and aspirations through legal needs surveys and also examined how bargaining works in plural legal contexts. The capability to strategize and be valued are further understood through their indicators as follows:

Basic Capability	Dimensions of capability
Strategize outcomes	• Capability to think freely about the potential solutions to the dispute • Capability to deliberate on and bargain over any decisions made between parties • Capability to determine how the dispute is resolved without coercion

(Contd)

Bhattacharya, 'Timor-Leste: Q&A with a Maubere Fisherman on Reviving Depleted Fisheries', *Mongabay Environmental News*, 31 October 2018, https://news.mongabay.com/2018/10/timor-leste-qa-with-a-maubere-fisherman-on-reviving-depleted-fisheries/ (accessed 22 April 2020).

90 Siddharth Peter de Souza, 'India's Parallel Justice Systems: Engaging with Lok Adalats, Gram Nyayalayas, Nari Adalats and Khap Panchayats through Human Rights', in *Human Rights in India*, edited by Satvinder Juss, 80–101 (London: Routledge, 2019). As demonstrated in essays in this collection, a sense of personal belonging to a community often triumphs desires for individual autonomy. See Marie-Claire Foblets, Michele Graziadei and Alison Dundes Renteln, *Personal Autonomy in Plural Societies: A Principle and Its Paradoxes* (London: Routledge, 2017).

(*Contd*)

Basic Capability	Dimensions of capability
Be Valued	• Capability to participate and be heard during a negotiation process • Capability to ensure equal treatment and reciprocity before deciding on a dispute process • Capability to speak about the outcomes of such a resolution

At the stage of negotiation, the justice user is required to strategize about how to think freely about the ways to resolve the dispute, how to bargain for a satisfactory outcome and how to make a decision to participate in a forum without coercion. At this stage, it is also important that the justice user is able to choose a forum where they are heard, experience fair and reciprocal treatment, and feel secure to speak during and after the decision to go to a forum has been made. The stage of negotiation is an important juncture because it is the point at which the trajectory of the dispute can take many different shapes, whether it goes to a state court or a non-state court. Depending upon which forum the justice user goes to, the dispute will be designed keeping in mind the institutional and socio-cultural specificities.[91] This step thus requires not just the capability to strategize but also to make a meaningful decision because this will have an impact on the kind of processes and structures that later determine the trajectory of the dispute.

Capability to navigate a procedure

The third stage of procedure in the path to access to justice is the capabilities that the individual requires to navigate and participate in the procedure.

---

[91] In their work on an analytic approach to dispute system design, Smith and Martinez introduce a framework that includes thinking through the goals of the system and what kind of disputes it seeks to resolve, what are the processes, structures and incentives to resolve such disputes, who are the stakeholders, what are the resources at hand, and finally how to think in terms of success and accountability. These factors provide a sense of how, in order to negotiate a future course of action, there are several dynamic issues at play. See also Stephanie Smith and Janet Martinez, 'An Analytic Framework for Dispute Systems Design', *Harvard Negotiation Law Review* 14 (2009): 123–169; Lisa Blomgren Amsler, Janet Martinez and Stephanie E. Smith, *Dispute System Design: Preventing, Managing, and Resolving Conflict* (Stanford, CA: Stanford University Press, 2020).

In order to arrive at the capabilities for this stage, I examine legal needs surveys that provided details of how people resolve their disputes, as well as studies on the translation and localisation of human rights to examine the issue of whether people are able to understand as well as correspondingly use such forums.[92] The first aspect is the familiarity of the forum and the ability of a person to relate to how it functions. This is critical because one of the key reasons people choose forums is the need to be comfortable with how the forum is run, the concepts of justice that are used and the processes and structures employed. The second aspect is that the justice user should be able to share their thoughts, experiences and anxieties, which, in a hierarchical or particularly formal court with procedures that can be alienating, would not be possible. Thus, for evaluating capabilities at the procedure stage, the two key issues required are the capability to relate to the processes in the forum and the capability to share their own understanding within the forum. Both these factors connect to the issue of the functionality of a dispute resolution forum and the processes and structures that go into their design. They also connect to the notion of legitimacy and authority that such factors of relating and sharing evoke among justice users, and the influence these have on choices between forums.[93]

---

[92] Eve Darian-Smith, 'Reimagining Legal Geographies', in *Laws and Societies in Global Contexts: Contemporary Approaches*, 167–242 (Cambridge: Cambridge University Press, 2013); K. Patrick Glenn, 'Preface', in *The Cosmopolitan State*, vii–viii (Oxford: Oxford University Press, 2013); Mark Goodale, 'Introduction: Locating Rights, Envisioning Law between the Global and the Local', in *The Practice of Human Rights: Tracking Law between the Global and the Local*, ed. Mark Goodale and Sally Engle Merry, 1–38 (Cambridge: Cambridge University Press, 2007); Sally Engle Merry, 'Transnational Human Rights and Local Activism: Mapping the Middle', *American Anthropologist* 108, no. 1 (2006): 38–51; Brian Z. Tamanaha, Caroline Sage and Michael Woolcock (eds.), *Legal Pluralism and Development: Scholars and Practitioners in Dialogue* (Cambridge: Cambridge University Press, 2012); Danish Institute for Human Rights, 'Informal Justice Systems'.

[93] Dispute system design influences the choices people make. See also Miranda Forsyth, 'A Typology of Relationships between State and Non-State Justice Systems', *The Journal of Legal Pluralism and Unofficial Law* 39, no. 56 (2007): 67–112; Brian Z. Tamanaha, 'Introduction: A Bifurcated Theory of Law in Hybrid Societies', in *Non-State Justice Institutions and the Law: Decision-Making at the Interface of Tradition, Religion and the State*, ed. M. Kötter, Tilmann J. Röder, Gunnar Folke Schuppert and Rüdiger Wolfrum,

These aspects are further understood as follows:

Basic Capability	Dimensions of capability
Relate to the procedures of the forum	• Capability to know the procedures of the forum • Capability to understand how a resolution would play out and predict certain outcomes • Capability to feel comfortable and familiar during the procedures
Share needs and anxieties	• Capability to make needs known • Capability to contest and articulate any unjustified decision • Capability to make known any anxieties about the nature of the process and its outcomes

The capability to relate is a key aspect of navigating a procedure because it deals with a wide variety of aspects that concern the agency and freedom of an individual to make informed decisions within the forum. These include certain knowledge about procedures, a familiarity of contexts and the ability to predict how outcomes will play out. Similarly, the idea of sharing also assumes importance because it involves the stage after understanding the nature of injury to also articulating it in a way to ensure that there is a space to be safe and make anxieties about the nature of the process known, and challenge unjustified decisions. Sharing is thus proactive in articulating needs but also in challenging abuses of power.

Capabilities to obtain a resolution

In dealing with plural legal systems, it is clear that different institutions have different degrees of legitimacy and authority, and each have different approaches towards resolving disputes, from finding compromises and restorative justice solutions to adversarial positions as with formal courts.

The capability to obtain a resolution draws from different concepts, from *ubuntu* to *sumak kawsay* and principles of restorative justice.[94] The ability to

---

1–21 (London: Springer, 2015) ; Amsler, Martinez and Smith, *Dispute System Design*; Smith and Martinez, 'An Analytic Framework for Dispute Systems Design'.

[94] The idea of a common humanity and oneness, and the importance of community in *ubuntu*. See also Mluleki Mnyaka and Mokgethi Motlhabi, 'The African Concept

enforce a resolution also corresponds closely with the how the justice user is able to function after a decision has been arrived at. In the final stage of a path to justice, the emphasis is on understanding the after-effects and the impact of the previous three stages, and in particular the last stage of navigating a procedure. For justice users, what this stage seeks to evaluate is whether they have the capability to obtain just and fair outcomes not just in fact but in reality. This assumes importance when judgments or decisions of formal courts are not understandable or impactful on the ground, or in situations where non-state courts also meet similar challenges from community and social sanctions.[95]

At this stage of resolution of disputes, two aspects are important: the first is the capability to enforce a decision, and the second is the capability to belong in one's community after a decision has been made. It is further understood as follows:

---

of Ubuntu/Botho and Its Socio-Moral Significance', *Black Theology* 3, no. 2 (2005): 215–237. See also '… a commission is a necessary exercise to enable South Africans to come to terms with their past on a morally accepted basis and advance the cause of reconciliation' in 'Truth and Reconciliation Commission', https://www.justice. gov.za/trc/ (accessed 22 April 2020). The idea of *sumak kawsay* and *buen virir* and the idea of living together with each other and with nature assume importance here when resolving disputes. Boaventura de Sousa Santos, 'Gandhi, An Archivist of the Future', in *The End of the Cognitive Empire: The Coming of Age of Epistemologies of the South*, 209–246 (Durham: Duke University Press, 2018). As also the idea of self-governance in *swaraj* by Gandhi in Bhikhu Parekh, *Gandhi: A Very Short Introduction* (Oxford: Oxford University Press, 2001). See also in these essays the need for alternative life worlds, life cyles, and interlocutors who can bring together different ways of resolving a dispute. Bhikhu Parekh, *Ethnocentric Political Theory: The Pursuit of Flawed Universals* (Cham: Springer International Publishing, 2019); Shiv Visvanathan, 'Alternative Science', *Theory, Culture and Society* 23, nos. 2–3 (2006): 164–169. See also the *Fair Trial Manual* from Amnesty International (London: Amnesty International Publication, 2014); United Nations, 'Basic Principles on the Use of Restorative Justice Programmes in Criminal Matters', E COSOC Res. 2000/14, U.N. Doc. E/2000/INF/2/Add.2 at 35 (2000), https://www.un.org/ruleoflaw/blog/ document/basic-principles-on-the-use-of-restorative-justice-programmes-in-criminal-matters/ (accessed 8 October 2020).

[95] This relates to the discussion of the Sabarimala case in Chapter 4, where the decision of the Supreme Court to allow women to enter a temple was not enforced on the ground.

Basic Capability	Dimensions of capability
Enforce decisions	• Capability to implement the resolution of a forum • Capability to contest the decision without fear or sanction • Capability to settle or find compromises that are satisfactory
Belong to the community	• Capability for truth sharing and reconciliation • Capability to participate in a community after the dispute concludes, socially and culturally • Capability to be able to access basic necessities like food, clothing, shelter and jobs

In obtaining a resolution, the idea of enforcement becomes relevant because it is not enough that a decision has been reached, it must also be implemented, and this can depend on whether there is pressure or compromise. Along with the capability to enforce a resolution is the capability of belonging. In this aspect, questions of living harmoniously in the community become important along with being able to continue to have basic well-being. In order to think of enforcement, therefore, it is important to delve into fair trial standards, but it is equally important to think of other legal systems, which encourage non-adversarial resolutions such

Table 5.1 Basic capabilities organized around the four stages

Understand (Stage 1)	Negotiation (Stage 2)	Decision (Stage 3)	Resolution (Stage 4)
Name	**Strategize**	**Relate**	**Enforce**
Capability to name an injury and acknowledge one's hurt	Capability to adopt a strategy in a negotiation	Capability to relate to the procedure for the dispute resolution	Capability to enforce a resolution
Choose	**Value**	**Share**	**Belong**
Capability to choose how to resolve the dispute	Capability to feel valued during the negotiation	Capability to share one's grievances	Capability to belong after the resolution of the dispute

Source: Author.

that oftentimes individual and community needs are placed in balance. Therefore, in this regard, attention is also given to the aspect of belonging, which considers the social, political and cultural implications of decisions from dispute resolution forums.

This section has examined the eight basic capabilities across four stages that a justice user needs in order to participate and obtain meaningful outcomes to enhance access to justice in a plural legal system. It further went into the details of each capability, identifying three dimensions or indicators for each capability.

A table of the eight basic capabilities are summarized for easy reference in Table 5.1.

Data: What we need and how to collect it

The JCF introduced in this chapter provides an opportunity to engage with some of the gaps and silences that currently are not evaluated or conceived as categories for measurement when evaluating plural legal systems. In providing a framework for identifying the key capabilities for a user to obtain access to justice, there is also an expectation of how to collect data in order to carry out this evaluation.

This section explores what kind of data the capability instrument requires for it to be able to map different capabilities that would enable an individual to have better access to justice. It also provides an overview of how to collect this data and introduces the methods as well as the questionnaire that I have developed in order to collect data, which is provided in the appendix.

Data required for the JCF

By focusing on people and their needs and capabilities, the kind of data required will focus on the demand for justice. This is in the tradition of legal needs surveys and surveys that capture justiciable events.[96] I extend the work on legal needs surveys by including different categories and concepts that reflect the focus on access to justice, capabilities and legal pluralism.

---

[96] Pleasence, Balmer and Sandefur, *Paths to Justice*; Genn, 'The Landscape of Justiciable Problems'; Pleasence and Balmer, *Legal Needs Surveys and Access to Justice*.

In doing so, this research engages with whether people understand the nature of their disputes, know how to negotiate it, are able to participate in the forums and can enforce the decisions. By focusing on stages that make up an access to justice process, and attributing particular capabilities to negotiate each stage, the focus of this kind of data is to map people's path to justice.[97]

In addition to focusing on demand-based justice data, talking in terms of capabilities offers a different kind of vocabulary to think about the functioning of a legal system as well as the challenges of access to justice. With capabilities, the focus shifts from dialogues on administrative performance to understanding what people need in order to flourish and attain particular objectives. In turn, the focus extends beyond matters related to efficiency to those related to security, stability, participation—each of which offers a different view from where to evaluate the legal system. In this sense, there is a distinction to be made between judicial performance and justice capabilities. Whereas the former is concerned with matters of administration and is influenced by technocratic considerations, the latter is reflected by more substantive considerations and is centred on people's perspectives and what matters to them when they face a dispute and have to resolve it. By focusing on capabilities, the vocabulary of justice shifts from the perspectives of institutions to the perspectives of people. Doing so will help bridge gaps where those whose voices are marginalized or suppressed, by virtue of being constructed in administrative terminologies, will now be understood more actively. There is also a conscious attempt to move beyond a state-centred imagination to one that instead incorporates the plurality of institutions for people. In this sense, there is an opportunity to examine where people go when they wish to resolve their disputes and not a presumption that they will go to courts or similar formal institutions. This will also help to rethink the rule of law as a statist concept and instead think in terms of being part of the more expansive concept of access to justice.

The kind of data required for the JCF should capture the capabilities of people to negotiate the different stages in order to have access to justice. This can draw on the legal needs surveys and allow for an understanding of how justice problems emerge and subside, and the factors behind their permanence. It should also include data that examines plural legal institutions and not just those that are related to the state. In this sense, when

---

[97] TISCO et al., *Measuring the Costs and Quality of Access to Justice*; HiiL, 'HiiL Justice Dashboard: Justice Data at Your Fingertips'.

we are measuring access to justice, it is important to capture the competing nature of legal institutions and how some are more legitimate, acceptable and more entrenched than others. Finally, there is a need for data to move beyond only administrative aspects of justice delivery to also capture the substantive aspects of justice, which looks at ideas of participation, security and fairness of the dispute resolution process for the justice user. This will allow for more bottom-up and user-focused approaches to understanding challenges and opportunities to addressing questions of access to justice.[98] The capability instrument will require new categories of data and new priorities for measurement. The benefit of this is that it will offer a more responsive and reflexive understanding of justice.

Populating the JCF through random sampling, cross-sectional study and interviewing methods

A key challenge of ensuring that the JCF is populated is to identify users of plural justice systems who have already been through the four stages of the access to justice rectangle. For this purpose, it is important to identify an area, district or city where it is likely that plural justice systems are commonly found. On identifying such an area, the next step would be to draw a random sample from the general population in that agreed upon area. The purpose of the sample being random is to capture how different people at different stages of the justice process evaluate whether they are able to find outcomes that they consider valuable.

For the purpose of validating the JCF, a small sample of 200 persons could be considered, though this figure depends on the size and structure of the population, the level of detail required and the available resources.[99] It

---

[98] HiiL, 'HiiL Justice Dashboard: Justice Data at Your Fingertips'; CLEP and UNDP, *Making the Law Work for Everyone, Vol. 1: Report of the Commission on Legal Empowerment of the Poor* (New York: CLEP and UNDP, 2008), https://www.un.org/ruleoflaw/blog/document/making-the-law-work-for-everyone-vol-1-report-of-the-commission-on-legal-empowerment-of-the-poor/ (accessed 7 August 2019); Martin Gramatikov and Robert B. Porter, 'Yes, I Can: Subjective Legal Empowerment—Tisco Working Paper Series on Civil Law and Conflict Resolution Systems', *Georgetown Journal on Poverty Law and Policy* 18, no. 2 (Spring 2010): 169–200.

[99] In their work on measuring access to justice, TISCO et al. provide an overview of suitable sample sizes for pilot studies. See generally TISCO et al., *Measuring the Costs and Quality of Access to Justice*, 52.

is envisaged that a cross-sectional study will be undertaken. This typically means that the data will be analysed from one specific point in time.[100] In the case of the JCF, we will be able to capture different cases through the sample, in some cases where the user has completed the four stages of access to justice or in others where they have completed a particular stage.

While there is no one strategy to collect data, it is envisaged that the use of an in-person questionnaire, where individual users fill up a survey, or face-to-face interviews, where the users answer questions by an interviewer, will be adopted for the survey. Alternatively, a combination of face-to-face interviews with a web-based questionnaire might be adopted to ensure reliability and facilitate easier tabulation of information.[101] A detailed questionnaire is available in the appendix section that can be used for the purposes of collecting data for the framework.

Conclusion

This chapter has offered reflections on thinking of new ways of evaluating data on the legal system, and argues how, through the use of the capability approach in the JCF, one is able to study less examined aspects of legal systems, focusing on the needs, capabilities and challenges of people when they resolve their disputes. The capability approach acknowledges that people are complex and have different motivations. It thereby evaluates not just the resources that people have to engage in a legal system but also how they convert those resources into opportunities and realized outcomes. There is a need for more people-centred data to understand systemic challenges to the legal system. The informational asymmetry between people and legal systems needs to be bridged, and this chapter argues that if such a bridge is made, then justice data will be able to provide a more reflective understanding of access to justice.

---

[100] Frans L. Leeuw and Hans Schmeets, 'Research Designs: Raisons d'être, Examples and Criteria', in *Empirical Legal Research: A Guidance Book for Lawyers, Legislators and Regulators* (Cheltenham: Edward Elgar Publishing, 2016).

[101] For more on building a survey questionnaire, see Laura Beth Nielsen, 'The Need for Multi-Method Approaches in Empirical Legal Research', in *The Oxford Handbook of Empirical Legal Research*, ed. Peter Cane and Herbert M Kritzer, 951–975 (Oxford: Oxford University Press, 2010).

This chapter offers various elements of a people-centred justice capabilities framework and proposed a set of capabilities and indicators to measure access to justice in plural legal systems. It argues for a flexible, realization-centred approach that focuses on the capabilities of the individual, and it captures a plurality of experiences and interactions that are central to achieving access to justice, particularly when seen in light of the competing institutions, norms and values. This is relevant because, as has been argued in much of this book, it is important to capture how people in diverse legal contexts are able to resolve their disputes and analyse the methods they undertake to find an effective resolution for their problems. The chapter further undertakes a detailed examination of how to choose and identify a basic set of capabilities. In the appendix it also provides an example of a potential questionnaire as a model to be used in any jurisdictions for a pilot study.

To conclude, it has sought to demonstrate a framework for measuring justice that draws from plural, multi-locational ecologies of knowledge and aims to study how transcending justice barriers can be assessed through understanding the capabilities of people to navigate a legal system.

6

Conclusion

The aim of this book has been to understand the role of quantification in law and its impact on law and development, and judicial reform. It has sought to examine how different institutions shape the making and use of legal indicators. The relevance of this research is evident in that, at the 51st Session of the UN Statistical Commission in March 2020, the issue of indicators and data related to governance was on the agenda.[1] One of the items for discussion within this agenda was a report, which suggested developing a new indicator to measure access to justice and also articulated that any measurement must start from 'the perspective of people and communities'.[2]

This book aspired to shed light on the limitations of existing quantification tools, which measure the rule of law, and their lack of engagement with concepts and frameworks from plural legal worlds. In addition to a critique of existing frameworks of legal indicators, the book also offers an alternative framework for the measurement of the dispute resolution processes in plural legal orders. This expands beyond an

---

[1] At the 51st Session of the UN Statistical Commission in March 2020, the issue of indicators and data related to governance was on the agenda. See 'UNSD—United Nations 51st Statistical Commission', https://unstats.un.org/unsd/statcom/51st-session/documents/#background (accessed 26 April 2020).

[2] Praia City Group, *Handbook on Governance Statistics (Draft for Global Consultation)* (Praia City Group, 2020), https://unstats.un.org/unsd/statcom/51st-session/documents/Handbook_on_GovernanceStatistics-Draft_for_global_consultation-E.pdf (accessed 8 February 2022). The Praia group was set up to develop and compile international standards on different dimensions of governance in 2015.

institutional approach to the rule of law to a bottom-up, user-centred approach that places importance on the legal needs and challenges of people through adopting the wider concept of access to justice. Keeping in mind the interdisciplinary nature of the research, the book adopted a socio-legal approach to unpacking not just the frameworks behind rule of law indicators, but also how they impact the social worlds around them. In particular, the book has advanced the idea that we need to incorporate the rule of law as a concept within the more expansive idea of access to justice. This argument is made because access to justice is broader and more flexible as a concept and is able to include different narratives and life worlds.

Through the course of the book, I have examined the views of critics on how quantification simplifies the functioning and complexity with which disputes in legal systems are evaluated. Engaging with these critical challenges to the use of indicators, I have aimed to build a consolidated response to these criticisms by looking at how to build legal indicators that are cognizant of diverse epistemologies of knowledge around justice and the variety and diverse nature of how disputes are resolved in plural legal systems.

The argument developed in this book acknowledges that the development and use of indicators is a complex and contested process, especially with respect to issues of the efficacy, accountability and impartiality of these frameworks to measure how justice systems function across the world and at the same time being conscious of the material worlds in which disputes arise and are resolved.

In keeping with building legal indicators that acknowledge the contexts of the Global South, I have stressed the importance of examining legal pluralism and the existence of competing forums for dispute resolution, in addition to that of the State, when evaluating legal systems. In doing so, the book has argued for a new vocabulary to understand how legal systems function in plural contexts, and what users need when they are faced with competing options, which have different procedures and values.

In dealing with the pervasiveness of quantification, the book argues for a need to engage with new cosmologies of knowledge, particularly drawing from the Global South, which is expansive enough to accommodate this wider plurality. It argues for a new method of persistence with quantification, one that allows for the inclusion of new histories, experiences and categories into the development of legal indicators. The framework that this book proposes is based on examining justice capabilities, which is an understanding of the ways in which justice users are able to find resolutions for their disputes. This is a significant departure from the past, where the emphasis of legal indicators has been on how justice institutions function in terms of efficiency and managerial paradigms. This is, thereafter, followed by ways to reform these systems from an administrative and institutional perspective.

In this concluding chapter, I draw together the main findings and contributions of the book. The next section presents an account of the methodology used in this book; it engages with various critiques of indicators but argues for their necessity, and the importance of pluralizing them. The third section highlights the epistemological contribution in terms of the concepts, vocabularies and values that this book brings to the legal indicators debate. The final section highlights the substantive contribution of the book in constructing a justice capabilities framework that is grounded in examining access to justice for a plural legal system.

From critique to persistence of quantification

In the discussions on legal indicators, much has been written about the power of these tools to simplify, standardize and reduce complex situations into reductive and often superficial assessments.[3] This book has attempted to systemize these critiques by studying them through the lens of the 'meanings' that are embodied in indicators, the 'trust' that is embedded and

---

[3]   Debora Valentina Malito, Gaby Umbach and Nehal Bhuta (eds.), *The Palgrave Handbook of Indicators in Global Governance* (Cham: Springer, 2017); Kevin Davis, Angelina Fisher, Benedict Kingsbury and Sally Engle Merry (eds.), *Governance by Indicators: Global Power through Classification and Rankings* (Oxford: Oxford University Press, 2012); Sally Engle Merry, 'A World of Quantification', in *The Seductions of Quantification: Measuring Human Rights, Gender Violence, and Sex Trafficking*, 1–33 (Chicago: University of Chicago Press, 2016); Sally Engle Merry, Kevin E. Davis and Benedict Kingsbury (eds.), *The Quiet Power of Indicators: Measuring Governance, Corruption, and Rule of Law* (Cambridge: Cambridge University Press, 2015); Richard Rottenburg, Sally E. Merry, Sung-Joon Park and Johanna Mugler, *The World of Indicators: The Making of Governmental Knowledge through Quantification* (Cambridge: Cambridge University Press 2015); Alexander Cooley and Jack Snyder (eds.), *Ranking the World: Grading States as Tools of Global Governance* (Cambridge: Cambridge University Press 2015).; Theodore M. Porter, *Trust in Numbers: The Pursuit of Objectivity in Science and Public Life* (Princeton: Princeton University Press, 1996).

evoked through their narratives, and the influencing 'power' that they have to create different types of responses from stakeholders and institutions.[4] Focusing on the meanings, trust and power of indicators provided an understanding of how indicators and numbers build regimes of knowledge and sustain existing power structures and information asymmetries between those that produce and those that consume such information.

From this vantage point, it then became possible to build a response to the critiques, which, while critiquing the existing development of legal indicators, also offered pragmatic and persistent arguments for their use.[5] The reason for such pragmatism stems from the recognition of the pervasive use of indicators in policy-making and development work and, additionally, the fact that we live in a quantified society wherein decision-making is data driven at an economic, social and political level.[6] It follows, therefore, that in an environment where the articulation of problems and solutions is made in terms of numbers, we must develop an imagination for how to use and produce these numbers differently to serve the objectives of acknowledging and evaluating a heterogeneous and plural world, rather than the homogenous one often envisioned by existing indicators.

I have used several examples for how justice is articulated in terms of numbers. To reiterate this point, an example is the following extract from a UN Report in 2018 on Goal 16 of the Sustainable Development Goals, on promoting peaceful and inclusive societies and access to justice.

In 2014, the majority of detected trafficking victims were women and girls (71 per cent), and about 28 per cent were children (20 per cent girls and 8 per cent boys). Over 90 per cent of victims detected were trafficked

---

[4] Please refer to discussions in Chapter 2 for a consolidation of critiques of legal indicators.

[5] Chapter 4 of this book provides arguments for how legal indicators are pervasive in our understanding of legal systems, and there is a need to persist with them and pluralize the discourse to prevent it from becoming hegemonic.

[6] See Amartya Sen's contribution, 'Human Development and Mahbub Ul Haq', in the *Human Development Report 2020*, page xi, on why quantification and even a single simple index proved useful to deliver a message on quality of human life in contrast to the Gross Domestic Product figures. See Amartya Sen, 'Human Development and Mahbub Ul Haq', in *Human Development Report 2020: Human Development and the Anthropocene*, xi (New York: UNDP, 2020), http://hdr.undp.org/en/2020-report (accessed 17 December 2020).

for sexual exploitation or forced labour. The proportion of prisoners held in detention without being sentenced for a crime remained almost constant in the last decade: from 32 per cent in 2003–2005 to 31 per cent in 2014–2016.[7]

The framing of this assessment indicates a language of justice that is well entrenched in its quantitative form. It is for this reason that this book has made a case for persistence with quantification and advanced the argument that this act of persistence with quantification is a deeply political act because it allows the raising of questions about the kind of narratives that are erased or silenced when promoting ideas of a global law. Erasure, inattention and silence about other forms of diversities of legal systems will become apparent if practices of the rule of law without an acknowledgment of plurality continues to take place. In this light, I offer access to justice as a broader and more inclusive concept that can take into account the material ways in which legal systems function and people resolve their disputes, while including principles of the rule of law.

In order to counter the prevailing managerial approach that has dominated the development of indicators, this book has emphasized the need to look at law from below, to examine how the law is realized in its everyday manifestations and how its use impacts the lives of people. In engaging with a world that is beyond legal centralism, where the focus is purely on state institutions, this book has argued for an engagement with law's plurality, in terms of the procedures, structures and values that emerge when we begin to acknowledge that there is a diversity of law and legal systems beyond the state.

In order to do so, the idea of access to justice is developed as one that is people centred and which focuses on how justice users realize and resolve their legal disputes.[8] This engagement with the concept of access to justice seeks to reorient the discussion away from a preoccupation with how to reform institutions from the top down to instead ask *how can we understand*

---

[7]   United Nations, *The Sustainable Development Goals Report 2018* (New York: United Nations, 2018), https://unstats.un.org/sdgs/report/2018 (accessed 26 April 2020).

[8]   The Praia Group 2020 report serves as a timely affirmation of the need to move towards measuring access to justice, and in a people-centred manner as has been discussed and argued for in this book. See Praia City Group, *Handbook on Governance Statistics*.

how people make choices, and achieve justice outcomes that are based on their needs and capabilities. Justice capabilities is the concept of what people can do and what resources they have at their disposal, and whether they have the opportunity to utilize their freedoms to be able to access justice.[9] Through developing and offering a methodological path for the use of this concept, this book has emphasized a need to think beyond managerial notions of numbers and efficiencies when evaluating legal systems, which are often very technocratic. These indicators, I have argued, offer a limited imagination and cannot accommodate the sheer breadth of socio-political and cultural factors that impact the functioning of people and the institutions they access and frequent.[10] This drive to push for thinking in terms of access to justice has also emerged from the clear evidence that rule of law promotion as a top-down institutional approach is insufficient to understand law in its plurality.[11] We need a bottom-up approach that considers voices from the ground that represent the realities, cultures and contexts of where law and development reform are taking place, and how disputes are resolved in those contexts.

Plural epistemologies and designing for a changing world

A key element in the design of legal indicators has been the rule of law framework, which has determined how legal indicators have been defined and quantified, and used as tools in development work. In this book, I have argued that while the rule of law as a concept has value, it is an essentially contested concept, politically and ethically.[12] Through narrating the different forms that rule of law reform has taken, it is clear that the rule of law, as a statist, highly Eurocentric framework, requires substantial reframing to embrace the realities of a plural legal world. Can it take on another avatar?

The discussions on experimentalism and legal empowerment suggests a more grounded approach to rule of law reform in plural contexts where there is an emphasis on agency, participation and epistemic diversity in

---

9   Please refer to Chapter 5 for an exploration of a capability approach to access to justice.
10 Further discussions on managerialism are made in Chapter 4 of this book.
11 Please refer to the discussions on these matters in Chapter 3.
12 Please refer to Chapter 3 for discussions on the rule of law.

building projects and programmes. Further, as we have seen in discussions on the Sustainable Development Goals, there has been a move from a rule of law framework in favour of a more plural concept of access to justice.[13] This is recognition not of countries' unwillingness to engage with the rule of law and its institutions but a statement that there is a need to recognize its limited use when many countries do not have the institutional and cultural contexts to administer such a framework. It further suggests that the concept should be more representative of legal pluralism across the world.

In this book, I look at how to engage with legal indicators from the perspective and location of the Global South. This is to find a way to persist with quantification because of its ubiquity, but to do so in a way that displays a more plural and diverse mindset. Through an examination of the different approaches of persistence, from replication to transformation in local contexts of legal indicator frameworks from elsewhere, this book argues for the idea of co-production.[14] This idea requires one to draw on the knowledge of people from across the world and adopt a more collaborative approach when developing concepts, policies and frameworks around indicators. As opposed to other approaches, this method acknowledges the need to engage with different ecologies of knowledge if we are to build an indicator framework that can work for cross-country comparisons.

Much of this work is inspired by adopting a people-centred understanding of legal systems and legal needs. To do this, I have looked at a wide variety of legal needs surveys, ethnographic literature from cases of non-state justice systems (NSJS), and material on concepts of truth and reconciliation, *swaraj* or *ubuntu*, that emerge from communities in the Global South.[15] These departures are to emphasize that a plurality of sources is required when we engage with legal systems that are diverse

---

[13] Margaret L. Satterthwaite and Sukti Dhital, 'Measuring Access to Justice: Transformation and Technicality in SDG 16.3', *Global Policy* 10, no. 1 (2019): 96–109. Please also refer to the discussion in Chapter 3 on access to justice.

[14] Chapter 4 deals with the different ways in which we can persist with quantification from replication to transformation and co-production.

[15] In Chapter 4, I discuss the argument presented by de Sousa Santos, that for global social justice, you need global cognitive justice.

and multifaceted. In order for these diverse legal systems to be understood better, and in order for them to function better, we need to understand why people use them, why they give different institutions legitimacy and authority, and what triggers make people change their decisions between using one institution and the next. Doing so helps us question the universal nature of concepts that are shaped and justified through the collection and analysis of data and also acknowledge the complexity of how concepts emerge in reality.

In earlier chapters, I have argued that not only is data not neutral but the ways in which it is collected and processed are also not ideologically neutral. It is important to ask questions about the processes and methods that have led to the creation of data and the purposes for which it is used and examine the forms of power that emanate from this data, whether at international organizations or governments or people themselves.

In Chapter 4, through analysing the different sources of data that measure justice in India, I sought to examine the narratives that drive conceptions of justice in an Indian context.[16] The purpose of examining the narratives behind the data was to highlight the messages and priorities that are currently taking precedence in India when it comes to analysing, reforming and studying justice. By examining the data sources of judicial institutions, law commissions, academics and civil society organizations, I sought to produce an understanding of the narratives around data and justice in India. I argued that through the framing of the categories that conceptualize data in the Indian context, a particular imagination of institutions and managerialism is offered, which then influences reform and shapes policy in the judicial system and inspires academic work.

Further, as examples in this book have shown, legal indicators have politics associated with them, and this impacts the ways in which countries engage with each other.[17] Building a framework that is centred in a plural consciousness is a step towards recognizing diversity and ensuring that different countries are given representation in framing and developing

---

[16] Chapter 4 examines the sources of data from India and how this speaks to the managerial nature of legal indicators.

[17] Chapter 2 of this book examines the life cycle of indicators, and the impact they have and the reactions they extract from entities that they measure.

ways to measure justice, and are not merely recipients of such indicator frameworks.[18]

This book has highlighted not only a clear gap in the landscape of legal indicators around the world when they engage with plural legal systems, but it has also offered a way to rectify this limitation.

Substantive aspects of the JCF

In building a framework that counters managerialism and a technocratic approach to evaluation, I have sought to elaborate on the concept of access to justice by examining how the term 'access' signifies different attributes—networks, processes and ability—and how each of these attributes determines how an individual is able to attain justice. A common theme in this book is to move beyond measurement of justice as an institution-focused approach and instead make it realization focused, inspired by the work of Amartya Sen.[19]

To develop this alternative framework for measurement of justice, I deconstructed the resolution of disputes in terms of a path to justice of an individual to constitute stages: stage 1 is to understand the nature of the dispute, stage 2 is to negotiate and react to it, stage 3 is to navigate the procedure, and stage 4 is the enforce the decision that emerges from the dispute resolution process. As this framework recognizes that dispute resolution systems are designed differently and are inherently plural in nature, it focuses less on the attributes of the institutions and relies more on understanding what people's needs are when they seek to resolve a dispute.

The capability approach is adopted as a conceptual framework for designing legal indicators because it offers a language that focuses on people and their experiences, and therefore offers an alternative to the existing managerial legal indicator frameworks. It is not grounded in a particular legal tradition and, instead, can be adapted to reflect the plurality of expressions in legal systems that this project seeks to highlight. Further, the framework is iterative by design, which means that it is not built for perpetuity but is open to change through deliberative processes.

---

[18] Chapters 4 and 5 of this book examine how to build a legal indicator that considers the intricacies of concepts and values of a plural legal system.

[19] Chapters 4 and 5 speak in detail about this approach.

The proposed Justice Capabilities Framework (JCF) has eight basic capabilities aligned to the stages described above: the capabilities to name the injury and choose how to proceed at the stage of understanding the contours of the dispute (stage 1); the capabilities to strategize and find value when negotiating the details of the dispute (stage 2); the capabilities to relate and share when deciding on a process (stage 3); and the capabilities to enforce and belong when managing a resolution to the dispute (stage 4). These eight basic capabilities are central to navigating a dispute resolution process. Twenty-four indicators are then identified that correspond to these eight basic capabilities. A template to collect this alternative data is offered in the appendix.

This JCF, based on capabilities, seeks to interact with a plurality of knowledge centres and with different ecologies of knowledge that capture resistances, struggles and sufferings of people as they resolve their disputes.[20] It is a clear departure from other indicator frameworks because it fundamentally acknowledges the plurality that exists in legal systems around the world. To deepen this acknowledgment, it is essential to think of law in its cosmopolitan form, to move beyond common sites of knowledge formation and common influences of international law, and instead explore law from below.[21]

It is also envisaged that such an instrument will induce stakeholders to suggest informed reform and allow both users and suppliers of justice

---

[20] For more on this please refer to Chapter 5. See Boaventura de Sousa Santos, 'Introduction: Why the Epistemologies of the South? Artisanal Paths for Artisanal Futures', in *The End of the Cognitive Empire: The Coming of Age of Epistemologies of the South*, 1–35 (Durham: Duke University Press, 2018); Luis Eslava and Sundhya Pahuja, 'Beyond the (Post)Colonial: TWAIL and the Everyday Life of International Law', *Verfassung und Recht n Übersee/Law and Politics in Africa, Asia and Latin America* 45, no. 2 (2012): 195–221; Siddharth Peter de Souza, 'Towards a User-Centered Engagement with Law', *Südasien-Chronik/South Asia Chronicle* 2018, no. 8 (2019): 238–291, https://edoc.hu-berlin.de/handle/18452/20489 (accessed 31 July 2019).

[21] See also Chapters 3 and 4 of this book, which cover these issues in detail. Further, please also look at Balakrishnan Rajagopal, 'Introduction', in *International: Development, Social Movements and Third World Resistance*, 1–6 (Cambridge: Cambridge University Press, 2003); Siddharth Peter de Souza, 'Beyond Best Practices: How to Use Design Thinking in Rule of Law Promotion', Peace Lab Blog, 2019, https://peacelab.blog/2019/03/beyond-best-practices-how-to-use-design-thinking (accessed 29 August 2019).

to respond and adapt to benchmarks that are required in order to improve the quality of access and opportunity within the justice system. The results from the framework will also be able to show variability within similar geographical contexts.

The JCF will be able to give an overall picture of the challenges for access to justice when negotiating a plural legal landscape such as that of India. It will provide an outlook on justice experiences and user stories across the plural systems that exist in the country.

Moving forward

This book sought to combine literature from law, anthropology, politics and sociology. It does so by engaging with literature that is, on one hand, doctrinal and institutional in nature and, on the other hand, is shaped through ethnographic reflections and policy interventions. By doing so, the goal of the book is to produce a dialogue between academics and practitioners. It adopts a plural understanding of the law, particularly as it seeks to amplify understandings and epistemologies of knowledge that exist in the Global South.

Looking ahead, a key future course of the research from the book is to find ways to engage with policy makers to validate, adapt and use the indicator framework proposed in this book. This will help to assess how different kinds of data can be collected and used to understand the nature of legal systems around the world, and why people make the choices that they do in seeking justice. In building a framework that is responsive, it is also hoped that the methodological, epistemological and substantive contributions of this project will spark future debate into how to conceive indicators that are reflective and conscious of people, the politics of knowledge, and the impact this has on building legal indicators.

Appendix

Sample Questionnaire

This questionnaire is an attempt to trace how the respondent has made the journey through four stages in the search for access to justice that includes understanding a dispute, negotiating a solution, navigating a procedure and obtaining a resolution. The purpose of this questionnaire is to evaluate and record the experiences of the justice user in using a plural justice system. It seeks to showcase the kind of data that will be collected using this method.

This questionnaire is about eight main capabilities:

1 The capacity to name a dispute and acknowledge an injury
2 The capacity to choose how to resolve a dispute
3 The capacity to strategize in a negotiation
4 The capacity to feel and be valued during the negotiation
5 The capacity to relate to the manner of the procedures being used
6 The capacity to share during the procedure
7 The capacity to be enforce a resolution
8 The capacity to belong after a decision at the time of resolution

The questionnaire is anonymous and confidential.

Profile of the user

Field	Categories			
Gender				
Age				
Marital status	Single	Married	Widowed	Separated
Education level	No education	Primary school (class 8)	High school (class 12)	Graduate
Employment	Self-employed		Full-time employed	Unemployed
Income				
Native language				
Language of the forum				

Profile of the case

Field	Categories			
1. Type of the dispute	Describe the type of case depending on whether it was related to family, neighbours, property, work, crime, finance, religion or some other occurrence.			
2. Duration of the dispute	From the time it occurred to when it was resolved			
3. Result of the dispute	Consensus	Enforced	Compromise	Other
4. Money and time spent on the dispute	Money		Time	
5. Details of the resolution				

Sr. No	Questions	Unable	Partially able	Able	Not Applicable
1.	Were you able to recognize the nature of the injury?				
2.	Were you able to know how to proceed with remedying the injury?				
3.	Were you aware of the consequences of decisions taken?				
4	Were you able to determine the best dispute forum for addressing the injury?				
5	Were you able to act freely to resolve the dispute without bodily or mental injury?				
6	Were you able to have access to the forum keeping in mind cost and time?				
7	Were you able to think freely about the potential solutions?				
8	Were you able to deliberate on and bargain over any decisions between parties?				
9	Were you able to join the forum for resolution without coercion?				
10	Were you able to participate and be heard during a dispute resolution process?				
11	Were you able to ensure equal treatment in any resolution and ensure reciprocity?				
12	Were you able to speak about the outcomes of such a resolution?				
13	Were you able to know the procedures of the forum?				

Sr. No	Questions	Unable	Partially able	Able	Not Applicable
14	Were you able to understand how a resolution would play out and predict certain outcomes?				
15	Were you able to feel comfortable and familiar during the procedures?				
16	Were you able to make legal needs known?				
17	Were you able to contest any unjustified decision such as lack of information or persons appointed to adjudicate the dispute?				
18	Were you able to make known any anxieties about the nature of the process and its outcomes?				
19	Were you able to enforce the resolution of a forum?				
20	Were you able to accept the decision without fear or sanction?				
21	Were you able to settle or find compromises that are satisfactory?				
22	Were you able to do truth sharing and engage in reconciliation?				
23	Were you able to participate in the community after the dispute concluded, socially and culturally?				
24	Were you able to access basic necessities like food, clothing, shelter and jobs?				

Bibliography

Adcock, Robert, and David Collier. 'Measurement Validity: A Shared Standard for Qualitative and Quantitative Research'. *American Political Science Review* 95, no. 3 (September 2001): 529–546.

Adelman, Sam, and Abdul Paliwala. 'Voicing Suffering and Commitment of the Intellectual'. *Jindal Global Law Review* 9 (2018): 315–325.

Adler, Daniel, and Sokbunthoeun So. 'Towards Equity in Development When the Law Is Not the Law: Reflections on Legal Pluralism in Practice'. In *Legal Pluralism and Development: Scholars and Practitioners in Dialogue*, edited by Brian Z. Tamanaha, Caroline Sage and Michael Woolcock, 83–92. Cambridge: Cambridge University Press, 2012.

Agrast, Mark David, Juan Carlos Botero and Alejandro Ponce. *The World Justice Project: Rule of Law Index*. Washington, DC: World Justice Project, 2010. https://worldjusticeproject.org/sites/default/files/WJP_Rule_of_Law_Index_2010_Report.pdf. Accessed 5 July 2020.

Albiston, Catherine R., Lauren B. Edelman and Joy Milligan. 'The Dispute Tree and the Legal Forest'. *Annual Review of Law and Social Science* 10, no. 1 (2014): 105–131.

Albiston, Catherine R., and Rebecca L. Sandefur. 'Expanding the Empirical Study of Access to Justice'. *Wisconsin Law Review* 2013, no. 1 (2013): 101–120.

Albrecht, Peter, Helene Maria Kyed, Deborah Isser and Erica Harper, eds. *Perspectives on Involving Non-State and Customary Actors in Justice and Security Reform*. Rome: IDLO and DIIS, 2011.

Albrecht, Peter, and Helena Maria Kyed. 'Introduction: Non-State and Customary Actor in Developing Programs'. In *Perspectives on Involving Non-State and Customary Actors in Justice and Security Reform*, edited by Peter

Albrecht, Helene Maria Kyed, Deborah Isser and Erica Harper, 3–22. Rome: IDLO and DIIS, 2011.

Alkire, Sabina. 'Why the Capability Approach?' *Journal of Human Development* 6, no. 1 (2005): 115–135.

———. 'Choosing Dimensions: The Capability Approach and Multidimensional Poverty'. Chronic Poverty Research Centre Working Paper No. 88, 1 August 2007. https://papers.ssrn.com/sol3/papers.cfm?abstract_id=1646411. Accessed 17 February 2022.

Alkire, Sabina, and Séverine Deneulin. 'The Human Development and Capability Approach'. In *An Introduction to the Human Development and Capability Approach: Freedom and Agency*, edited by Séverine Deneulin and Lila Shahani, 22–48 London: Earthscan and IDRC, 2009.

Alkire, Sabina, Mozaffar Qizilbash and Flavio Comim. 'Introduction'. In *The Capability Approach: Concepts, Measures and Applications*, edited by Flavio Comim, Mozaffar Qizilbash and Sabina Alkire, 1–25. Cambridge: Cambridge University Press, 2008.

Alsop, Ruth, Mette Frost Bertelsen and Jeremy Holland. 'Empowerment: An Analytic Framework'. In *Empowerment in Practice: From Analysis to Implementation*, 9–28. Washington, DC: The World Bank, 2006.

Alston, Philip. 'Does the Past Matter? On the Origins of Human Rights'. *Harvard Law Review* 126, no. 7 (2013): 2043–2081.

Altmann, Philipp. 'Plurinationality and Interculturality in Ecuador: Indigenous Movement and the Development of Political Concepts'. *Iberoamericana – Nordic Journal of Latin American and Caribbean Studies* 43, nos. 1–2 (2014): 47–66.

Amariles, David Restrepo. 'Legal Indicators, Global Law and Legal Pluralism: An Introduction'. *The Journal of Legal Pluralism and Unofficial Law* 47, no. 1 (2015): 9–21.

———. 'Transnational Legal Indicators: The Missing Link in a New Era of Law and Development'. In *Law and Policy in Latin America*, edited by Pedro Borges Fortes, Larissa Boratti, Andres Palacios Lleras and Tom Gerald Daly, 95–111. London: Palgrave Macmillan, 2016.

———. 'Supping with the Devil? Indicators and the Rise of Managerial Rationality in Law'. *International Journal of Law in Context* 13, no. 4 (2017): 465–484.

American Bar Association. *Access to Justice Assessment Tool: A Guide to Analyzing Access to Justice for Civil Society Organizations*. ABA, 2012. https://www.americanbar.org/content/dam/aba/directories/roli/misc/

aba_roli_access_to_justice_assessment_manual_2012.authcheckdam.pdf. Accessed 19 April 2020.

Amnesty International. *Fair Trial Manual*. London: Amnesty International Publications, 2014.

Amsler, Lisa Blomgren, Janet Martinez and Stephanie E. Smith. *Dispute System Design: Preventing, Managing, and Resolving Conflict*. Stanford, CA: Stanford University Press, 2020.

Anderson, Elizabeth. 'Justifying the Capabilities Approach to Justice'. In *Measuring Justice: Primary Goods and Capabilities*, edited by Harry Brighouse and Ingrid Robeyns, 81–100. Cambridge: Cambridge University Press, 2010.

Andrews, Edmund L. 'The Science Behind Cambridge Analytica: Does Psychological Profiling Work?' Stanford Graduate School of Business, 12 April 2018. https://www.gsb.stanford.edu/insights/science-behind-cambridge-analytica-does-psychological-profiling-work. Accessed 13 September 2019.

Andrews, Matt, Lant Pritchett and Michael Woolcock. 'Escaping Capability Traps through Problem-Driven Iterative Adaptation (PDIA)'. Working paper 299, CGDEV, 22 June 2012. https://www.cgdev.org/publication/escaping-capability-traps-through-problem-driven-iterative-adaptation-pdia-working-paper. Accessed 7 May 2020.

Angwin, Julia, Jeff Larson, Surya Mattu and Lauren Kirchner. 'Machine Bias'. *ProPublica*, 23 May 2016. https://www.propublica.org/article/machine-bias-risk-assessments-in-criminal-sentencing. Accessed 16 February 2018.

Arajärvi, Noora Johanna. 'The Rule of Law in the 2030 Agenda'. KFG Working Paper Series, No. 9, Berlin Potsdam Research Group "The International Rule of Law – Rise or Decline?", 2017. https://www.ssrn.com/abstract=2992016 Accessed 10 April 2020.

Arora, Payal. *The Next Billion Users: Digital Life beyond the West*. Cambridge, MA: Harvard University Press, 2019.

Asia Foundation. 'Tara Bandu: Its Role and Use in Community Conflict Prevention in Timor-Leste'. Asia Foundation, 2013. https://asiafoundation.org/publication/tara-bandu-its-role-and-use-in-community-conflict-prevention-in-timor-leste/. Accessed 9 April 2020.

Avila, Keymer. 'Use of Lethal Force in Latin America: A Sinister Political Priority'. *openDemocracy*, 2019. https://www.opendemocracy.net/en/demo craciaabierta/uso-de-la-fuerza-letal-en-am%C3%A9rica-latina-una-siniestra -prioridad-pol%C3%ADtica-en/. Accessed 13 September 2019.

Banakar, Reza. *Normativity in Legal Sociology: Methodological Reflections on Law and Regulation in Late Modernity*. Cham: Springer, 2014.

Banakar, Reza, and Max Travers. 'Introduction to Theory and Method in Socio-Legal Research'. Social Science Research Network, SSRN Scholarly Paper ID 1511112, 2005. https://papers.ssrn.com/abstract=1511112. Accessed 18 February 2018.

Barendrecht, Maurits. 'In Search of Microjustice: Five Basic Elements of a Dispute System'. Tilburg University Legal Studies Working Paper No. 02/2009, 2009. http://www.ssrn.com/abstract=1334644. Accessed 2 September 2019.

——. 'Understanding the Market for Justice'. Tilburg University Legal Studies Working Paper No. 009/2009, 2009. http://www.ssrn.com/abstract=1416841. Accessed 10 October 2019.

Barendrecht, Maurits, Peter Kamminga and Jin Ho Verdonschot. 'Priorities for the Justice System: Responding to the Most Urgent Legal Problems of Individuals'. TISCO Working Paper, 2008. https://papers.ssrn.com/abstract=1090885. Accessed 7 August 2019.

Baruah, Padmini, Shruthi Naik, Surya Prakash B. S. and Kishore Mandyam. 'Paths to Justice: Surveying Judicial and Non-Judicial Dispute Resolution in India'. In *Approaches to Justice: A Report by Daksh*, edited by Shruti Vidyasagar, Harish Narasappa and Ramya Sridhar Tirumalai. Lucknow: Eastern Book Company, 2018. https://dakshindia.org/Daksh_Justice_in_India/12_chapter_02.xhtml#_idTextAnchor011. Accessed 20 February 2022.

Basu, Kaushik. 'India Can Hide Unemployment Data, but Not the Truth'. *New York Times*, 1 February 2019. https://www.nytimes.com/2019/02/01/opinion/india-unemployment-jobs-blackout.html. Accessed 13 September 2019.

Baxi, Pratiksha. 'Access to Justice and Rule-of (Good) Law: The Cunning of Judicial Reform in India'. *Indian Journal of Human Development* 2, no. 2 (2008): 279–302.

Baxi, Upendra. 'From Human Rights to the Right to Be Human: Some Heresies'. *India International Centre Quarterly* 13, no. 3/4 (December 1986): 185–200.

——. '"The State's Emissary": The Place of Law in Subaltern Studies'. In *Subaltern Studies VII: Writings on South Asian History and Society*, edited by Partha Chatterjee and Gyanendra Pandey, 247–262. New Delhi: Oxford University Press, 1992.

——. 'Voices of Suffering and the Future of Human Rights'. *Transnational Law and Contemporary Problems* 8 (Fall 1998):125–169.

———. 'Constitutionalism as a Site of State Formative Practices'. *Cardozo Law Review* 21 (1999): 1183–1210.

———. 'The Rule of Law in India'. *Sur - Revista Internacional De Direitos Humanos* 6 (2007): 7–27. http://socialsciences.scielo.org/scielo.php?script=sci_abstract &pid=S1806-64452007000100001&lng=en&nrm=iso&tlng=en. Accessed 2 June 2021.

———. 'Access, Development and Distributive Justice: Access Problems of the "Rural" Population'. *Journal of the Indian Law Institute* 18, no. 3 (1976): 375–430.

Beebeejaun, Yasminah, Catherine Durose, James Rees, Joanna Richardson and Liz Richardson. '"Beyond Text": Exploring Ethos and Method in Co-Producing Research with Communities'. *Community Development Journal* 49, no. 1 (January 2014): 37–53.

Benda-Beckmann, Franz von. 'Who's Afraid of Legal Pluralism?' *The Journal of Legal Pluralism and Unofficial Law* 34, no. 47 (2002): 37–82.

———. 'The Multiple Edges of Law: Dealing with Legal Pluralism in Development Practice'. In *The World Bank Legal Review: Law, Equity and Development*, edited by Caroline Mary Sage and Michael Woolcock, vol. 2, 51–86. Washington, DC: The World Bank, 2006.

Benda-Beckmann, Keebet von, and Bertram Turner. 'Legal Pluralism, Social Theory, and the State'. *Journal of Legal Pluralism and Unofficial Law* 50, no. 3 (2018): 255–274.

Benda-Beckmannn, Franz von, and Keebet von Benda-Beckmannn. 'The Dynamics of Change and Continuity in Plural Legal Orders'. *The Journal of Legal Pluralism and Unofficial Law* 38, nos. 53–54 (2006): 1–44.

Bennett, Luke, and Antonia Layard. 'Legal Geography: Becoming Spatial Detectives'. *Geography Compass* 9, no. 7 (2015): 406–422.

Berg, Louis-Alexandre, and Deval Desai. 'Background Paper: Overview on the Rule of Law and Sustainable Development for the Global Dialogue on Rule of Law and the Post-2015 Development Agenda'. UNDP, 2013. https:// tijpublicforum.org/wp-content/uploads/2018/06/4-20130801-READING_ Global-Dialogue-Background-Paper-Rule-of-Law-and-Sustainable-Developme....pdf. Accessed 22 February 2022.

Berg, Louis-Alexandre, Deborah Isser D and Doug Porter. 'Beyond Deficit and Dysfunction: Three Questions toward Just Development in Fragile and Conflict-Affected Settings'. In *The International Rule of Law Movement: A Crisis of Legitimacy and the Way Forward*, edited by David Marshall, 267–294. Cambridge, MA: Harvard Law School, 2014.

Berger, Tobias. 'Linked in Translation: International Donors and Local Fieldworkers as Translators of Global Norms'. *Third World Thematics: A TWQ Journal* 2, no. 5 (2017): 606–620.

———. 'The "Global South" as a Relational Category: Global Hierarchies in the Production of Law and Legal Pluralism'. *Third World Quarterly* 42, no. 9 (2020): 2001–2017.

Bernstorff, Jochen von, and Philipp Dann. 'The Battle for International Law: An Introduction'. In *The Battle for International Law: South-North Perspectives on the Decolonization Era*, edited by Jochen von Bernstorff and Philipp Dann, 1–21. Oxford: Oxford University Press, 2019.

Bhattacharya, Bikash Kumar. 'Timor-Leste: Maubere Tribes Revive Customary Law to Protect the Ocean'. *Mongabay Environmental News*, 26 October 2018. https://news.mongabay.com/2018/10/timor-leste-maubere-tribes-revive-customary-law-to-protect-the-ocean/. Accessed 9 April 2020.

———. 'Timor-Leste: Q&A with a Maubere Fisherman on Reviving Depleted Fisheries'. *Mongabay Environmental News*, 31 October 2018. https://news.mongabay.com/2018/10/timor-leste-qa-with-a-maubere-fisherman-on-reviving-depleted-fisheries/. Accessed 22 April 2020.

———. 'Timor-Leste: With Sacrifice and Ceremony, Tribe Sets Eco Rules' (*Mongabay Environmental News*, 8 November 2018) <https://news.mongabay.com/2018/11/timor-leste-with-sacrifice-and-ceremony-tribe-sets-eco-rules/. Accessed 22 April 2020.

Bhuta, Nehal, Debora Valentina Malito and Gaby Umbach. 'Introduction: Of Numbers and Narratives—Indicators in Global Governance and the Rise of a Reflexive Indicator Culture'. In *The Palgrave Handbook of Indicators in Global Governance*, edited by Debora Valentina Malito, Gaby Umbach and Nehal Bhuta, 1–29. Cham: Springer, 2017.

Blomley, Nicholas. 'From "What?" To "So What?": Law and Geography in Retrospect'. In *Law and Geography*, edited by Jane Holder and Carolyn Harrison, 8–14. Oxford: Oxford University Press, 2003.

BMZ. 'Rule of Law: Protecting Citizens from Arbitrary Rule by the State'. Federal Ministry for Economic Cooperation and Development.http://www.bmz.de/en/issues/rule_of_law/hintergrund/index.html. Accessed 10 April 2020.

Boje, David Michael. 'Narrative Analysis'. In *Encyclopedia of Case Study Research*, edited by Albert Mills, Gabrielle Durepos and Elden Wiebe, 591–594. Thousand Oaks, CA: SAGE Publications, 2012. http://methods.sagepub.com/reference/encyc-of-case-study-research/n220.xml. Accessed 19 February 2022.

Boje, David Michael, and Grace Ann Rosile. 'Storytelling'. In *Encyclopedia of Case Study Research*, edited by Albert Mills, Gabrielle Durepos and Elden Wiebe, 899–901. Thousand Oaks, CA: SAGE Publications, 2012. http://methods.sagepub.com/reference/encyc-of-case-study-research/n331.xml. Accessed 28 August 2019.

Maldonado, Daniel Bonilla. 'Introduction: Toward a Constitutionalism of the Global South'. In *Constitutionalism of the Global South: The Activist Tribunals of India, South Africa, and Colombia*, edited by Daniel Bonilla Maldonado, 1–36. Cambridge: Cambridge University Press, 2013.

———. 'The Political Economy of Legal Knowledge'. In *Constitutionalism in the Americas*, edited by Daniel Bonilla Maldonado and Colin Crawford, 29–78. Cheltenham: Edward Elgar, 2018.

Botero, Juan Carlos, and Alejandro Ponce. 'Measuring the Rule of Law'. Social Science Research Network, SSRN Scholarly Paper ID 1966257, 2011. https://papers.ssrn.com/abstract=1966257. Accessed 7 May 2020.

Bowker, Geoffrey C., and Susan Leigh Star. 'Introduction: To Classify Is Human'. In *Sorting Things Out: Classification and Its Consequences*, 1–32. Cambridge, MA: MIT Press, 2000.

Brandsen, Taco, and Marlies Honingh. 'Distinguishing Different Types of Coproduction: A Conceptual Analysis Based on the Classical Definitions'. *Public Administration Review* 76 (2016): 427–435.

Brinks, Daniel M. 'Access to What? Legal Agency and Access to Justice for Indigenous Peoples in Latin America'. *Journal of Development Studies* 55, no. 3 (2019): 348–365.

Broome, André, Alexandra Homolar and Matthias Kranke. 'Bad Science: International Organizations and the Indirect Power of Global Benchmarking'. *European Journal of International Relations* 24, no. 3 (2018): 514–539.

Broome, André, and Joel Quirk. 'Governing the World at a Distance: The Practice of Global Benchmarking'. *Review of International Studies* 41, no. 5 (2015): 819–841.

———. 'The Politics of Numbers: The Normative Agendas of Global Benchmarking'. *Review of International Studies* 41, no. 5 (2015): 813–818.

Brown, Mark. '"An Unqualified Human Good"? On Rule of Law, Globalization, and Imperialism'. *Law and Social Inquiry* 43, no. 4 (2018): 1391–1426.

Bühlmann, Marc, Wolfgang Merkel, Lisa Müller and Bernhard Weßels. 'The Democracy Barometer: A New Instrument to Measure the Quality of Democracy and Its Potential for Comparative Research'. *European Political Science* 11 (2012): 519–536.

Burchardt, Tania, and Polly Vizard. '"Operationalizing" the Capability Approach as a Basis for Equality and Human Rights Monitoring in Twenty-First-Century Britain'. *Journal of Human Development and Capabilities* 12, no. 1 (2011): 91–119.

Burchi, Francesco, Pasquale De Muro and Eszter Kollar. 'Which Dimensions Should Matter for Capabilities? A Constitutional Approach'. *Ethics and Social Welfare* 8, no. 3 (2014): 233–247.

Cadena, Marisol de la, and Mario Blaser. 'Pluriverse: Proposals for a World of Many Worlds', In *A World of Many Worlds*, 1–22. Durham: Duke University Press, 2018.

Canadian Bar Association. 'Access to Justice Metrics: A Discussion Paper'. 2013. http://www.cba.org/CBAMediaLibrary/cba_na/images/Equal%20 Justice%20-%20Microsite/PDFs/Access_to_Justice_Metrics.pdf. Accessed 28 September 2018.

———. *Reaching Equal Justice: An Invitation to Envision and Act*. Ottawa: Canadian Bar Association, 2013.

Cappelletti, Mauro. 'Alternative Dispute Resolution Processes within the Framework of the World-Wide Access-to-Justice Movement'. *The Modern Law Review* 56, no. 3 (May 1993): 282–296.

Cappelletti, Mauro, and Bryant Garth. 'Access to Justice as a Focus of Research Foreword'. *Windsor Yearbook of Access to Justice* 1 (1981): ix–xxv.

Carothers, Thomas. 'The Rule of Law Revival'. *Foreign Affairs*, 1998. https://www.foreignaffairs.com/articles/1998-03-01/rule-law-revival. Accessed 13 August 2018.

———. *Aiding Democracy Abroad: The Learning Curve*. Washington, DC: Carnegie Endowment, 1999.

———. 'The Problem of Knowledge'. In *Promoting the Rule of Law Abroad: The Problem of Knowledge*, edited by Thomas Carothers, 15–30. (Washington, DC: Carnegie Endowment. 2006.

Chan, Anita. *Networking Peripheries: Technological Futures and the Myth of Digital Universalism*. Cambridge, MA: MIT Press, 2013.

Chandra, Aparna. 'Indian Judiciary and Access to Justice: An Appraisal of Approaches'. In *State of the Indian Judiciary*, edited by Harish Narasappa and Shruti Vidyasagar. Lucknow: Eastern Book Company, 2016. https://dakshindia.org/state-of-the-indian-judiciary/33_chapter_18.html#_idTextAnchor412 (accessed 20 February 2022).

Chandra, Aparna, William H. J. Hubbard and Sital Kalantry. 'The Supreme Court of India: A People's Court?'. *Indian Law Review* 1, no. 2 (2017): 145–181.

Chandra, Aparna, and Rishabh Sharma. 'The Indian Judicial System by Numbers (Part I)'. *Daksh*, 30 August 2016. http://dakshindia.org/indian-judicial-system-numbers-part/ Accessed 12 August 2019.

———. 'The Indian Judicial System by Numbers (Part II)'. *Daksh*, 8 September 2016. http://dakshindia.org/indian-judicial-system-numbers-part-ii/. Accessed 12 August 2019.

Chatterjee, Promit, and Sreerupa Chowdhury. 'A Capabilities Approach to Access to Justice'. *Journal of Indian Law and Society* 20, no. 5 (Winter 2012): 107–129.

Cheesman, Nick. 'Rule-of-Law Ethnography'. *Annual Review of Law and Social Science* 14, no. 1 (2018): 167–184.

Chiba, Masaji. 'Other Phases of Legal Pluralism in the Contemporary World'. *Ratio Juris* 11 (1998): 228.

Chimni, B. S. 'Third World Approaches to International Law: A Manifesto'. *International Community Law Review* 8, no. 1 (2006): 3–27.

CLEP and UNDP. *Making the Law Work for Everyone, Vol. 1: Report of the Commission on Legal Empowerment of the Poor*. New York: CLEP and UNDP, 2008. https://www.un.org/ruleoflaw/blog/document/making-the-law-work-for-everyone-vol-1-report-of-the-commission-on-legal-empowerment-of-the-poor/. Accessed 7 August 2019.

Comim, Flavio. 'Measuring Capabilities'. In *The Capability Approach: Concepts, Measures and Applications*, edited by Flavio Comim, Mozaffar Qizilbash and Sabina Alkire, 157–200. Cambridge: Cambridge University Press, 2008.

Connolly, Brynna. 'Non-State Justice Systems and the State: Proposals for a Recognition Typology'. *Connecticut Law Review* 38, no. 2 (2005): 239–294.

Constitute. 'Bolivia (Plurinational State of)'s Constitution of 2009'. Constitute. https://www.constituteproject.org/constitution/Bolivia_2009?lang=en. Accessed 10 December 2020.

Cooley, Alexander. 'The Emerging Politics of International Rankings and Ratings'. In *Ranking the World: Grading States as a Tool of Global Governance*, edited by Alexander Cooley and Jack Snyder, 1–38. Cambridge: Cambridge University Press, 2015.

Costanza-Chock, Sasha. *Design Justice: Community-Led Practices to Build the Worlds We Need*. Cambridge, MA: MIT Press, 2020.

Cott, Donna Lee Van. 'A Political Analysis of Legal Pluralism in Bolivia and Colombia'. *Journal of Latin American Studies* 32, no. 1 (February 2000): 207–234.

Cotterrell, Roger. 'Why Must Legal Ideas Be Interpreted Sociologically?' *Journal of Law and Society* 25, no. 2 (June 1998): 171–192. https://onlinelibrary.wiley.com/doi/abs/10.1111/1467-6478.00086. Accessed 8 February 2022.

Creutzfeldt, Naomi, Marc Mason and Kirsten McConnachie. *Routledge Handbook of Socio-Legal Theory and Methods*. Oxon: Routledge, 2019.

DANIDA. 'Informal Justice Systems'. 2009. http://um.dk/en/~/media/UM/English-site/Documents/Danida/Activities/Strategic/Human%20rights%20and%20democracy/Human%20rights/Informal%20Justice%20Systems%20final%20print.jpgH. Accessed 5 November 2020.

Danish Institute for Human Rights. 'Informal Justice Systems: Charting a Course for Human Rights-Based Engagement'. UNDP, UNICEF and UN Women, 2013. http://www.undp.org/content/undp/en/home/librarypage/democratic-governance/access_to_justiceandruleoflaw/informal-justice-systems.html. Accessed 7 December 2017.

Dann, Philipp. 'Introduction'. In *The Law of Development Cooperation: A Comparative Analysis of the World Bank, the EU and Germany*, 1–32. Cambridge: Cambridge University Press, 2013.

———. 'Institutional Law and Development Governance: An Introduction'. *Law and Development Review* 12, no. 2 (2019): 537–560.

Dann, Philipp, Michael Riegner and Maxim Bönnemann. 'The Southern Turn in Comparative Constitutional Law: An Introduction'. SSRN Electronic Journal, 2020. https://www.ssrn.com/abstract=3553852. Accessed 16 April 2020.

Dann, Philipp, and Arun K. Thiruvengadam. 'Comparing Constitutional Democracy in the European Union and India: An Introduction'. In *Democratic Constitutionalism in India and the European Union: Comparing the Law of Democracy in Continental Polities*, edited by Philipp Dann and Arun K. Thiruvengadam, 1–11. Cheltenham: Edward Elgar Publishing, 2021.

Darian-Smith, Eve. 'Reimagining Legal Geographies'. In *Laws and Societies in Global Contexts: Contemporary Approaches*, 167–242. Cambridge: Cambridge University Press, 2013.

———. 'Introduction: Sociolegal Scholarship in the Twenty-First Century'. In *Laws and Societies in Global Contexts: Contemporary Approaches*, 1–38. Cambridge: Cambridge University Press, 2013.

———. 'Producing Legal Knowledge'. In *Laws and Societies in Global Contexts: Contemporary Approaches*, 97–166. Cambridge: Cambridge University Press, 2013.

———. 'Mismeasuring Humanity: Examining Indicators through a Critical Global Studies Perspective'. *New Global Studies* 10, no. 1 (2016): 73–99.

Davies, William. 'Spirits of Neoliberalism: "Competitiveness" and "Wellbeing" Indicators as Rival Orders of Worth'. In *The World of Indicators: The Making of Governmental Knowledge through Quantification*, edited by Richard Rottenburg, Sally E. Merry, Sung-Joon Park and Johanna Mugler. Cambridge: Cambridge University Press, 2015.

Davis, Kevin, Angelina Fisher, Benedict Kingsbury and Sally Engle Merry, eds. *Governance by Indicators: Global Power through Classification and Rankings*. Oxford: Oxford University Press, 2012.

Davis, Kevin E., Benedict Kingsbury, and Sally Engle Merry. 'Indicators as a Technology of Global Governance'. *Law and Society Review* 46 (2012): 71–104.

Davis, Kevin E., Benedict Kingsbury and Sally Engle Merry. 'Introduction: Global Governance by Indicators'. In *Governance by Indicators: Global Power through Quantification and Rankings*, edited by Kevin E. Davis, Angelina Fisher, Benedict Kingsbury and Sally Engle Merry, 3–28. Oxford: Oxford University Press, 2012.

———. 'Introduction: The Local-Global Life of Indicators: Law, Power, and Resistance'. In *The Quiet Power of Indicators: Measuring Governance, Corruption, and Rule of Law*, edited by Sally Engle Merry, Kevin E. Davis and Benedict Kingsbury, 1–24. Cambridge: Cambridge University Press, 2015.

de Langen, Mike, and Maurits Barendrecht. 'Legal Empowerment of the Poor: Innovating Access to Justice'. In *The State of Access: Success and Failure of Democracies to Create Equal Opportunities*, edited by Jorrit de Jong and Gowher Rizvi, 250–271. Washington, DC: Brookings Institution Press, 2009.

de Souza, Peter Ronald. 'The Recolonization of the Indian Mind'. *Revista Crítica de Ciências Sociais* 114 (2017): 137–160.

———. 'Epilogue'. In *Keywords for India: A Conceptual Lexicon for the 21st Century*, edited by Rukmini Bhaya Nair and Peter Ronald de Souza, 415–419. London: Bloomsbury Academic, 2020.

de Souza, Siddharth. 'Unpacking the Black Box: Addressing the "Social" to Make Construction of AI-Powered Legal Technologies More Transparent and Unbiased'. *Journal of the Oxford Centre for Socio-Legal Studies* 2018. https://joxcsls.com/2018/06/18/unpacking-the-black-box-addressing-the-social-to-make-construction-of-ai-powered-legal-technologies-more-transparent-and-unbiased/. Accessed 20 March 2019.

de Souza, Siddharth Peter. 'Evaluating "Access to Justice" in Informal Justice Systems: A Suggestive Framework'. *Max Planck Yearbook of United Nations Law Online* 19, no. 1 (2016): 469–504.

———. 'Beyond Best Practices: How to Use Design Thinking in Rule of Law Promotion'. Peace Lab Blog, 2019. https://peacelab.blog/2019/03/beyond-best-practices-how-to-use-design-thinking. Accessed 29 August 2019.

———. 'India's Parallel Justice Systems: Engaging with Lok Adalats, Gram Nyayalayas, Nari Adalats and Khap Panchayats through Human Rights'. In *Human Rights in India*, edited by Satvinder Juss, 80–101. London: Routledge, 2019.

———. 'Towards a User-Centered Engagement with Law'. *Südasien-Chronik/ South Asia Chronicle* 2018, no. 8 (2019): 238–291. https://edoc.hu-berlin.de/ handle/18452/20489. Accessed 31 July 2019.

———. 'Non-State Justice Systems'. In *Max Planck Encyclopedia of Comparative Constitutional Law*, 2020. https://oxcon.ouplaw.com/view/10.1093/law-mpeccol/law-mpeccol-e650. Accessed 9 April 2020.

Deakin, Simon, David Gindis, Geoffrey M. Hodgson, Kainan Huang and Katharina Pistor. 'Legal Institutionalism: Capitalism and the Constitutive Role of Law'. *Journal of Comparative Economics* 45, no. 1 (2017): 188–200. http:// uhra.herts.ac.uk/handle/2299/17715. Accessed 13 August 2018.

Dean, Mitchell. 'Putting the Technological into Government'. *History of the Human Sciences* 9, no. 3 (1996): 47–68.

Delaney, David. 'Beyond the Word: Law as a Thing of This World'. In *Law and Geography*, edited by Jane Croft and Carolyn Harrison, 67–83. Oxford: Oxford University Press, 2003.

Democracy Barometer. http://www.democracybarometer.org/dataset_en.html. Accessed 7 May 2020.

———. 'Project Description: WZB'. https://www.wzb.eu/en/node/4858/ subpage/7494. Accessed 6 November 2020.

———. 'Democracy Barometer Project Background'. 9 September 2020. https:// democracybarometer.org/team/. Accessed 6 November 2020.

Deneulin, Séverine, and Lila Shahani, eds. *An Introduction to the Human Development and Capability Approach: Freedom and Agency*. London: Earthscan and IDRC, 2009.

Desai, Deval. 'In Search of "Hire" Knowledge'. In *The International Rule of Law Movement: A Crisis of Legitimacy and the Way Forward*, edited by David Marshall, 42–83. Cambridge, MA: Harvard University Press, 2014.

Desai, Deval, Deborah Isser and Michael Woolcock. 'Rethinking Justice Reform in Fragile and Conflict-Affected States: Lessons for Enhancing the Capacity of Development Agencies'. *Hague Journal on the Rule of Law* 4, no. 1 (2012): 54–75.

Desai, Deval, and Michael Woolcock. 'Experimental Justice Reform: Lessons from the World Bank and Beyond'. *Annual Review of Law and Social Science* 11, no. 1 (2015): 155–174.

Design Justice Network. 'Read the Principles'. https://designjustice.org/read-the-principles. Accessed 4 May 2020.

Desrosières, Alain. 'Introduction: Arguing from Social Facts'. In *The Politics of Large Numbers: A History of Statistical Reasoning*, 1–15. Cambridge, MA: Harvard University Press, 1998.

———. 'Retroaction: How Indicators Feed Back onto Quantified Actors'. In *The World of Indicators: The Making of Governmental Knowledge through Quantification*, edited by Richard Rottenburg, Sally E. Merry, Sung-Joon Park and Johanna Mugler, 329–353. Cambridge: Cambridge University Press, 2015.

Deutsche Gesellschaft für and Internationale Zusammenarbeit (GIZ) GmbH. 'The ABC for Human Rights for Development Cooperation'. GIZ, 2013. https://www.institut-fuer-menschenrechte.de/fileadmin/user_upload/ Publikationen/E-Info-Tool/e-info-tool_abc_of_human_rights_for_ development_cooperation.pdf. Accessed 30 July 2021.

DFID Briefing. 'Non-State Justice and Security Systems'. DFID, 2004. http:// www.gsdrc.org/docs/open/ssaj101.pdf. Accessed 7 May 2020.

Dhavan, Rajeev. *The Supreme Court under Strain: The Challenge of Arrears*. Bombay: N. M. Tripathi, 1978.

———. *Litigation Explosion in India*. Bombay: N. M. Tripathi, 1986.

D'Ignazio, Catherine, and Lauren F. Klein. 'Introduction: Why Data Science Needs Feminism'. In *Data Feminism*, 1–20. Cambridge, MA: MIT Press, 2020.

Dupret, Baudouin. 'What Is Plural in the Law? A Praxiological Answer'. *Égypte/ Monde Arabe* 1 (2005): 159–172.

———. 'Legal Pluralism, Plurality of Laws, and Legal Practices'. *European Journal of Legal Studies* 1, no. 1 (2007): 1–26. http://cadmus.eui.eu//handle/1814/6852. Accessed 7 December 2017.

Durose, Catherine, Yasminah Beebeejaun, James Rees, Jo Richardson and Liz Richardson. *Towards Co-Production in Research with Communities*. Arts and Humanities Research Council Connected Communities Programme, 2011. https://ahrc.ukri.org/documents/project-reports-and-reviews/connected-communities/towards-co-production-in-research-with-communities/. Accessed 15 September 2019.

Dutta, Debolina. 'Another Story of the Open Letter: An Inheritance of Relationship-Making'. *Jindal Global Law Review* 9, no. 2 (2018): 181–201.

Dutta, Nikhil K. 'Tradeoffs in Accountability: Conditionality Processes in the European Union and Millennium Challenge Corporation'. In *The Quiet Power of Indicators: Measuring Governance, Corruption, and Rule of Law*, edited by Benedict Kingsbury, Kevin E. Davis and Sally Engle Merry, 156–196. Cambridge: Cambridge University Press, 2015.

Eckert, Julia, Zerrin Özlem Biner, Brian Donahoe and Christian Strümpell. 'Law's Travels and Transformations'. In *Law against the State: Ethnographic Forays into Law's Transformations*, edited by Julia Eckert, Brian Donahoe, Christian Strümpell and Zerrin Özlem Biner, 1–22. Cambridge: Cambridge University Press, 2012.

Economic Survey of India. 'Chapter 9: Ease of Doing Business' Next Frontier: Timely Justice'. In *Economic Survey of India 2017–18*, 131–143. New Delhi, 2018. https://mofapp.nic.in/economicsurvey/economicsurvey/pdf/131-144_Chapter_09_ENGLISH_Vol%2001_2017-18.pdf. Accessed 20 February 2022.

Economic Times. 'Big Thumbs-up to Modinomics: India Jumps 30 Places to 100th Rank in Ease of Doing Business Report', 31 October 2017. https://economictimes.indiatimes.com/news/economy/indicators/big-thumbs-up-to-modinomics-india-jumps-30-places-to-100th-rank-in-ease-of-doing-business-report/articleshow/61363995.cms?from=mdr. Accessed 17 December 2020.

ECourt India Services. https://ecourts.gov.in/ecourts_home/. Accessed 12 August 2019

Erbeznik, Katherine. 'Money Can't Buy You Law: The Effects of Foreign Aid on the Rule of Law in Developing Countries'. *Indiana Journal of Global Legal Studies* 18 (2011): 873–900.

Escobar, Arturo. *Designs for the Pluriverse: Radical Interdependence, Autonomy, and the Making of Worlds*. Durham: Duke University Press, 2018.

Eslava, Luis. 'The Teaching of (Another) International Law: Critical Realism and the Question of Agency and Structure'. *The Law Teacher* 54, no. 3 (2020): 368–384.

Eslava, Luis, and Sundhya Pahuja. 'Beyond the (Post)Colonial: TWAIL and the Everyday Life of International Law'. *Verfassung und Recht in Übersee/Law and Politics in Africa, Asia and Latin America* 45, no. 2 (2012): 195–221.

Espeland, Wendy. 'Narrating Numbers'. In *The World of Indicators: The Making of Governmental Knowledge through Quantification*, edited by Richard Rottenburg, Sally E. Merry, Sung-Joon Park and Johanna Mugler, 56–75. Cambridge: Cambridge University Press, 2015.

Espeland, Wendy Nelson, and Michael Sauder. 'Rankings and Reactivity: How Public Measures Recreate Social Worlds'. *American Journal of Sociology* 113, no. 1 (2007): 1–40.

Espeland, Wendy Nelson, and Michael Sauder. 'The Dynamism of Indicators'. In *Governance by Indicators: Global Power Through Classification and Rankings*, edited by Kevin Davis, Angelina Fisher, Benedict Kingsbury and Sally Engle Merry, 86–109. Oxford: Oxford University Press, 2012.

Espeland, Wendy Nelson, and Mitchell L. Stevens. 'Commensuration as a Social Process'. *Annual Review of Sociology* 24, no. 1 (1998): 313–343.

———. 'A Sociology of Quantification'. *European Journal of Sociology / Archives Européennes de Sociologie* 49, no. 3 (2008): 401–436.

Evans, Peter. 'Collective Capabilities, Culture, and Amartya Sen's Development as Freedom'. *Studies in Comparative International Development* 37 (2002): 54–60.

Ewick, Patricia, and Susan S. Silbey. *The Common Place of Law: Stories from Everyday Life*. University of Chicago Press, 1998.

Faundez, Julio. 'Non-State Justice Systems in Latin America Case Studies: Peru and Colombia'. DFID, 2003.

———. 'The Rule of Law Enterprise: Promoting a Dialogue between Practitioners and Academics'. *Democratization* 12, no. 4 (2005): 567–586.

———. 'Should Justice Reform Projects Take Non-State Justice Systems Seriously? Perspectives from Latin America'. In *The World Bank Legal Review: Law, Equity and Development*, edited by Caroline Mary Sage and Michael Woolcock. Vol. 2, 113–139. Washington, DC: The World Bank, 2006.

———. 'Legal Pluralism and International Development Agencies: State Building or Legal Reform?' *Hague Journal on the Rule of Law* 3, no. 1 (2011): 18–38.

Felstiner, William L. F., Richard L. Abel and Austin Sarat. 'The Emergence and Transformation of Disputes: Naming, Blaming, Claiming ....' *Law and Society Review* 15, no. 3/4 (1980): 631–654.

Ferguson, Neil M., Daniel Laydon, Gemma Nedjati-Gilani, Natsuko Imai, Kylie Ainslie, Marc Baguelin, Sangeeta Bhatia, Adhiratha Boonyasiri, Zulma Cucunubá, Gina Cuomo-Dannenburg, Amy Dighe, Ilaria Dorigatti, Han Fu, Katy Gaythorpe, Will Green, Arran Hamlet, Wes Hinsley, Lucy C. Okell, Sabine van Elsland, Hayley Thompson, Robert Verity, Erik Volz, Haowei Wang, Yuanrong Wang, Patrick G. T. Walker, Caroline Walters, Peter Winskill, Charles Whittaker, Christl A. Donnelly, Steven Riley and Azra C. Ghani. *Report 9: Impact of Non-Pharmaceutical Interventions (NPIs) to Reduce COVID-19 Mortality and Healthcare Demand*. 16 March 2020. http://www.imperial.ac.uk/medicine/departments/school-public-health/infectious-disease-epidemiology/mrc-global-infectious-disease-analysis/covid-19/report-9-impact-of-npis-on-covid-19/. Accessed 19 December 2020.

Fioramonti, Lorenzo. 'The Politics of Statistics'. In *How Numbers Rule the World: The Use and Abuse of Statistics in Global Politics*, 1–9. London: ZED Books, 2014.

Foblets, Marie-Claire, Michele Graziadei and Alison Dundes Renteln. *Personal Autonomy in Plural Societies: A Principle and Its Paradoxes*. London: Routledge, 2017.

Fontana, Lorenza. 'Plurinational Citizenship in the Making'. OxPol, 19 February 2015. https://blog.politics.ox.ac.uk/plurinational-citizenship-making/. Accessed 10 December 2020.

Forsyth, Miranda. 'A Typology of Relationships between State and Non-State Justice Systems'. *The Journal of Legal Pluralism and Unofficial Law* 39, no. 56 (2007): 67–112.

———. *A Bird That Flies with Two Wings: Kastom and State Justice Systems in Vanuatu*. Canberra: ANU E Press, 2009.

Fortes, Pedro Rubim Borges. 'How Legal Indicators Influence a Justice System and Judicial Behavior: The Brazilian National Council of Justice and "Justice in Numbers"'. *The Journal of Legal Pluralism and Unofficial Law* 47, no. 1 (2015): 39–55.

Francioni, Francesco. *Access to Justice as a Human Right*. Oxford: Oxford University Press, 2007.

Freedom House. 'Freedom in the World 2019: Democracy in Retreat'. 3 January 2019. https://freedomhouse.org/report/freedom-world/freedom-world-2019. Accessed 13 September 2019.

Freudenberg, Michael. 'Composite Indicators of Country Performance: A Critical Assessment'. Working paper no. 2003/16, OECD, 2003. https://www.oecd-ilibrary.org/science-and-technology/composite-indicators-of-country-performance_405566708255. Accessed 22 May 2020.

Frydman, Benoît. 'From Accuracy to Accountability: Subjecting Global Indicators to the Rule of Law'. *International Journal of Law in Context* 13, no. 4 (2017): 450–464.

Frydman, Benoît, and Twining. 'A Symposium on Global Law, Legal Pluralism and Legal Indicators'. *The Journal of Legal Pluralism and Unofficial Law* 47 (2015): 1–8. DOI: 10.1080/07329113.2015.1030210.

Fukuda-Parr, Sakiko. 'The Human Development Paradigm: Operationalizing Sen's Ideas on Capabilities'. *Feminist Economics* 9, nos. 2–3 (2003): 301–317.

Fukuda-Parr, Sakiko, and Desmond McNeill. 'Knowledge and Politics in Setting and Measuring the SDGs: Introduction to Special Issue'. *Global Policy* 10 (2019): 5–15.

Fuller, Lon Luvois. *The Morality of Law*. New Haven: Yale University Press, 1969.

Galanter, Marc. 'The Displacement of Traditional Law in Modern India'. *Journal of Social Issues* 24, no. 4 (1968): 65–90.

———. 'Justice in Many Rooms: Courts, Private Ordering, and Indigenous Law'. *The Journal of Legal Pluralism and Unofficial Law* 13, no. 19 (1981): 1–47.

———. 'Reading the Landscape of Disputes: What We Know and Don't Know (and Think We Know) about Our Allegedly Contentious and Litigious Society'. *UCLA Law Review* 31, no. 1 (October 1983): 4–71.

Galanter, Marc, and Jayanth K. Krishnan. 'Bread for the Poor: Access to Justice and the Rights of the Needy in India'. *Hastings Law Journal* 55 (2004): 789–834.

Gandomi, Amir, and Murtaza Haider. 'Beyond the Hype: Big Data Concepts, Methods, and Analytics'. *International Journal of Information Management* 35, no. 2 (2015): 137–144.

Garth, Bryant, and Mauro Cappelletti. 'Access to Justice: The Newest Wave in the Worldwide Movement to Make Rights Effective'. *Buffalo Law Review* 27, no. 2 (1978): 181–292.

Gauri, Varun. 'Public Interest Litigation in India: Overreaching or Underachieving?' World Bank Policy Research Working Paper No. 5109, The World Bank, 22 June 2013. https://elibrary.worldbank.org/doi/abs/10.1596/1813-9450-5109. Accessed 20 August 2019.

Geetha, V. 'Justice in the Name of God: Organizing Muslim Women in Tamil Nadu'. In *Indian Feminisms: Individual and Collective Journeys*, edited by Poonam Kathuria and Abha Bhaiya. New Delhi: Zubaan, 2018.

Genn, Hazel. 'The Landscape of Justiciable Problems'. In *Paths to Justice: What People Do and Think about Going to Law*, 21–66. Oxford: Hart Publishing, 1999.

Ghai, Yash, and Jill Cottrell. 'The Rule of Law and Access to Justice'. In *Marginalized Communities and Access to Justice*, edited by Yash Ghai and Jill Cottrell, 1–22. London: Routledge, 2009.

Ghani, Norjihan Binti Abdul, Suraya Binti Hamid, Ibrahim Abaker Targio Hashem and Ejaz Ahmed. 'Social Media Big Data Analytics: A Survey'. *Computers in Human Behavior* 101 (2019): 417–428.

Gisselquist, Rachel M. 'Developing and Evaluating Governance Indexes: 10 Questions'. *Policy Studies* 35, no. 5 (2014): 513–531.

Glenn, H. Patrick. 'Preface'. In *The Cosmopolitan State*, vii–viii. Oxford: Oxford University Press, 2013.

Global Forest Coalition. 'Intervention by the Women's Major Group on Land Degradation, Desertification and Drought at the UN OWG SDG Meeting 23 May 2013'. 23 May 2013. https://globalforestcoalition.org/es/intervention-by-the-womens-major-group-on-land-degradation

-desertification-and-drought-at-the-un-owg-sdg-meeting-23-may-2013/. Accessed 5 May 2020.

Goldstein, Daniel M. 'Whose Vernacular? Translating Human Rights in Local Contexts'. In *Human Rights at the Crossroads*, edited by Mark Goodale, 111–121. Oxford: Oxford University Press, 2014.

Goldston, James A. 'New Rules for the Rule of Law'. In *The International Rule of Law Movement: A Crisis of Legitimacy and the Way Forward*, edited by David Marshall, 1–42. Cambridge, MA: Harvard Law School, 2014.

Golub, Stephen. 'Legal Empowerment: Impact and Implications for the Development Community and the World Bank'. In *The World Bank Legal Review: Law, Equity and Development*, edited by Caroline Mary Sage and Michael Woolcock. Vol. 2, 167–184. Washington, DC: The World Bank, 2006.

———. 'Make Justice the Organizing Principle of the Rule of Law Field'. *Hague Journal on the Rule of Law* 1, no. 1 (2009): 61–66.

———. 'What Is Legal Empowerment? An Introduction'. In *Legal Empowerment: Practitioners' Perspectives*, edited by Stephen Golub, 9–18. Rome: IDLO, 2010.

———. 'Beyond Rule of Law Orthodoxy: The Legal Empowerment Alternative'. Carnegie Endowment for International Peace, 14 October 2003. http://carnegieendowment.org/2003/10/14/beyond-rule-of-law-orthodoxy-legal-empowerment-alternative-pub-1367. Accessed 7 December 2017.

Goodale, Mark. 'Introduction: Locating Rights, Envisioning Law between the Global and the Local'. In *The Practice of Human Rights: Tracking Law between the Global and the Local*, edited by Mark Goodale and Sally Engle Merry, 1–38. Cambridge: Cambridge University Press, 2007.

———. *Anthropology and Law: A Critical Introduction*. New York: NYU Press, 2017.

Goodwin, Laura, and Vivek Maru. 'What Do We Know about Legal Empowerment? Mapping the Evidence'. *Hague Journal on the Rule of Law* 9 (2017): 157–194.

Goodwin, Morag. 'The Poverty of Numbers: Reflections on the Legitimacy of Global Development Indicators'. *International Journal of Law in Context* 13, no. 4 (2017): 485–497.

Gore, Charles. 'Irreducibly Social Goods and the Informational Basis of Amartya Sen's Capability Approach'. *Journal of International Development* 9 (1997): 235–250.

Gramatikov, Martin, Maurits Barendrecht and Jin Ho Verdonschot. 'Measuring the Costs and Quality of Paths to Justice: Contours of a Methodology'. *Hague Journal on the Rule of Law* 3 (2011): 349–379.

Gramatikov, Martin, and Malini Laxminarayan. 'Weighting Justice: Constructing an Index of Access to Justice'. Tilburg University Legal Studies Working Paper No. 18/2008, 2009. https://papers.ssrn.com/abstract=1344418. Accessed 28 September 2018.

Gramatikov, Martin, and Robert B. Porter. 'Yes, I Can: Subjective Legal Empowerment—Tisco Working Paper Series on Civil Law and Conflict Resolution Systems'. *Georgetown Journal on Poverty Law and Policy* 18, no. 2 (Spring 2010): 169–200.

Greco, Salvatore, Alessio Ishizaka, Menelaos Tasiou and Gianpiero Torrisi. 'On the Methodological Framework of Composite Indices: A Review of the Issues of Weighting, Aggregation, and Robustness'. *Social Indicators Research* 141 (2019): 61–94.

Grek, Sotiria. 'Prophets, Saviours and Saints: Symbolic Governance and the Rise of a Transnational Metrological Field'. *International Review of Education* 66, nos. 2–3 (2020): 139–166.

Griffiths, John. 'What Is Legal Pluralism?' *The Journal of Legal Pluralism and Unofficial Law* 18, no. 24 (1986): 1–55.

Grundmann, Reiner. 'The Problem of Expertise in Knowledge Societies'. *Minerva* 55 (2017): 25–48.

Hagan, Margaret. 'Legal Design as a Thing: A Theory of Change and a Set of Methods to Craft a Human-Centered Legal System'. *Design Issues* 36, no. 3 (2020): 3–15.

Hahn, Lisa, and Siddharth de Souza. 'Self-Reflecting, Constructing and Positioning: Intersecting Debates in Socio-Legal Studies'. Rechtswirklichkeit, 14 March 2019. https://barblog.hypotheses.org/2988. Accessed 7 December 2020.

Hall, Margaux, Nicholas Menzies and Michael Woolcock. 'From HiPPOs to "Best Fit" in Justice Reform: Experimentalism in Sierra Leone'. In *The International Rule of Law Movement: A Crisis of Legitimacy and the Way Forward*, edited by David Marshall, 243–266. Cambridge, MA: Harvard Law School, 2014.

Hammergren, Linn. 'Indices, Indicators and Statistics: A View from the Project Side as to Their Utility and Pitfalls'. *Hague Journal on the Rule of Law* 3 (2011): 305.

Hansen, Hans Krause, and Tony Porter. 'What Do Numbers Do in Transnational Governance?' *International Political Sociology* 6, no. 4 (December 2012): 409–426.

Haus der Kulturen der Welt. 'Nervous Systems'. 11 February 2016. https://www. hkw.de/en/programm/projekte/2016/nervoese_systeme/nervoese_ systeme_mehr.php. Accessed 5 February 2019.

Hawthorne, Omar E. *Do International Corruption Metrics Matter? The Impact of Transparency International's Corruption Perception Index*. Maryland: Lexington Books, 2015.

Hazra, Arnab Kumar, and Maja B. Micevska. 'The Problem of Court Congestion: Evidence from Indian Lower Courts'. In *Judicial Reforms in India: Issues and Aspects*, edited by Arnab Kumar Hazra and Bibek Debroy, 137–156. New Delhi: Academic Foundation, in association with Rajiv Gandhi Institute for Contemporary Studies, 2007. https://trove.nla.gov.au/version/38793678. Accessed 17 August 2019.

Hemrajani, Rahul, and Himanshu Agarwal. 'A Temporal Analysis of the Supreme Court of India's Workload'. *Indian Law Review* 3, no. 2 (2019): 125–158.

Heredia, Rudolf C. 'Interpreting Gandhi's Hind Swaraj'. *Economic and Political Weekly* 34, no. 24 (12 June 1999): 1497–1502.

Herklotz, Tanja. 'Dead Letters? The Uniform Civil Code through the Eyes of the Indian Women's Movement and the Indian Supreme Court'. *Verfassung in Recht und Übersee* 49, no. 2 (2016): 148–174.

Hertogh, Marc. 'A Sociology of the Rule of Law: Why, What, Where? And Who Cares?' Social Science Research Network, SSRN Scholarly Paper ID 2285996, 2013. https://papers.ssrn.com/abstract=2285996. Accessed 6 November 2020.

———. 'Your Rule of Law Is Not Mine: Rethinking Empirical Approaches to EU Rule of Law Promotion'. *Asia Europe Journal* 14 (2016): 43–59.

HiiL, *Understanding Justice Needs: The Elephant in the Courtroom*. The Hague: HiiL, 2018. https://www.hiil.org/wp-content/uploads/2018/11/HiiL-Understanding-Justice-Needs-The-Elephant-in-the-Courtroom.pdf. Accessed 9 December 2020.

———. 'HiiL Justice Dashboard: Justice Data at Your Fingertips'. https://justice-dashboard.hiil.org/. Accessed 6 May 2020.

Hoekema, André J. 'European Legal Encounters between Minority and Majority Cultures: Cases of Interlegality'. *The Journal of Legal Pluralism and Unofficial Law* 37, no. 51 (2005): 1–28.

Humphreys, Stephen. 'Introduction'. In *Theatre of the Rule of Law: Transnational Legal Intervention in Theory and Practice*, 1–26. Cambridge: Cambridge University Press, 2010.

Husa, Jaakko. 'Developing Legal System, Legal Transplants, and Path Dependence: Reflections on the Rule of Law'. *The Chinese Journal of Comparative Law* 6, no. 2 (December 2018): 129–150.

Ibrahim, Solava S. 'From Individual to Collective Capabilities: The Capability Approach as a Conceptual Framework for Self-Help'. *Journal of Human Development* 7, no. 3 (2006): 397–416.

ICIJ. 'Explore 10 Years of World Bank Resettlement Data'. https://www.icij. org/investigations/world-bank/explore-10-years-world-bank-resettlement-data/. Accessed 28 March 2020.

IDLO. 'Comparative Justice Policy Workshop'. Rome: IDLO, 2015. https://www. idlo.int/sites/default/files/pdfs/events/Report%20-%20Comparative%20 Justice%20Policy%20Workshop.pdf. Accessed 26 August 2019.

———. 'HIV-Related Legal Services for Adolescent Girls, Young Women'. IDLO: International Development Law Organization, 20 December 2016. https:// www.idlo.int/news/highlights/hiv-related-legal-services-adolescent-girls-and-young-women. Accessed 6 April 2020.

———. *Legal and Judicial Development Assistance: Global Report 2010*. Rome: IDLO, 2010. https://www.files.ethz.ch/isn/139312/LJAnnualReport.pdf. Accessed 30 July 2021.

———. 'The 2nd Generation of Rule of Law Reform'. https://www.idlo.int/ news/events/2nd-generation-rule-law-reform. Accessed 6 April 2020.

Indian Express. 'Lok Adalats Settled over 8 Crore Cases in Last 20 Years: T S Thakur'. 10 November 2015. https://indianexpress.com/article/india/india -news-india/lok-adalats-settled-over-8-crore-cases-in-last-20-years-t-s -thakur/. Accessed 26 August 2019.

Inda, Jonathan Xavier. 'Government and Numbers'. In *Targeting Immigrants: Government, Technology, and Ethics*, 63–66. Oxford: John Wiley & Sons, 2008.

———. 'Introduction: Government and Immigration'. In *Targeting Immigrants: Government, Technology, and Ethics*, 1–26. Oxford: John Wiley & Sons, 2008.

International Council on Human Rights Policy. *When Legal Worlds Overlap: Human Rights, State and Non-State Law*. Geneva: International Council on Human Rights Policy, 2009.

International Labour Organization. 'Indigenous and Tribal Peoples Convention (No. 169)'. 1989. https://www.ilo.org/dyn/normlex/en/f?p=NORMLEXPUB :12100:0::NO::P12100_ILO_CODE:C169. Accessed 7 May 2020.

Isser, Deborah H. 'The Problem with Problematizing Legal Pluralism'. In *Legal Pluralism and Development: Scholars and Practitioners in Dialogue*, edited by Brian Z. Tamanaha, Caroline Sage and Michael Woolcock, 237–248. Cambridge: Cambridge University Press, 2012.

Jackson, Sherman. 'Legal Pluralism between Islam and the Nation-State: Romantic Medievalism or Pragmatic Modernity?' *Fordham International Law Journal* 30, no. 1 (2006): 158–176.

Janse, Ronald. 'A Turn to Legal Pluralism in Rule of Law Promotion?' *Erasmus Law Review* 6 (2013): 181–190.

Jasanoff, Sheila. *The Fifth Branch: Science Advisors as Policy Makers.* Cambridge, MA: Harvard University Press, 1998.

———. 'The Idiom of Co-Production'. In *States of Knowledge: The Co-Production of Science and the Social Order*, edited by Sheila Jasanoff, 1–12. London: Routledge, 2004.

———. 'Virtual, Visible, and Actionable: Data Assemblages and the Sightlines of Justice'. *Big Data and Society* 4 (December 2017). doi:10.1177/2053951717724477.

Jodoin, Sébastien, and Katherine Lofts. 'What's Critical about Critical International Law? Reflections on the Emancipatory Potential of International Legal Scholarship'. In *Critical International Law: Postrealism, Postcolonialism and Transnationalism*, edited by Prabhakar Singh and Benoit Mayer, 326–345. New Delhi: Oxford University Press, 2014.

Joseph Mbembe, Achille. 'Decolonizing the University: New Directions'. *Arts and Humanities in Higher Education* 15, no. 1 (2016): 29–45.

Kalberg, Stephen. 'Max Weber's Types of Rationality: Cornerstones for the Analysis of Rationalization Processes in History'. *American Journal of Sociology* 85, no. 5 (1980). 1145–1179.

Kannabiran, K. 'The Contexts of Criminology: A Brief Restatement'. In *Challenging the Rule(s) of Law: Colonialism, Criminology and Human Rights in India*, edited by Kalpana Kannabiran and Ranbir Singh, 451–476. New Delhi: SAGE Publications, 2008.

Kaufmann, Daniel, Aart Kraay and Massimo Mastruzzi. 'The Worldwide Governance Indicators: Methodology and Analytical Issues'. *Hague Journal on the Rule of Law* 3 (2011): 220–246.

Kelley, Judith G., and Beth A. Simmons. 'Politics by Number: Indicators as Social Pressure in International Relations'. *American Journal of Political Science* 59 (2015): 55–70.

Kennedy, David. 'Introduction: Could This Be 1648?' In *A World of Struggle: How Power, Law, and Expertise Shape Global Political Economy*, 1–20. Princeton: Princeton University Press, 2016.

Kleinfeld, Rachel. 'How to Advance the Rule of Law Abroad'. Carnegie Endowment for International Peace, 2013. https://carnegieendowment.org/files/how_to_advance_ROL.pdf. Accessed 24 December 2020.

———. 'Competing Definitions of the Rule of Law: Implications for Practitioners'. Carnegie Endowment for International Peace, Washington, DC, 21 January 2005. https://carnegieendowment.org/2005/01/21/competing-definitions-of-rule-of-law-implications-for-practitioners-pub-16405. Accessed 2 August 2018.

Klikauer, Thomas. 'What Is Managerialism?' *Critical Sociology* 41, nos. 7–8 (2015): 1103–1119.

Kokal, Kalindi. 'Tamāshā: The Theatrics of Disputing and Non-State Dispute Processing'. In *Normative Pluralism and Human Rights*, edited by Kyriaki Topidi, 189–206. Oxon: Routledge, 2018.

———. 'Many Laws, Many Orders: Disputes and Their Processing in the Non-State Arena'. In *State Law, Dispute Processing, and Legal Pluralism: Unspoken Dialogues from Rural India*, 58–72. Oxon: Routledge, 2019.

———. *State Law, Dispute Processing and Legal Pluralism: Unspoken Dialogues from Rural India*. Routledge, 2019.

Kosinski, Michal, David Stillwell and Thore Graepel. 'Private Traits and Attributes Are Predictable from Digital Records of Human Behavior'. *Proceedings of the National Academy of Sciences of the United States of America* 110, no. 15 (April 2013): 5802–5805. DOI: 10.1073/pnas.1218772110.

Kothari, Ashish, Ariel Salleh, Arturo Escobar, Federico Demaria, and Alberto Acosta, eds. *Pluriverse: A Post-Development Dictionary*. New Delhi: Tulika Books, 2019.

Kötter, Matthias. 'Better Access to Justice by Public Recognition of Non-State Justice Systems?' Social Science Research Network, SSRN Scholarly Paper ID 2613408, 2015. https://papers.ssrn.com/abstract=2613408. Accessed 7 May 2020.

———. 'Non-State Justice Institutions: A Matter of Fact and a Matter of Legislation'. SFB Governance Working Paper Series, 2012. https://www.sfb-governance.de/en/publikationen/sfb-700-working_papers/wp34/index.html. Accessed 30 July 2021.

Kötter, Matthias, Tilmann J. Röder, Gunnar Folke Schuppert and Rüdiger Wolfrum, eds. *Non-State Justice Institutions and the Law: Decision-Making at the Interface of Tradition, Religion and the State*. London: Springer, 2015.

Krever, Tor. 'Quantifying Law: Legal Indicator Projects and the Reproduction of Neoliberal Common Sense'. *Third World Quarterly* 34, no. 1 (2013): 131–150.

Krishnan, Jayanth K., Shirish N. Kavadi, Azima Girach, Dhanaji Khupkar, Kilindi Kokal, Satyajeet Mazumdar, Nupar, Gayatri Panday, Aatreyee Sen, Aqseer Sodhi, and Bharati Takale Shukla. 'Grappling at the Grassroots: Access to Justice in India's Lower Tier'. *Harvard Human Rights Journal* 27 (2014): 151–189.

Krishnaswamy, Sudhir, Sindhu K. Sivakumar and Shishir Bail. 'Legal and Judicial Reform in India: A Call for Systemic and Empirical Approaches'. *Journal of National Law University Delhi* 2 (2014): 1.

Krygier, Martin. 'The Rule of Law: Legality, Teleology, Sociology'. In *Relocating the Rule of Law*, edited by Gianluigi Palombella and Neil Walker, 45–70. London: Hart Publishing, 2008.

———. 'Four Puzzles about the Rule of Law: Why, What, Where and Who Cares?' *Nomos* 50 (2011): 64–104.

———. 'The Rule of Law: Pasts, Presents, and Two Possible Futures'. *Annual Review of Law and Social Science* 12, no. 1 (2016): 199–229.

Kumar, Vidya. 'Towards a Constitutionalism of the Wretched'. Völkerrechtsblog, 27 July 2017. https://voelkerrechtsblog.org/towards-a-constitutionalism-of-the-wretched/. Accessed 16 April 2020.

Kumm, Mattias. 'The Cosmopolitan Turn in Constitutionalism: An Integrated Conception of Public Law'. *Indiana Journal of Global Legal Studies* 20, no. 2 (2013): 605–628.

———. 'Global Constitutionalism and the Rule of Law'. In *Handbook on Global Constitutionalism*, edited by Anthony F. Lang and Antje Wiener, 167–190. Cheltenham: Edward Elgar Publishing, 2017.

———. 'On the History and Theory of Global Constitutionalism'. In *Global Constitutionalism from European and East Asian Perspectives*, edited by Takao, Suami, Anne Peters, Dimitri Vanoverbeke and Mattias Kumm, 168–200. Cambridge: Cambridge University Press, 2018.

———. 'The Rule of Law, Legitimate Authority and Constitutionalism'. In *Legal Positivism, Institutionalism and Globalization Vienna Lectures on Legal Philosophy*, edited by Christoph Bezemek, Michael Potacs and Alexander Somek, vol. 1, 113–126. Oxford: Hart Publishing, 2018.

Lapowsky, Issie. 'The Man Who Saw the Dangers of Cambridge Analytica Years Ago'. *Wired*. https://www.wired.com/story/the-man-who-saw-the-dangers-of-cambridge-analytica/. Accessed 13 September 2019.

Law Commission of India. *Delay and Arrears in Trial Courts*. Report no. 77. New Delhi, 1978. https://lawcommissionofindia.nic.in/51-100/Report77.pdf.

Accessed 20 February 2022. https://lawcommissionofindia.nic.in/51-100/report79.pdf. Accessed 20 February 2022.

———. *Delay and Arrears in High Courts and Other Appellate Courts.* Report no. 79. New Delhi, 1979. https://lawcommissionofindia.nic.in/51-100/report79.pdf (accessed 20 February 2022).

———. *Manpower Planning in the Judiciary: A Blueprint.* Report no. 120. New Delhi, 1987. https://lawcommissionofindia.nic.in/101-169/Report120.pdf. Accessed 20 February 2022.

———. *Need for Division of the Supreme Court into a Constitution Bench at Delhi and Cassation Benches in Four Regions at Delhi, Chennai/Hyderabad, Kolkata and Mumbai.* Report no. 229. New Delhi, 2009. https://lawcommissionofindia.nic.in/reports/report229.pdf. Accessed 20 February 2022.

———. *Need for Speedy Justice: Some Suggestions.* Report no. 221. New Delhi, 2009. https://lawcommissionofindia.nic.in/reports/report221.pdf. Accessed 20 February 2022.

———. *Arrears and Backlog: Creating Additional Judicial (Wo)Manpower.* Report no. 245. New Delhi, 2014. https://lawcommissionofindia.nic.in/reports/Report245.pdf. Accessed 20 February 2022.

Leeuw, Frans L., and Hans Schmeets. 'Research Designs: Raisons d'être, Examples and Criteria'. In *Empirical Legal Research: A Guidance Book for Lawyers, Legislators and Regulators.* Cheltenham: Edward Elgar Publishing, 2016.

Legal Aid BC. 'First Nations Court: Aboriginal Legal Aid in BC'. https://aboriginal.legalaid.bc.ca/courts-criminal-cases/first-nations-court. Accessed 11 September 2019.

Lemke, Thomas. *Foucault, Governmentality, and Critique.* London: Routledge, 2015.

Lynch, Kathleen. 'Managerialism'. In *Encyclopedia of Educational Theory and Philosophy*, edited by D. C. Phillips, 507–511. Thousand Oaks, CA: SAGE Publications, 2014. http://sk.sagepub.com/reference/encyclopedia-of-education-theory-and-philosophy/n211.i1.xml. Accessed 20 August 2019.

Malito, Debora Valentina, Nehal Bhuta and Gaby Umbach. 'Conclusions: Knowing and Governing'. In *The Palgrave Handbook of Indicators in Global Governance*, edited by Debora Valentina Malito, Gaby Umbach and Nehal Bhuta, 503–512. Cham: Springer, 2017.

Malito, Debora Valentina, Gaby Umbach and Nehal Bhuta, eds. *The Palgrave Handbook of Indicators in Global Governance.* Cham: Springer, 2017.

Marshall, David. 'Introduction'. In *The International Rule of Law Movement A Crisis of Legitimacy and the Way Forward*, edited by David Marshall. Harvard University Press, 2014.

Maru, Vivek. 'Between Law and Society: Paralegals and the Provision of Justice Services in Sierra Leone and Worldwide'. *Yale Journal of International Law* 31 (2006): 427–476.

————. 'Access to Justice and Legal Empowerment: A Review of World Bank Practice'. *Hague Journal on the Rule of Law* 2, no. 2 (2010): 259–281.

Massoud, Mark Fathi. 'Ideals and Practices in the Rule of Law: An Essay on Legal Politics'. *Law and Social Inquiry* 41, no. 2 (2016): 489–501.

Mattei, Ugo, and Marco de Morpurgo. 'Global Law and Plunder: The Dark Side of the Rule of Law'. IUC Research Commons 1–10, International University College of Turin, 2010. https://ideas.repec.org/p/iuc/rpaper/1-10.html. Accessed 9 April 2020.

Mattei, Ugo, and Laura Nader. 'Plunder and the Rule of Law'. In *Plunder: When the Rule of Law Is Illegal*, 10–34. Oxford: John Wiley & Sons, 2008.

Mau, Steffen. *The Metric Society: On the Quantification of the Social*. Cambridge: John Wiley & Sons, 2019.

May, Christopher. 'The Rule of Law and Technocratisation'. *Hague Journal on the Rule of Law* 11 (2019): 321–326.

McCann, Michael. 'Law and Social Movements: Contemporary Perspectives'. *Annual Review of Law and Social Science* 2, no. 1 (2006): 17–38.

McMurrin, Sterling M. (ed.). *Tanner Lectures on Human Values*. Vol. 1. Cambridge: Cambridge University Press, 1980.

Menski, Werner F. 'Comparative Law and Legal Theory from a Global Perspective'. In *Comparative Law in a Global Context: The Legal Systems of Asia and Africa*, 25–81. Cambridge: Cambridge University Press, 2006.

Merino, Roger. 'Reimagining the Nation-State: Indigenous Peoples and the Making of Plurinationalism in Latin America'. *Leiden Journal of International Law* 31, no. 4 (2018): 773–792.

Merkel, Wolfgang. 'Measuring the Quality of Rule of Law'. In *Rule of Law Dynamics: In an Era of International and Transnational Governance*, edited by Michael Zürn, André Nollkaemper and Randy Peerenboom, 21–47. Cambridge: Cambridge University Press, 2012.

Merry, Sally Engle. 'Legal Pluralism'. *Law and Society Review* 22, no. 5 (1988): 869–896.

————. 'Transnational Human Rights and Local Activism: Mapping the Middle'. *American Anthropologist* 108, no. 1 (2006): 38–51.

———. *Human Rights and Gender Violence: Translating International Law into Local Justice*. Chicago: University of Chicago Press, 2009.

———. 'Measuring the World: Indicators, Human Rights, and Global Governance'. *Current Anthropology* 52 (2011): S83–S95.

———. 'A World of Quantification'. In *The Seductions of Quantification: Measuring Human Rights, Gender Violence, and Sex Trafficking*, 1–33. Chicago: University of Chicago Press, 2016.

———. 'Conclusions'. In *The Seductions of Quantification: Measuring Human Rights, Gender Violence, and Sex Trafficking*, 207–222. Chicago: University of Chicago Press, 2016.

———. *The Seductions of Quantification: Measuring Human Rights, Gender Violence, and Sex Trafficking*. Chicago: University of Chicago Press, 2016.

Merry, Sally Engle, Kevin E. Davis and Benedict Kingsbury, eds. *The Quiet Power of Indicators: Measuring Governance, Corruption, and Rule of Law*. Cambridge: Cambridge University Press, 2015.

Merryman, John Henry. 'Law and Development Memoirs II: SLADE'. *The American Journal of Comparative Law* 48, no. 4 (2000): 713–727.

Michaels, Ralf. 'Global Legal Pluralism'. *Annual Review of Law and Social Science* 5, no. 1 (2009): 243–262.

Milan, Stefania. 'Techno-Solutionism and the Standard Human in the Making of the COVID-19 Pandemic'. *Big Data and Society* 7 (2020). https://doi.org/10.1177/2053951720966781. Accessed 30 October 2020.

Milan, Stefania, and Emiliano Treré. 'Big Data from the South(s): Beyond Data Universalism'. *Television and New Media* 20, no. 4 (2019): 319–335.

Miller, Richard E., and Austin Sarat. 'Grievances, Claims, and Disputes: Assessing the Adversary Culture Special Issue on Dispute Processing and Civil Litigation: Part Two – The Civil Litigation Research Project: A Dispute-Focused Approach: Surveying Disputes'. *Law and Society Review* 15, no. 3/4 (1980): 525–566.

M. K., Nidheesh. '"Jobs Report Can't Be Called a Draft, It Is Final Once I Approve It"'. *Mint*, 11 February 2019. https://www.livemint.com/news/india/the-jobs-report-can-t-be-called-a-draft-it-is-final-once-i-approve-it-mohanan-1549824555045.html. Accessed 15 March 2019.

Mnookin, Robert H., and Lewis Kornhauser. 'Bargaining in the Shadow of the Law: The Case of Divorce'. *The Yale Law Journal* 88, no. 5 (April 1979): 950–997.

Mnyaka, Mluleki, and Mokgethi Motlhabi. 'The African Concept of Ubuntu/Botho and Its Socio-Moral Significance'. *Black Theology* 3, no. 2 (2005): 215–237.

Mo Ibrahim Foundation. 'Ibrahim Index of African Governance (IIAG)'. http://mo.ibrahim.foundation/iiag. Accessed 7 May 2020.

Modi, Chowkidar Narendra (@narendramodi). 'Historic Jump in "Ease of Doing Business" Rankings Is the Outcome of the All-Round & Multi-Sectoral Reform Push of Team'. Twitter, 31 October 2017. https://twitter.com/narendramodi/status/925371481437044737/photo/1?ref_src=twsrc%5Etfw%7Ctwcamp%5Etweetembed%7Ctwterm%5E925371481437044737&ref_url=https%3A%2F%2Fwww.cgdev.org%2Fblog%2Fchange-world-bank-methodology-not-reform-explains-indias-rise-doing-business. Accessed 16 May 2019.

Møller, Jørgen, and Svend-Erik Skaaning. 'Evaluating Extant Rule of Law Measures'. In *The Rule of Law: Definitions, Measures, Patterns and Causes*, edited by Jørgen Møller and Svend-Erik Skaaning, 41–61. London: Palgrave Macmillan, 2014.

Moog, Robert. 'Indian Litigiousness and the Litigation Explosion: Challenging the Legend'. *Asian Survey* 33, no. 12 (1 December 1993): 1136–1150.

Moretti, Franco, and Dominique Pestre. 'Bankspeak'. *New Left Review* 92 (2015): 75–99.

Muralidhar, S. *Law, Poverty, and Legal Aid: Access to Criminal Justice*. New Delhi: LexisNexis Butterworth, 2004.

Murphy, Michael. 'Self-Determination as a Collective Capability: The Case of Indigenous Peoples'. *Journal of Human Development and Capabilities* 15, no. 4 (2014): 320–334.

Musaraj, Smoki. 'Indicators, Global Expertise, and a Local Political Drama: Producing and Deploying Corruption Perception Data in Post-Socialist Albania'. In *The Quiet Power of Indicators: Measuring Governance, Corruption, and Rule of Law*, edited by Sally Engle Merry, Kevin E. Davis and Benedict Kingsbury, 222–247. Cambridge: Cambridge University Press, 2015.

Mutua, Makau. 'What Is TWAIL?' *Proceedings of the ASIL Annual Meeting* 94 (2000): 31–38.

Narasappa, Harish. 'India's Rule of Law: A Theoretical Analysis'. In *Rule of Law in India: A Quest for Reason*, 37–62. New Delhi: Oxford University Press, 2019.

Narasappa, Harish, Kavya Murthy, Surya Prakash B. S. and Yashas C. Gowda. 'Access to Justice Survey: Introduction, Methodology, and Findings'. In *State of the Indian Judiciary: A Report by Daksh*, edited by Harish Narasappa and Shruti Vidyasagar. Lucknow: Eastern Book Company, 2016. https://dakshindia.org/state-of-the-indian-judiciary/28_chapter_15.html#_idTextAnchor320. Accessed 20 February 2022.

National Crime Records Bureau. *Crime in India*. New Delhi: National Crime Records Bureau, 2016. https://nalsa.gov.in/services/lok-adalat/national-lok-adalat/national-lok-adalat-2018. Accessed 20 February 2022.

———. *Prison Statistics in India*. New Delhi: National Crime Records Bureau, 2016.

National Legal Services Authority. 'Disposal of National Lok Adalat Held on 8th December 2018'. https://nalsa.gov.in/services/lok-adalat/national-lok-adalat/national-lok-adalat-2018. Accessed 20 February 2022.

———.'Lok Adalat: National Legal Services Authority'. http://nalsa.gov.in/lok-adalat. Accessed 3 November 2017.

———. 'National Lok Adalat 2018: National Legal Services Authority'. 2018. https://nalsa.gov.in/services/lok-adalat/national-lok-adalat/national-lok-adalat-2018. Accessed 22 February 2022.

Nelken, David. 'Eugen Ehrlich, Living Law, and Plural Legalities'. *Theoretical Inquiries in Law* 9, no. 2 (2008): 443–471.

———. 'Conclusion: Contesting Global Indicators'. In *The Quiet Power of Indicators: Measuring Governance, Corruption, and Rule of Law*, edited by Sally Engle Merry, Kevin E. Davis and Benedict Kingsbury, 317–388. Cambridge: Cambridge University Press, 2015.

———. 'The Legitimacy of Global Social Indicators: Reconfiguring Authority, Accountability and Accuracy'. *Les Cahiers De Droit* 59, no. 1 (2018): 35–84.

———. 'Whose Best Practices? The Significance of Context in and for Transnational Criminal Justice Indicators'. *Journal of Law and Society* 46, no. S1 (2019): S31–S50.

Newell, William H. 'A Theory of Interdisciplinary Studies'. *Issues in Integrative Studies* 19 (2001): 1–25. https://our.oakland.edu/handle/10323/4378. Accessed 4 December 2020.

Nicolaidis, Kalypso, and Rachel Kleinfeld. 'Rethinking Europe's Rule of Law and Enlargement Agenda: The Fundamental Dilemma'. SIGMA Papers, No. 49, OECD Publishing, Paris. https://www.oecd-ilibrary.org/governance/rethinking-europe-s-rule-of-law-and-enlargement-agenda_5k4c42jmn5zp-en. Accessed 6 November 2020.

Nielsen, Laura Beth. 'The Need for Multi-Method Approaches in Empirical Legal Research'. In *The Oxford Handbook of Empirical Legal Research*, edited by Peter Cane and Herbert M Kritzer, 951–975. Oxford: Oxford University Press, 2010.

NITI Aayog. 'Overview'. https://niti.gov.in/content/overview. Accessed 9 December 2020.

NJDG. 'National Judicial Data Grid'. https://njdg.ecourts.gov.in/njdgnew/ index.php. Accessed 12 August 2019.

Norman, Donald A. 'The Psychopathology of Everyday Things'. In *The Design of Everyday Things*, 1–36. New York: Basic Books, 1990.

Noronha, Ligia and Subrahmanya Nairy. 'Assessing Quality of Life in a Mining Region'. *Economic and Political Weekly* 40 (2005): 72–78.

North, Douglass C. 'Institutions, Ideology, and Economic Performance'. *Cato Journal* 11, no. 3 (1991): 477–496.

Nussbaum, Martha. 'Capabilities as Fundamental Entitlements: Sen and Social Justice'. *Feminist Economics* 9, nos. 2–3 (2003): 33–59.

Nussbaum, Martha, and Amartya Sen. *The Quality of Life*. Oxford: Oxford University Press, 1993.

Nussbaum, Martha C. 'Capabilities across National Borders'. In *Frontiers of Justice: Disability, Nationality, Species Membership*, 273–324. Cambridge, MA: Harvard University Press, 2009.

———. 'The Central Capabilities'. In *Creating Capabilities: The Human Development Approach*, 17–45. Cambridge, MA: Harvard University Press, 2011.

———. 'Capabilities, Entitlements, Rights: Supplementation and Critique'. *Journal of Human Development and Capabilities* 12, no. 1 (2011): 23–37.

Oberoi, Geeta. 'The Curious Case of Court Manager in India: From Its Creation to Its Desertion'. *International Journal for Court Administration* 9, no. 1 (2017): 1–9.

OCHCR. 'Statement by the UN High Commissioner for Human Rights, Navi Pillay to the Security Council Open Debate on Maintenance of International Peace and Security'. https://www.ohchr.org/EN/ NewsEvents/Pages/DisplayNews.aspx?NewsID=14958&LangID=E. Accessed 7 May 2020.

OECD. 'Paris Declaration on Aid Affectiveness and Accra Agenda for Action'. https://www.oecd.org/dac/effectiveness/parisdeclarationandaccraagenda foraction.htm. Accessed 7 May 2020.

———. *Equal Access to Justice for Inclusive Growth: Putting People at the Centre*. Paris: OECD,2019. https://www.oecd.org/governance/equal-access-to-justice-for-inclusive-growth-597f5b7f-en.htm. Accessed 31 July 2019.

OECD and Joint Research Centre European Commission. *Handbook on Constructing Composite Indicators: Methodology and User Guide*. Paris: OECD, 2008. https://ictlogy.net/bibliography/reports/projects.php?idp=2308& lang=es. Accessed 17 May 2019.

Okafor, Obiora. 'Critical Third World Approaches to International Law (TWAIL): Theory, Methodology, or Both?' *International Community Law Review* 10, no. 4 (2008): 371–378.

Open Society Foundations. 'Life in a Quantified Society'. May 2019. https://www.opensocietyfoundations.org/explainers/life-quantified-society. Accessed 30 July 2021.

Ostrom, Elinor. 'Crossing the Great Divide: Coproduction, Synergy, and Development'. *World Development* 24, no. 6 (1996): 1073–1087.

OPHI. 'Global Multidimensional Poverty Index'. https://ophi.org.uk/multidimensional-poverty-index/. Accessed 14 December 2020.

Pahuja, Sundhya. 'Development and the Rule of (International Law)'. In *Decolonising International Law: Development, Economic Growth and the Politics of Universality*, 172–253. Cambridge: Cambridge University Press, 2011.

Palombella, G. 'Two Threats to the Rule of Law: Legal and Epistemic (Between Technocracy and Populism)'. *Hague Journal on the Rule of Law* 11 (2019): 383–388.

Parcell, Erin Sahlstein, and Benjamin M. A. Baker. 'Narrative Analysis'. In *The SAGE Encyclopedia of Communication Research Methods*, edited by Mike Allen, 1069–1072. Thousand Oaks: SAGE Publications, 2018. http://methods.sagepub.com/reference/the-sage-encyclopedia-of-communication-research-methods/i9374.xml. Accessed 28 August 2019.

Parekh, Bhikhu. *Gandhi: A Very Short Introduction*. (Oxford: Oxford University Press, 2001.

———. *Ethnocentric Political Theory: The Pursuit of Flawed Universals*. Cham: Springer International Publishing, 2019.

Patrignani, Emma. *Otherness, Pluralism and Context: Underground Issues in Comparative Legal Studies*. Rovaniemi: Lapland University Press, 2017.

Peerenboom, Randall. 'Varieties of Rule of Law: An Introduction and Provisional Conclusion'. In *Asian Discourses of Rule of Law*, edited by Randall Peerenboom, 1–55. London: Routledge, 2003.

Peerenboom, Randall, Michael Zürn and André Nollkaemper. 'Conclusion: From Rule of Law Promotion to Rule of Law Dynamics'. In *Rule of Law Dynamics: In an Era of International and Transnational Governance*, edited by Michael Zürn, André Nollkaemper and Randy Peerenboom, 305–324. Cambridge: Cambridge University Press, 2012.

Perry-Kessaris, Amanda. 'Prepare Your Indicators: Economics Imperialism on the Shores of Law and Development'. *International Journal of Law in Context* 7, no. 4 (2011): 401–421.

————. 'The Re-Co-Construction of Legitimacy of/through the Doing Business Indicators'. *International Journal of Law in Context* 13, no. 4 (2017): 498–511.

————. 'Legal Design for Practice, Activism, Policy, and Research'. *Journal of Law and Society* 46, no. 2 (June 2019): 185–210.

Pirie, Fernanda. *The Anthropology of Law*. Oxford: Oxford University Press, 2013.

Pleasence, Pascoe, and Nigel Balmer. *How People Resolve 'Legal' Problems*. Cambridge: Legal Services Board, 2014. https://legalservicesboard.org.uk/wp-content/media/How-People-Resolve-Legal-Problems.pdf/. Accessed 20 February 2022.

————. *Legal Needs Surveys and Access to Justice*. Paris: OECD, 2018. https://iris.ucl.ac.uk/iris/publication/1620815/1. Accessed 7 August 2019.

Pleasence, Pascoe, Nigel Balmer and Rebecca Sandefur. *Paths to Justice: A Past, Present and Future Roadmap*, London: Nuffield Foundation, 2013. https://www.nuffieldfoundation.org/sites/default/files/files/PTJ%20Roadmap%20NUFFIELD%20Published.pdf. Accessed 8 October 2020.

Pohl, Christian, Stephan Rist, Anne Zimmermann, Patricia Fry, Ghana S Gurung, Flurina Schneider, Chinwe Ifejika Speranza, Boniface Kiteme, Sébastian Boillat, Elvira Serrano, Gertrude Hirsch Hadorn and Urs Wiesmann. 'Researchers' Roles in Knowledge Co-Production: Experience from Sustainability Research in Kenya, Switzerland, Bolivia and Nepal'. *Science and Public Policy* 37, no. 4 (2010): 267–281.

Porter, Robert B. 'Measurement of Legal Empowerment through the Subjective Perceptions of Individuals'. *Impact Assessment and Project Appraisal* 32, no. 3 (2014): 213–221.

Porter, Theodore M. 'Introduction: Cultures of Objectivity'. In *Trust in Numbers: The Pursuit of Objectivity in Science and Public Life*, 3–8. Princeton: Princeton University Press, 1995.

————. 'Preface'. In *Trust in Numbers: The Pursuit of Objectivity in Science and Public Life*, vii–xii. Princeton: Princeton University Press, 1995.

————. 'The Political Philosophy of Quantification'. In *Trust in Numbers: The Pursuit of Objectivity in Science and Public Life*, 73–86. Princeton: Princeton University Press, 1995.

————. *Trust in Numbers: The Pursuit of Objectivity in Science and Public Life*. Princeton: Princeton University Press, 1996.

————. 'The Flight of the Indicator'. In *The World of Indicators: The Making of Governmental Knowledge through Quantification*, edited by Richard Rottenburg, Sally E. Merry, Sung-Joon Park and Johanna Mugler, 34–55. Cambridge: Cambridge University Press, 2015.

Pound, Roscoe. 'Law in Books and Law in Action'. *American Law Review* 44 (1910): 12–36.

Power, Michael. *The Audit Explosion*. Oxford: Oxford University Press, 1999.

Praia City Group. *Handbook on Governance Statistics (Draft for Global Consultation)*. Praia City Group, 2020. https://unstats.un.org/unsd/statcom/51st-session/documents/Handbook_on_GovernanceStatistics-Draft_for_global_consultation-E.pdf. Accessed 8 February 2022.

Press Trust of India (PTI). 'CJI Dattu Asks Lok Adalats to Settle at Least 10 Lakh Cases This Year'. *Mint*. https://www.livemint.com/Politics/3oNDFuIL1MXcHqpg45NRTL/CJI-Datta-asks-Lok-Adalats-to-settle-at-least-10-lakh-cases.html. Accessed 20 August 2019.

———. 'CJI T. S. Thakur Laments Lack of Judges, Pendency in His Farewell Speech'. *Mint*, 3 January 2017. https://www.livemint.com/Politics/v4Z20q2nZf2AllrSzyat0O/CJI-TS-Thakur-laments-lack-of-judges-pendency-in-his-fare.html. Accessed 20 August 2019.

———. 'Narendra Modi Wants India among Top 50 on Ease of Doing Business Index, Double Economy to $5trillion'. *Hindustan Times*, 19 November 2018. https://www.hindustantimes.com/india-news/narendra-modi-wants-india-among-top-50-on-ease-of-doing-business-index-double-economy-to-5trillion/story-n9da7OmAzAJQQzfuxyOeTP.html. Accessed 15 March 2019.

———. 'Pendency of Cases Bound to Increase: CJI Altamas Kabir'. *Business Standard*, 2 March 2013. https://www.business-standard.com/article/pti-stories/pendency-of-cases-bound-to-increase-cji-altamas-kabir-113030200332_1.html. Accessed 20 February 2022.

Radebe, Sibusiso Blessing, and Moses Retselisitsoe Phooko. 'Ubuntu and the Law in South Africa: Exploring and Understanding the Substantive Content of Ubuntu'. *South African Journal of Philosophy* 36, no. 2 (2017): 239–251.

Rajagopal, Balakrishnan. 'Writing Third World Resistance into International Law'. In *International Law from Below: Development, Social Movements and Third World Resistance*, 9–23. Cambridge: Cambridge University Press, 2003.

———. 'Introduction'. In *International Law from Below: Development, Social Movements and Third World Resistance*, 1–6. Cambridge: Cambridge University Press, 2003.

Rajah, Jothie. '"Rule of Law" as Transnational Legal Order'. In *Transnational Legal Orders*, edited by Terence C. Halliday and Gregory Shaffer, 340–373. Cambridge: Cambridge University Press, 2015.

Rawls, John. 'Principles of Justice'. In *A Theory of Justice*, 47–101. Cambridge, MA: Harvard University Press, 1971.

Raz, Joseph. 'The Rule of Law and Its Virtue'. In *The Authority of Law: Essays on Law and Morality*, 210–229. Oxford: Oxford University Press.

Riegner, Michael. 'Cheating Chile'. Völkerrechtsblog, 19 January 2018. https://voelkerrechtsblog.org/cheating-chile/. Accessed 29 December 2018.

Roberts, Anthea. 'The Divisible College of International Lawyers'. In *Is International Law International?* 1–17 Oxford: Oxford University Press, 2017.

Robeyns, Ingrid. 'The Capability Approach: A Theoretical Survey'. *Journal of Human Development* 6 (2005): 93.

———. 'Selecting Capabilities for Quality of Life Measurement'. *Social Indicators Research* 74 (2005): 191–215.

———. 'The Capability Approach'. In *The Stanford Encyclopedia of Philosophy*, edited by Edward N. Zalta. Winter 2016 edition, Metaphysics Research Lab, Stanford University, 2016. https://plato.stanford.edu/archives/win2016/entries/capability-approach/. Accessed 11 October 2019.

———. 'Core Ideas and the Framework'. In *Wellbeing, Freedom and Social Justice: The Capability Approach Re-Examined*, 21–88. Cambridge: Open Book Publishers, 2017.

———. *Wellbeing, Freedom and Social Justice: The Capability Approach Re-Examined*. Cambridge: Open Book Publishers, 2017.

Robeyns, Ingrid, and Harry Brighouse. 'Introduction: Social Primary Goods and Capabilities as Metrics of Justice'. In *Measuring Justice: Primary Goods and Capabilities*, edited by Harry Brighouse and Ingrid Robeyns, 1–14. Cambridge: Cambridge University Press, 2010.

Robinson, Nick. 'A Quantitative Analysis of the Indian Supreme Court's Workload'. *Journal of Empirical Legal Studies* 10, no. 3 (2013): 570–601.

Rosga, Ann Janette, and Margaret L. Satterthwaie. 'The Trust in Indicators: Measuring Human Rights'. *Berkeley Journal of International Law* 27, no. 2 (2009): 253–315.

Rottenburg, Richard, Sally E. Merry, Sung-Joon Park and Johanna Mugler, eds. *The World of Indicators: The Making of Governmental Knowledge through Quantification*. Cambridge: Cambridge University Press, 2015.

Rottenburg, Richard, and Sally Engle Merry. 'A World of Indicators: The Making of Governmental Knowledge through Quantification'. In *The World of Indicators: The Making of Governmental Knowledge through Quantification*, edited by Richard Rottenburg, Sally E. Merry, Sung-Joon Park and Johanna Mugler, 1–33. Cambridge: Cambridge University Press, 2015.

RSF Hub. 'User-Centred Law: What Law, Which Rights Do People in Fragile Contexts Need?' Impulse Paper No. 2, November 2018. https://www.

fu-berlin.de/sites/rsf-hub/_medien/RSF_Hub_IP02.pdf. Accessed 30 July 2021.

Rudolph, Susanne Hoeber. 'The Imperialism of Categories: Situating Knowledge in a Globalizing World'. *Perspectives on Politics* 3, no. 1 (2005): 5–14.

Ruskola, T. *Legal Orientalism*. Harvard University Press, 2013.

State v. Makwanyane and Another, (CCT3/94) [1995] ZACC 3; 1995 (6) BCLR 665; 1995 (3) SA 391; [1996] 2 CHRLD 164; 1995 (2) SACR 1 (6 June 1995). http://www.saflii.org/za/cases/ZACC/1995/3.html. Accessed 8 October 2019.

Sachs, Jeffrey, Guido Schmidt-Traub, Christian Kroll, Guillaume Lafortune and Grayson Fuller. *Sustainable Development Report 2019: Transformations to Achieve the Sustainable Development Goals*. New York: Bertelsmann Stiftung and Sustainable Development Solutions Network (SDSN). https://www.sustainabledevelopment.report. Accessed 13 September 2019.

Sachs, Wolfgang. 'Preface'. In *The Development Dictionary*, edited by Wolfgang Sachs, vi–vii. New York: ZED Books, 2009.

Sage, Caroline, Nicholas Menzies and Michael Woolcock. 'Taking the Rules of the Game Seriously: Mainstreaming Justice in Development - the World Bank's Justice for the Poor Program'. Justice and Development Working Paper Series no. 7, 51845, The World Bank, 2009. http://documents.worldbank.org/curated/en/431161468331052929/Taking-the-rules-of-the-game-seriously-mainstreaming-justice-in-development-the-World-Banks-justice-for-the-poor-program. Accessed 7 May 2020.

Sage, Caroline, and Michael Woolcock. 'Introduction: Legal Pluralism and Development Policy – Scholars and Practitioners in Dialogue'. In *Legal Pluralism and Development: Scholars and Practitioners in Dialogue*, edited by Brian Z. Tamanaha, Caroline Sage and Michael Woolcock, 1–18. Cambridge: Cambridge University Press, 2012.

Salevao, Iutisone. 'The Rule of Law: Principles, Issues and Challenges'. In *Rule of Law, Legitimate Governance and Development in the Pacific*, 1–35. Canberra: ANU Press, 2005.

Sandefur, Justin, and Divyanshi Wadhwa. 'A Change in World Bank Methodology (Not Reform) Explains India's Rise in Doing Business Rankings'. Center for Global Development. https://www.cgdev.org/blog/change-world-bank-methodology-not-reform-explains-indias-rise-doing-business. Accessed 29 December 2018.

———. 'Chart of the Week #3: Why the World Bank Should Ditch the "Doing Business" Rankings—in One Embarrassing Chart'. Center for Global Development. https://www.cgdev.org/blog/chart-week-3-why-world-bank

-should-ditch-doing-business-rankings-one-embarrassing-chart. Accessed 16 May 2019.

Santos, Alvaro. 'The World Bank's Uses of the "Rule of Law" Promise in Economic Development'. In *The New Law and Economic Development*, edited by David M. Trubek and Alvaro Santos, 253–300. Cambridge: Cambridge University Press, 2006.

Santos, Boaventura de Sousa. 'Law: A Map of Misreading—Toward a Postmodern Conception of Law'. *Journal of Law and Society* 14, no. 3 (Autumn 1987): 279–302.

———. 'Legal Plurality and the Time-Spaces of Law: The Local, the National, and the Global'. In *Toward a New Legal Common Sense: Law, Globalization, and Emancipation*, 99–120. Cambridge: Cambridge University Press, 2002.

———. *Toward a New Legal Common Sense: Law, Globalization, and Emancipation*. Cambridge: Cambridge University Press, 2002.

———. 'The Heterogeneous State and Legal Pluralism in Mozambique'. *Law and Society Review* 40, no. 1 (March 2006): 39–75.

———. *Epistemologies of the South: Justice Against Epistemicide*. London: Routledge, 2015.

———. 'Introduction: Why the Epistemologies of the South? Artisanal Paths for Artisanal Futures'. In *The End of the Cognitive Empire: The Coming of Age of Epistemologies of the South*, 1–35. Durham: Duke University Press, 2018.

———. 'From University to Pluriversity and Subversity'. In *The End of the Cognitive Empire: The Coming of Age of Epistemologies of the South*, 269–292. Durham: Duke University Press, 2018.

———. 'Gandhi, An Archivist of the Future'. In *The End of the Cognitive Empire: The Coming of Age of Epistemologies of the South*, 209–246. Durham: Duke University Press, 2018.

Santos, Boaventura de Sousa, João Arriscado Nunes and Maria Paula Meneses. 'Introduction: Opening Up the Canon of Knowledge and Recognition of Difference'. In *Another Knowledge Is Possible: Beyond Northern Epistemologies*, edited by Boaventura de Sousa Santos, xxix–lxii. New York: Verso, 2008.

Santos, Boaventura de Sousa, and Cesar A. Rodríguez-Garavito. 'Law, Politics, and the Subaltern in Counter-Hegemonic Globalization'. In *Law and Globalization from Below: Towards a Cosmopolitan Legality*, edited by Boaventura de Sousa Santos and Cesar A. Rodríguez-Garavito, 1–26. Cambridge: Cambridge University Press, 2005.

Sarfaty, Galit A. 'Regulating through Numbers: A Case Study of Corporate Sustainability Reporting'. *Virgina Journal of International Law* 53, no. 3 (2013): 575–622.

Satterthwaite, Margaret L., and Sukti Dhital. 'Measuring Access to Justice: Transformation and Technicality in SDG 16.3'. *Global Policy* 10, no. 1 (2019): 96–109.

Sauder, Michael, and Wendy Nelson Espeland. 'The Discipline of Rankings: Tight Coupling and Organizational Change'. *American Sociological Review* 74, no. 1 (2009): 63–82.

Schiff, David N. 'Socio-Legal Theory: Social Structure and Law'. *The Modern Law Review* 39, no. 3 (1976): 287–310.

Schimmelfennig, Frank. 'A Comparison of the Rule of Law Promotion Policies of Major Western Powers'. In *Rule of Law Dynamics: In an Era of International and Transnational Governance*, edited by Michael Zürn, André Nollkaemper and Randy Peerenboom. Cambridge: Cambridge University Press, 2012.

Schomerus, Mareike. 'Policy of Government and Policy of Culture, Understanding the Rule of Law in the "Context" Of South Sudan's Western Equatoria State'. In *The International Rule of Law Movement: A Crisis of Legitimacy and the Way Forward*, edited by David Marshall, 167–190. Cambridge, MA: Harvard University Press, 2014.

Scroll.in. 'Chief Justice Designate Ranjan Gogoi Says Case Pendencies Bring Disrepute'. 30 September 2018. https://scroll.in/latest/896415/i-have-a-plan-says-chief-justice-designate-ranjan-gogoi-on-tackling-pendency-of-cases-in-courts. Accessed 20 August 2019.

———. 'Sabarimala: Women Who First Entered Shrine Were Escorted by Police in Civilian Clothes, Court Told'. 25 January 2019. https://scroll.in/latest/910838/sabarimala-women-who-first-entered-shrine-were-escorted-by-police-in-civilian-clothes-court-told. Accessed 16 September 2019.

Secretary General. 'The Rule of Law and Transitional Justice in Conflict and Post-Conflict Societies'. 2004. https://www.un.org/ruleoflaw/blog/document/the-rule-of-law-and-transitional-justice-in-conflict-and-post-conflict-societies-report-of-the-secretary-general/. Accessed 7 May 2020.

———. 'Report of the Secretary-General on Legal Empowerment of the Poor and Eradication of Poverty (A/64/133)'. 2009. https://www.un.org/ruleoflaw/blog/document/report-of-the-secretary-general-on-legal-empowerment-of-the-poor-and-eradication-of-poverty-a64133/ Accessed 7 May 2020.

Segatti, Marco. 'A Capabilities Approach to Access to Justice: Unfulfilled Promises, and Promising Strategies in the US and in Europe'. *Teoria Politica (Nuova serie Annali)* 6 (2016): 335–359.

Segatti, Marcos. 'The Point of Equal Access to Justice: On the Duty to, at All Times and Provisionally, Pause, Cool Down and Listen'. JSD diss., University of Chicago, 2019. https://chicagounbound.uchicago.edu/jsd_dissertations/69. Accessed 30 July 2021.

Sen, Amartya. 'Equality of What?'. In *Tanner Lectures on Human Values*, edited by S. McMurrin, vol. 1, 197–220. Cambridge: Cambridge University Press, 1980.

———. *Tanner Lectures on Human Values*. Vol. 1. Cambridge University Press, 1980.

———. 'Well-Being, Agency and Freedom: The Dewey Lectures 1984'. *The Journal of Philosophy* 82, no. 4 (April 1985): 169–221.

———. 'Capability and Well-Being'. In Martha Nussbaum and Amartya Sen, *The Quality of Life*, 30–53. Oxford: Oxford University Press, 1993.

———. 'Functionings and Capabilities'. In *Inequality Reexamined*, 39–55. Cambridge, MA: Harvard University Press, 1995.

———. 'Human Development and Mahbub Ul Haq'. In *Human Development Report 2020:Human Development and the Anthropocene*, xi. New York: UNDP, 2020. http://hdr.undp.org/en/2020-report. Accessed 17 December 2020.

———. 'Introduction: Questions and Themes'. In *Inequality Reexamined*. Harvard University Press, 1995.

———. 'Introduction: Development as Freedom'. In *Development as Freedom*, 3–12. Oxford: Oxford University Press, 2001.

———. 'Capabilities, Lists, and Public Reason: Continuing the Conversation'. *Feminist Economics* 10, no. 3 (2004): 77–80.

———. 'Human Rights and Capabilities'. *Journal of Human Development* 6, no. 2 (2005): 151–166.

———. 'Introduction: An Approach to Justice'. In *The Idea of Justice*, 1–27. Cambridge, MA: Harvard University Press, 2009.

———. 'Lives, Freedoms and Capabilities'. In *The Idea of Justice*, 225–252. Cambridge, MA: Harvard University Press, 2009.

———. *The Idea of Justice*. Cambridge, MA: Harvard University Press, 2011.

Serban, Mihaela. 'Rule of Law Indicators as a Technology of Power in Romania'. In *The Quiet Power of Indicators: Measuring Governance, Corruption, and Rule of Law*, edited by Sally Engle Merry, Kevin E. Davis and Benedict Kingsbury, 199–221. Cambridge: Cambridge University Press, 2015.

Sharma, Yogima. 'Niti Aayog Working on Proposal to Appraise Judges' Performance, Make Rankings Public'. *Economic Times*, 7 May 2019. https://economictimes.indiatimes.com/news/politics-and-nation/niti-aayog-working-on-proposal-to-appraise-judges-performance-make-rankings-public/articleshow/69210175.cms?from=mdr. Accessed 30 July 2021.

Shepherd, Sue. 'Managerialism: An Ideal Type'. *Studies in Higher Education* 43, no. 9 (2018): 1668–1678.

Shore, Cris, and Susan Wright. 'Governing by Numbers: Audit Culture, Rankings and the New World Order'. *Social Anthropology* 23 (2015): 22–28.

———. 'Audit Culture Revisited: Rankings, Ratings, and the Reassembling of Society'. *Current Anthropology* 56, no. 3 (2015): 421–444.

Siems, Mathias, and David Nelken. 'Global Social Indicators and the Concept of Legitimacy'. *International Journal of Law in Context* 13 (2017): 436.

Singh, Prabhakar, and Benoit Mayer. 'Introduction: Thinking International Law Critically One Attitude, Three Perspectives'. In *Critical International Law: Postrealism, Postcolonialism, and Transnationalism*, edited by Prabhakar Singh and Benoit Mayer, 1–26. New Delhi: Oxford University Press, 2014.

Sircar, Oishik. 'Professor of Pathos: Upendra Baxi's Minor Jurisprudence'. *Jindal Global Law Review* 9, no. 2 (2018): 203–222.

Skaaning, Svend-Erik. 'Measuring the Rule of Law'. *Political Research Quarterly* 63, no. 2 (2010): 449–460.

Smith, Stephanie, and Janet Martinez. 'An Analytic Framework for Dispute Systems Design' *Harvard Negotiation Law Review* 14 (2009): 123–169.

Snyder, Francis G. 'Anthropology, Dispute Processes and Law: A Critical Introduction'. *British Journal of Law and Society* 8, no. 2 (1981): 141–180.

Snyder, Jack, and Alexander Cooley. 'Conclusion'. In *Ranking the World: Grading States as a Tool of Global Governance*, edited by Alexander Cooley and Jack Snyder, 178–193. Cambridge: Cambridge University Press, 2015.

Sokhi-Bulley, Bal. 'Governing (Through) Rights: Statistics as Technologies of Governmentality' *Social & Legal Studies* 20, no. 2 (2011): 139–155.

Sridhar, Devi. 'Britain Had a Head Start on Covid-19, but Our Leaders Squandered It'. *The Guardian.* https://www.theguardian.com/commentisfree/2020/mar/23/britain-covid-19-head-start-squandered. Accessed 8 April 2020.

Srivastava, Medha, Shalini Seetharam and Sumathi Chandrashekaran. *Development and Enforcement of Performance Standards to Enhance Accountability of the Higher Judiciary in India.* New Delhi: Vidhi Centre for Legal Policy, 2017. https://doj.gov.in/sites/default/files/document%282%29.pdf. Accessed 30 July 2021.

Stepan, Alfred, Juan J. Linz and Yogendra Yadav. 'The Rise of "State-Nations"'. *Journal of Democracy* 21 (2010): 50–68.

Stewart, Frances. 'Groups and Capabilities'. *Journal of Human Development* 6, no. 2 (2005): 185–204.

Sundarajan, Priya. 'NITI Aayog for Judicial Performance Index to Check Pendency'. *Business Line*, 30 April 2017. https://www.thehindubusinessline.com/news/national/niti-aayog-for-judicial-performance-index-to-check-pendency/article9674596.ece. Accessed 13 August 2019.

Sundaresan, Somasekhar. 'Courts Need Business Process Reform'. *Business Standard India*, 10 May 2016. https://www.business-standard.com/article/opinion/somasekhar-sundaresan-courts-need-business-process-reform-116051001476_1.html. Accessed 20 August 2019.

Supreme Court of Canada. *Hryniak v. Maudlin* 2014 SCC 7. https://scc-csc.lexum.com/scc-csc/scc-csc/en/item/13427/index.do#_ftnref2. Accessed 19 May 2020.

Supreme Court of India. *Indian Judiciary: Annual Report 2017–2018*. New Delhi: Supreme Court of India, 2018. https://ncrb.gov.in/en/crime-india-2016-0 Accessed 20 February 2022.

Swenson, Geoffrey. 'Legal Pluralism in Theory and Practice'. *International Studies Review* 20, no. 3 (2018): 438–462.

Tachtical Tech. 'The Data Detox Kit: An 8 Day Data Detox'. https://theglassroomnyc.org/files/2016/12/DataDetoxKit_optimized_01.pdf. Accessed 30 July 2021.

Taekema, Sanne, and Wibren van der Burg. 'The Incorporation Problem in Interdisciplinary Legal Research, Part 1: Theoretical Discussions'. *Erasmus Law Review* 8, no. 2 (2015): 39–42.

Tamanaha, Brian Z. 'A Non-Essentialist Version of Legal Pluralism'. *Journal of Law and Society* 27, no. 2 (2000): 296–391.

———. 'Understanding Legal Pluralism: Past to Present, Local to Global'. *Sydney Law Review* 30, no. 3 (2008): 375–411.

———. 'The Rule of Law and Legal Pluralism in Development'. *Hague Journal on the Rule of Law* 3, no. 1 (2011): 1–17.

———. 'Introduction: A Bifurcated Theory of Law in Hybrid Societies'. In *Non-State Justice Institutions and the Law: Decision-Making at the Interface of Tradition, Religion and the State*, edited by Matthias Kötter, Tilmann J. Röder, Gunnar Folke Schuppert and Rüdiger Wolfrum, 1–21. London: Springer, 2015.

Tamanaha, Brian Z., Caroline Sage and Michael Woolcock, eds. *Legal Pluralism and Development: Scholars and Practitioners in Dialogue*. Cambridge: Cambridge University Press, 2012.

Task Force on Justice. *Justice for All Report: Final Report*. New York: Center on International Cooperation, 2019. https://www.justice.sdg16.plus/report. Accessed 2 July 2019.

Tata Trusts. *India Justice Report: Ranking States on Police, Judiciary, Prisons and Legal Aid*. New Delhi: Tata Trusts, 2019.

Taylor, Linnet. 'What Is Data Justice? The Case for Connecting Digital Rights and Freedoms Globally'. *Big Data and Society* 4 (December 2017). doi:10.1177/2053951717736335.

Taylor, Veronica L. 'The Mythology of (Rule of) Law'. *Hague Journal on the Rule of Law* 11 (2019): 331–339.

TechCrunch. '"The Great Hack": Netflix Doc Unpacks Cambridge Analytica, Trump, Brexit and Democracy's Death'. http://social.techcrunch.com/2019/07/23/the-great-hack-netflix-doc-unpacks-cambridge-analytica-trump-brexit-and-democracys-death/. Accessed 13 September 2019.

The White House. 'Remarks by the President at Cairo University, 6-04-09'. *whitehouse.gov*, 4 June 2009. https://obamawhitehouse.archives.gov/the-press-office/remarks-president-cairo-university-6-04-09. Accessed 10 April 2020.

Tilburg Institute for Interdisciplinary Studies of Civil Law and Conflict Resolution Systems (TISCO), Martin Gramatikov, Maurits Barendrecht, Malini Laxminarayan, Jin Ho Verdonschot, Laura Klaming and Corry van Zeeland. *A Handbook for Measuring the Costs and Quality of Access to Justice*. Apeldoorn, Antwerpen and Portland: Maklu Publishers, 2010.

Tonon, Graciela. 'Communities and Capabilities'. *Journal of Human Development and Capabilities* 19, no. 2 (2018): 121–125.

Transparency International. 'Corruption Perception Index: Overview'. https://www.transparency.org/research/cpi/overview. Accessed 13 September 2019.

Trubek, David M. 'The "Rule of Law" in Development Assistance: Past, Present, and Future'. In *The New Law and Economic Development: A Critical Appraisal*, edited by David M. Trubek and Alvaro Santos, 74–94. Cambridge: Cambridge University Press, 2006.

Trubek, David M., and Alvaro Santos. 'Introduction: The Third Moment in Law and Development Theory and the Emergence of a New Critical Practice'. In *The New Law and Economic Development: A Critical Appraisal*, edited by David M. Trubek and Alvaro Santos, 1–18. Cambridge: Cambridge University Press, 2006.

Tsui, Ming-sum, and Fernando C. H. Cheung. 'Gone with the Wind: The Impacts of Managerialism on Human Services'. *British Journal of Social Work* 34, no. 3 (2004): 437–442.

Tsutsui, Kiyoteru, Claire Whitlinger and Alwyn Lim. 'International Human Rights Law and Social Movements: States' Resistance and Civil Society's Insistence'. *Annual Review of Law and Social Science* 8, no. 1 (2012): 367–396.

Tuhiwai Smith, Linda. 'Introduction'. In *Decolonizing Methodologies: Research and Indigenous Peoples*, 1–41. New York: ZED Books, 2012.

———. 'Twenty-Five Indigenous Projects'. In *Decolonizing Methodologies: Research and Indigenous Peoples*, 142–161. New York: ZED Books, 2012.

Turner, Stephen. 'What Is the Problem with Experts?'. *Social Studies of Science* 31, no. 1 (2001): 123–149.

Twining, William. *Law in Context: Enlarging a Discipline*. Oxford: Clarendon Press, 1997.

———. 'Have Concepts, Will Travel: Analytical Jurisprudence in a Global Context'. *International Journal of Law in Context* 1, no. 1 (2005): 5–40.

———. *Human Rights, Southern Voices: Francis Deng, Abdullahi An-Na'im, Yash Ghai and Upendra Baxi*. Cambridge: Cambridge University Press, 2009.

UN Women. 'Facts and Figures: Ending Violence against Women—What We Do'. https://www.unwomen.org/en/what-we-do/ending-violence-against-women/facts-and-figures. Accessed 14 December 2020.

UNDP. 'Access to Justice Practice Note'. 2004. http://www.undp.org/content/undp/en/home/librarypage/democratic-governance/access_to_justiceandruleoflaw/access-to-justice-practice-note.html. Accessed 21 January 2018.

———. 'Human Development Index (HDI)'. *Human Development Reports*. http://hdr.undp.org/en/content/human-development-index-hdi. Accessed 19 April 2020.

———. *Programming for Justice: Access for All: A Practitioner's Guide to a Human-Right- Based Approach to Access to Justice*. UNDP, 2005. https://www.un.org/ruleoflaw/blog/document/programming-for-justice-access-for-all-a-practitioners-guide-to-a-human-rights-based-approach-to-access-to-justice/ Accessed 31 December 2020.

United Nations. 'Basic Principles on the Use of Restorative Justice Programmes in Criminal MattersE COSOC Res. 2000/14, U.N. Doc. E/2000/INF/2/Add.2 at 35 (2000)'. https://www.un.org/ruleoflaw/blog/document/basic-principles-on-the-use-of-restorative-justice-programmes-in-criminal-matters/. Accessed 8 October 2020.

———. 'International Covenant on Civil and Political Rights 1966'. United Nations Treaty Series no. 14688, 23 March 1976. https://treaties.un.org/

doc/publication/unts/volume%20999/volume-999-i-14668-english.pdf. Accessed 30 July 2021.

United Nations.

———. 'Introduction'. In *The United Nations Rule of Law Indicators: Implementation Guide and Project Tools*, v–vi. 2011. https://reliefweb.int/sites/reliefweb.int/files/resources/Full_Report_1653.pdf. Accessed 22 February 2022.

———. *The Sustainable Development Goals Report 2018*. New York: United Nations, 2018. https://unstats.un.org/sdgs/report/2018. Accessed 26 April 2020.

———. *The United Nations Rule of Law Indicators: Implementation Guide and Project Tools*. 2011. https://reliefweb.int/sites/reliefweb.int/files/resources/Full_Report_1653.pdf. Accessed 7 May 2020.

United Nations General Assembly. 'Human Rights and Cultural Diversity A/Res/60/167'. 22 February 2000. https://digitallibrary.un.org/record/404848?ln=en. Accessed 30 July 2021

——— 'United Nations Declaration on Rights of Indigenous Peoples 61/295'. 13 September 2007. https://www.un.org/esa/socdev/unpfii/documents/DRIPS_en.pdf. Accessed 7 May 2020.

———. 'Declaration of the High-Level Meeting of the General Assembly on the Rule of Law at the National and International Level A/Res/67/1'. 2012. https://www.un.org/ruleoflaw/files/A-RES-67-1.pdf. Accessed 7 May 2020.

United Nations Human Rights Committee. 'General Comment No. 32, Article 14: Right to Equality before Courts and Tribunals and to a Fair Trial'. 2007. http://hrlibrary.umn.edu/gencomm/hrcom32.html. Accessed 7 May 2020.

United States Government Accountability Office. *Rule of Law Assistance: Agency Efforts Are Guided by Various Strategies, and Overseas Missions Should Ensure That Programming Is Fully Coordinated*. Washington, DC: US GAO, 2020. https://www.gao.gov/assets/710/707442.pdf. Accessed 30 July 2021.

Unnithan, Maya, and Carolyn Heitmeyer. 'Challenges in "Translating" Human Rights: Perceptions and Practices of Civil Society Actors in Western India'. *Development and Change* 45 (2014): 1361–1384.

Unruh, David R. 'The Nature of Social Worlds'. *Pacific Sociological Review* 23, no. 3 (1980): 271–296.

Upham, Frank. 'Mythmaking in the Rule of Law Orthodoxy'. Carnegie Endowment for International Peace, 2002. https://carnegieendowment.org/2002/09/10/mythmaking-in-rule-of-law-orthodoxy-pub-1063. Accessed 11 April 2020.

Uribe, María Angélica Prada. 'The Quest for Measuring Development: The Role of the Indicator Bank'. In *The Quiet Power of Indicators: Measuring Governance, Corruption, and Rule of Law*, edited by Benedict Kingsbury, Kevin E. Davis and Sally Engle Merry, 133–155. Cambridge: Cambridge University Press, 2015.

Urueña, René. 'Indicators and the Law: A Case Study of the Rule of Law Index'. In *The Quiet Power of Indicators: Measuring Governance, Corruption, and Rule of Law*, edited by Sally Engle Merry, Kevin E. Davis and Benedict Kingsbury, 75–102. Cambridge: Cambridge University Press, 2015.

———. 'Activism through Numbers? The Corruption Perception Index and the Use of Indicators by Civil Society Organisations'. In *The Palgrave Handbook of Indicators in Global Governance*, edited by Debora Valentina Malito, Gaby Umbach and Nehal Bhuta, 371–387. Cham: Springer, 2017.

USAID. 'Democracy, Human Rights and Governance Strategy'. 7 May 2019. https://www.usaid.gov/democracy/democracy-human-rights-and-governance-strategy. Accessed 22 February 2022.

van Rooij, Benjamin. 'Bringing Justice to the Poor, Bottom-up Legal Development Cooperation'. *Hague Journal on the Rule of Law* 4, no. 2 (2012): 286–318.

Versteeg, Mila, and Tom Ginsburg. 'Measuring the Rule of Law: A Comparison of Indicators'. *Law and Social Inquiry* 42, no. 1 (2017): 100–137.

Neave, Marcia. 'Law Reform in the Age of Managerialism'. Speech delivered at the Australian Law Reform Agencies Conference, Darwin, 20 June 2002. https://www.lawreform.vic.gov.au/publications-and-media/speeches/law-reform-age-managerialism. Accessed 24 February 2019.

Vishwanath, Apurva. 'Indian Courts Need MBAs and Not Chief Justice to Deal with Pendency'. *The Print*, 5 October 2018. https://theprint.in/opinion/off-court/indian-courts-need-mbas-not-chief-justice-to-deal-with-pendency/129914/. Accessed 20 August 2019.

Visvanathan, Shiv. 'Alternative Science'. *Theory, Culture and Society* 23, nos. 2–3 (2006): 164–169.

———. 'The Search for Cognitive Justice'. *Seminar Magazine* 597 (May 2009). https://www.india-seminar.com/2009/597/597_shiv_visvanathan.htm. Accessed 30 September 2020.

Vizard, Polly. 'Specifying and Justifying a Basic Capability Set: Should the International Human Rights Framework Be Given a More Direct Role?' *Oxford Development Studies* 35, no. 3 (2007): 225–250.

Waldorf, Lars. 'Introduction: Legal Empowerment in Transitions'. *The International Journal of Human Rights* 19, no. 3 (2015): 229–241.

———. 'Legal Empowerment and Horizontal Inequalities after Conflict'. *The Journal of Development Studies* 55, no. 3 (2019): 437–455.

Waldron, Jeremy. 'Is the Rule of Law an Essentially Contested Concept (In Florida)?' *Law and Philosophy* 21, no. 2 (2002): 137–164.

Weeks, Sindiso Mnisi. 'South Africa Still Has a Long Way to Go to Settle Traditional Leadership Challenges'. *The Conversation*, 23 June 2019. http://theconversation.com/south-africa-still-has-a-long-way-to-go-to-settle-traditional-leadership-challenges-119009. Accessed 16 April 2020.

———. 'South Africa's Traditional Courts Bill 2.0: Improved but Still Flawed'. *The Conversation*, 23 June 2019. http://theconversation.com/south-africas-traditional-courts-bill-2-0-improved-but-still-flawed-74997. Accessed 16 April 2020.

Whitson, Sarah Leah. 'Neither Fish, nor Flesh, nor Good Red Herring Lok Adalats: An Experiment in Informal Dispute Resolution in India'. *Hastings International and Comparative Law Review* 15, no. 3 (1991): 391–445.

Wojkowska, Ewa. *Doing Justice: How Informal Justice Systems Can Contribute.* UNDP, 2006. https://www.un.org/ruleoflaw/blog/document/doing-justice-how-informal-justice-systems-can-contribute/. Accessed 3 February 2018.

Wolff, Jonathan, and Avner De-Shalit. 'Introduction'. In *Disadvantage*, 1–15. Oxford: Oxford University Press, 2007.

Woody, Christopher. 'The World Bank Says It Will Redo Its Competitiveness Rankings after Unfairly Influencing Them for Years'. *Business Insider*, 13 January 2018. https://www.businessinsider.in/the-world-bank-says-it-will-redo-its-competitiveness-rankings-after-unfairly-influencing-them-for-years/articleshow/62491966.cms. Accessed 29 December 2018.

World Bank. *Doing Business 2018: Reforming to Create Jobs.* 2018. https://www.doingbusiness.org/content/dam/doingBusiness/media/Annual-Reports/English/DB2018-Full-Report.pdf. Accessed 17 December 2020.

———. 'Doing Business Rankings'. https://www.doingbusiness.org/en/rankings. Accessed 13 September 2019.

———. 'Justice for the Poor'. https://www.worldbank.org/en/topic/governance/brief/justice-for-the-poor. Accessed 7 May 2020.

———. 'WGI 2020 Interactive: Documentation'. https://info.worldbank.org/governance/wgi/Home/Documents#wgiDataSources. Accessed 24 December 2020.

———. 'World Governance Indicators 2019'. https://info.worldbank.org/governance/wgi/. Accessed 7 May 2020.

World Justice Project. 'Advancing the Rule of Law Worldwide'. https://worldjusticeproject.org/. Accessed 6 November 2020.

———. *WJP Rule of Law Index 2020*. 2020. https://worldjusticeproject.org/our-work/research-and-data/wjp-rule-law-index-2020. Accessed 22 April 2020.

WP 373 of 2006, Supreme Court of India, '*Indian Young Lawyers Association v. State of Kerala*'

Xavier, Sujith. 'Learning from Below: Theorising Global Governance through Ethnographies and Critical Reflections from the Global South'. *Windsor Yearbook of Access to Justice* 33, no. 3 (2016): 229–255. https://papers.ssrn.com/sol3/papers.cfm?abstract_id=2979384&download=yes##. Accessed 31 August 2019.

Yadav, Bhupendra. 'Khap Panchayats: Stealing Freedom?' *Economic and Political Weekly* 44, no. 52 (2009):16–19.

Zainulbhai, Tameem. 'Justice for All: Improving the Lok Adalat System in India'. *Fordham International Law Journal* 35, no. 1 (2011): 248–278.

Zimmermann, Augusto. 'The Rule of Law as a Culture of Legality: Legal and Extra-Legal Elements for the Realization of the Rule of Law in Society'. *eLaw Journal: Murdoch University Electronic Journal of Law* 14, no. 1 (2007): 10–31.

Zumbansen, Peer. 'The Rule of Law, Legal Pluralism, and Challenges to a Western-Centric View: Some Very Preliminary Observations'. Osgoode Legal Studies Research Paper Series, 2017. https://digitalcommons.osgoode.yorku.ca/olsrps/193.

Zürn, Michael, André Nollkaemper and Randall Peerenboom. 'Introduction: Rule of Law Dynamics in an Era of International and Transnational Governance'. In *Rule of Law Dynamics: In an Era of International and Transnational Governance*, edited by Michael Zürn, André Nollkaemper and Randy Peerenboom, 1–18. Cambridge: Cambridge University Press, 2012.

Index